THE LAVENDER BANS

THE LAVENDER BANS

A CENTURY OF ANTI-LGBTQ+ POLICIES IN THE U.S. MILITARY

DORIAN RHEA DEBUSSY

Columbia University Press
New York

Columbia University Press
Publishers Since 1893
New York   Chichester, West Sussex
cup.columbia.edu
Copyright © 2026 Columbia University Press
All rights reserved

Cataloging-in-Publication Data is available from the Library of Congress.
ISBN 9780231205740 (hardback)
ISBN 9780231205757 (trade paperback)
ISBN 9780231556149 (ebook)
ISBN 9780231566056 (pdf)

LCCN 2025030975

Cover design: Elliott S. Cairns
Cover image: Maria Dryfhout / Shutterstock.com

GPSR Authorized Representative: Easy Access System Europe, Mustamäe tee 50,
10621 Tallinn, Estonia, gpsr.requests@easproject.com

FOR JUDITH SOPHRONIA NICHOLSON GUNTER

AND MY CHOSEN FAMILY

CONTENTS

Acknowledgments ix
Abbreviations xiii

INTRODUCTION 1

1. RESEARCHING WITH INTERDISCIPLINARY FRAMEWORKS 26

2. THE EARLY YEARS OF ANTI-LGBTQ+ MILITARY POLICY: WORLD WARS I AND II 49

3. THE COLD WAR, COMMUNISTS, AND QUEER BOOGEYMEN 70

4. IT'S MILITARY READINESS AND UNIT COHESION, *NOT* DISCRIMINATION 90

5. A MEANDERING PATH TOWARD TRANS INCLUSION 108

CONCLUSION 121

Afterword 131
Notes 133
Bibliography 179
Index 199

ACKNOWLEDGMENTS

First and foremost, I'd like to thank my ex-wife and best friend, Zoey Nicholson Decker, for supporting me during the decade of work that led to this manuscript. Without her love and friendship, I'd be much a more boring person. I'm also grateful for my partner, Lukas Grey, for providing ongoing love and support during the final phases of this project. More generally, I'm also thankful for my chosen family, who have helped to support me in so many ways. Without their love and support, I would not have found success in my life, and I'm forever grateful for Zoey, Celia Decker, James Decker, Judy Gunter, Raymond Campbell, Thomas Dunn, my nieces, Wino the dog, Prince the cat, and other members of my chosen family.

In addition to my chosen family, I'm also thankful for several mentors who supported me and this project during graduate school at the University of Connecticut. I'm especially grateful for Christine Sylvester of the University of Connecticut, who served as my doctoral adviser and mentor; Christine's guidance was absolutely essential during my graduate school years. I'm thankful for her ongoing support of me and her other mentees; we all owe her a debt of gratitude. Similarly, I'm grateful for Sherry Zane, formerly at the University of Connecticut, for nurturing this project and offering me guidance throughout graduate school; I cannot thank Sherry enough for her mentorship and friendship. I'm also appreciative of the other members of my doctoral committee—Kimberly

Gill of Columbus State University and Jeremy Pressman of the University of Connecticut. To Kim, thank you for that fateful call that set the trajectory for my doctoral research, and to Jeremy, thank you for the international security seminar, which provided the academic space to explore the history of "Don't Ask, Don't Tell" (DADT). And thank you to Jane Anna Gordon of the University of Connecticut, who provided support to me and so many other graduate students in the Department of Political Science.

I'd also like to offer appreciation for colleagues from my time at the University of Connecticut and beyond. To Ramona Peel of the Ohio State University, thank you for your friendship and support—both at OSU and far beyond—over the past several years. To Rob DuVall and Heather Llewellyn of Equitas Health, thank you both for the tireless encouragement and kindness. To Christopher Kennerly of Kenyon College, thank you for providing me with space to grow while at the Office of Diversity, Equity, and Inclusion. To Meredith Harper Bonham, formerly at Kenyon College, I'm immensely grateful that you brought me to the Hill in 2018. To H. Abbie Erler of Kenyon College, thank you for helping to keep me engaged with students and faculty in the Women's and Gender Studies Program. To Heather Peterson, formerly at Kenyon College, thank you for always being there with a positive outlook, even during the toughest times. To Kimberly Creasap of Wittenberg University, thank you for your support during the book proposal process. To Arnab Dutta Roy of Florida Gulf Coast University and Lyn Alexander of the University of Connecticut, thank you both for your friendship during my graduate school years and beyond. To Shalya Nunnally of the University of Tennessee, Knoxville, thank you for your support during my earliest years of graduate school. To Fleurette King, formerly at the University of Connecticut and the University of Northern Colorado, thank you for your guidance during some key moments in my early career. To Thomas Lawrence Long of the University of Connecticut, thank you for always offering your support to LGBTQ+ people, including me, on campus. To Fred Lee of the University of Connecticut, thank you for easing my mind about the peer review process; it helped more than you realize.

Thank you also to the team who brought this book from manuscript to production. To my editor, Stephen Wesley, at Columbia University Press, thank you for believing in this project. (Thank you, again, for the extension too!) To Lewis Gordon of the University of Connecticut, thank you for your indexing expertise. Thank you to the members of the project's editing and production team—Stephen, Alex Gupta, Leslie Kriesel, Peggy Tropp, and others—for your often invisible but exceedingly important work to make this book a success.

I'm also thankful for a close circle of friends who have helped me stay grounded throughout the writing, editing, and peer review process for this manuscript. While some of these friends have already been named, still others should be mentioned here. To Ari Toumpa, thank you for your caring friendship and for helping me to remain grounded. To Joshua Moretti, thank you for helping me find time to break away from writing for some much-needed breaks. To Steph Lumbra and Patrick Muro, thank you both for always being there for me. To Bri Bardos, thank you for always sharing your joy and positive outlook. To Lisa Nic An Bhreithimh, thank you for helping me to find my community in Storrs. To Nova Thayer and Ellis Cliff, thank you both for making sure that I'm never lonely in Washington, DC. And thank you to so many others—including Jes Evangelista, Asche Pooler, Chris McClung, Micah Mitchell, Tyson Crenshaw, Alex Ryan, Youssouf Gabriel Bellamy, Sara Ailshire, Felix Tunador, Coleen Spurlock, Isaac Sabelhaus, Jackie Frankovich, and those not named—for your support, kindness, and friendship.

Finally, thank you to Diet Cig, Japanese Breakfast, Howlin' Wolf, Margo Price, Bob Dylan, Sleater-Kinney, Sir Chloe, Tammy Wynette, Those Darlins, Janelle Monae, Kylie Minogue, Annie Mac, and Madonna for the albums often enjoyed during the writing and editing process. On a similar note, thank you to Martha Stewart for the many reruns on my sleepy, off days. And thank you to Kafe Kerouac and Cup O Joe in Columbus for the coffee.

ABBREVIATIONS

ACLU	American Civil Liberties Union
ACT UP!	AIDS Coalition to Unleash Power!
AIDS	Acquired immunodeficiency syndrome
APA	American Psychiatric Association
APD	American political development
APSA	American Political Science Association
CIA	Central Intelligence Agency
DADT	"Don't Ask, Don't Tell"
DCID	Director of Central Intelligence Directive
DHS	Department of Homeland Security
DoD	Department of Defense
DoDI	Department of Defense Instruction
DoJ	Department of Justice
DoS	Department of State
DoW	Department of War
DSM	*Diagnostic and Statistical Manual of Mental Disorders*
FBI	Federal Bureau of Investigation
FDA	Food and Drug Administration
GAO	Government Accountability Office
GRIDS	Gay-related immune deficiency syndrome
HHS	Department of Health and Human Services

HIV	Human immunodeficiency virus
IDF	Israeli Defense Forces
JAG	Judge Advocate General
LGBQ	Lesbian, gay, bisexual, queer
LGBTQ+	Lesbian, gay, bisexual, transgender, queer (plus)
MMAA	Modern Military Association of America
NARA	National Archives and Records Administration
NDAA	National Defense Authorization Act
NIH	National Institutes of Health
NME	National Military Establishment
NSA	National Security Agency
PERSEREC	Personnel Security Research Center
RAND Corp.	Research and Development Corporation
SLDN	Servicemembers Legal Defense Network
UCMJ	Uniform Code of Military Justice
VA	Department of Veterans Affairs
WAC	Women's Army Corps
WAAC	Women's Army Auxiliary Corps

INTRODUCTION

COLUMBUS, GEORGIA, 2017

During moments of national significance, people often recall where they were, what they were doing, and who they were with. For instance, many Americans of a certain age have this type of recall for September 11, 2001. Most people do not have this experience regarding July 26, 2017, but when reminded of what occurred on that date, they are likely to have some sort of response. This was the date on which President Donald Trump tweeted the following: "After consultation with my Generals and military experts, please be advised that the United States Government will not accept or allow . . . transgender individuals to serve in any capacity in the U.S. Military. Our military must be focused on decisive and overwhelming . . . victory and cannot be burdened with the tremendous medical costs and disruption that transgender [sic] in the military would entail. Thank you."[1] This series of tweets came largely out of nowhere, and it confused civilians and military personnel alike—especially since the Department of Defense (DoD) had announced a new and seemingly permanent trans-inclusion policy under the Obama administration more than a year earlier. These tweets, which were an increasingly common form of communication from Trump both on the campaign trail and during his first term in the White House, became the news of the day.

Unlike many people, I vividly remember where I was at that moment, what I was doing, and who I was with. The place was a front porch in

Columbus, Georgia, where I was drinking my morning coffee. Shortly into that daily ritual during my trips back to the Deep South, my then wife and still good friend Zoey walked outside to deliver the news. Throughout the day, mentors, colleagues, and friends—all people who knew that I was working on a project analyzing anti-LGBTQ+ military policies in the American military—texted and called to share their disappointment with the news. The day was emotionally exhausting and frustrating, and it marked a change in how people perceived my doctoral work. From that day onward, people outspokenly shared that my work was "so timely," "important," "relevant," and other such adjectives. For an academic, this is a very unusual experience, and ultimately, it altered my career path for years to come. Most obviously, this change in perception is partially responsible for this book's existence, but it is also responsible for my broader body of work, which evolved during the first Trump administration, into the Biden administration, and eventually into the second Trump administration.

As even the most casual readers of this book know, the broader LGBTQ+ community—and especially the transgender community—has faced an unprecedented number of legislative attacks in recent years. Many people are aware of public policy issues that have attempted to regulate who uses which bathroom, who plays on which sports team, and who gets what medical care. In summer 2017, the debate du jour was about who could serve in what military. Following that series of tweets, the average American began to form an opinion about open transgender service in the military—that is, allowing transgender people to serve, while providing them with the necessary resources for success in their service branch. Though not everyone recalls Trump's tweets about this topic, most recall what came of them: a ban against open service for transgender people in the military.

Reminiscent of the ban against lesbian, gay, bisexual, and queer (LGBQ) people during the era of "Don't Ask, Don't Tell" (DADT) from the Clinton to Obama administrations, the "trans ban," as it soon became known, was controversial from the beginning. Yet many people are not aware of the much deeper history of discrimination and exclusion connected to both the trans and the DADT-era bans. At the moment that Trump tweeted about the trans ban, I was actively working on this project, and in the moments thereafter, my project grew from an exclusively historical one to one that would require close attention to the nightly news, the DoD newsfeed, and occasionally Trump's Twitter feed. This change was an important distinction for me but also for my work: unlike other texts exploring the histories of LGBTQ+ exclusion in the military and/or intelligence community, my work would connect those histories with this specific cultural moment.[2] This connection would help to understand these policies, procedures, and bans not by treating them as isolated incidents throughout American history but by focusing on the ways in which they built upon and interacted with one another. In other words, I would step back for a wide-angle view of anti-LGBTQ+ discrimination in the American military and intelligence community, showing that the trans ban was just one period among many.

THE RESEARCH QUESTIONS AND MY INITIAL EXPECTATIONS

This book examines the major policy changes that the American military and intelligence community have implemented in the pursuit of LGBTQ+ exclusion from World War I to present (i.e., the second Trump administration). The book explores both these policies and the corresponding "logic" that supported their implementation, focusing specifically on the ways in which these anti-LGBTQ+ policies have shifted from the early twentieth century to the present. Since this covers more than a hundred years of American history, several questions came to my mind at the outset of this project: What has anti-LGBTQ+ discrimination in the military and intelligence community looked like over time? What were the major shifts in these policies over time? How did the rationale for these policies also develop? What other influences might have existed in these various cultural and historical settings? What have been the broader impacts of such policies? While this book will not and cannot answer all of these questions directly, all of these questions have influenced this work, how I interact with my source material, and what I present to you as a reader.

Although this book focuses on anti-LGBTQ+ discrimination, not all policies affected all portions of the broader LGBTQ+ community in the same way. For instance, some policies largely targeted men, especially during periods when women were disallowed from service in the American military. Similarly, some cultural factors and misconceptions about LGBTQ+ identities erroneously presumed that transgender women and intersex people were simply gay men. At the same time, intersectional identities related to race, ethnicity, class, and other factors resulted in policies that affected people differently. When possible, I draw attention to this important feature of this troubling history of anti-LGBTQ+ discrimination, but you, as the reader, should keep these complexities in mind too.

This book is ultimately an analysis of anti-LGBTQ+ policies, a discussion of the rationale for their development, and the story of how these policies have intertwined with one another through time. It is not a telling of individual histories; there are other authors far better qualified to tell those important stories. Instead, I identify six distinct periods of anti-LGBTQ+ exclusion from the American military and intelligence community: World War I, World War II, the early Cold War, the late Cold War, the DADT period (early 1990s to 2011), and the present period (2011 to the second Trump administration).[3] Each of these periods saw unique policy developments aimed at excluding LGBTQ+ people from the military and intelligence community, and this categorical discrimination, which I have collectively dubbed the "lavender bans," had a distinctly different rationale in each period. In examining these six periods, the book focuses specifically on two research questions: (1) What was the rationale for banning LGBTQ+ people from the military and intelligence community in each of these periods? (2) What were the policies that emerged in each period?

This project began during my doctoral studies, and in those early days, I expected to find a detailed history of anti-LGBTQ+ discrimination. I was not initially expecting to find as much information as I did, and I was surprised to learn that these anti-LGBTQ+ policies shifted so dramatically and clearly in the aforementioned six periods. I did not have many expectations for the apparent rationales that the government would offer at various points in history; I initially (and somewhat naively) presumed the rationale would be akin to what was offered during "Don't Ask, Don't Tell" (DADT). Obviously, these notions were incorrect. Instead, each period had a distinct rationale attached to the policies that emerged, and these rationales shifted dramatically over the course of more than a hundred years. While I expected that there would be some period-specific policies, that is just about where my initial expectations stopped proving correct. Finally, I was able to identify the policies and rationales for each of these six periods, though where the policies were administratively housed (as purely military policies, intelligence community policies, executive orders, etc.) differed across time.

In conducting this research, I have sought out historical data from key secondary sources; equally important, however, have been primary source materials from the National Archives and Research Administration (NARA), as well as from other sources and electronic archives such as the Central Intelligence Agency (CIA), presidential libraries, and others. Primary source materials include court-martial transcripts, internal memos from various federal agencies, executive orders, various documents and webpages from the Department of Defense, publicly available information from key intelligence agencies like the CIA and the Federal Bureau of Investigation (FBI), congressional testimony, federal court transcripts, and much more.

By relying upon a combination of both primary and secondary source material, I have constructed a detailed account of the developmental periods of LGBTQ+ military history in these six distinct phases from World War I to the present. Using these qualitative sources, I show the ever-shifting rationales—which the government readily offered—for banning LGBTQ+ people from the military and intelligence community. In doing so, I examine not only the major policies that resulted from the lavender bans throughout these six periods but also where and how they were administratively codified, whether as formal or informal policies. While the latter may not sound particularly exciting, it is especially important in telling this century-long history of anti-LGBTQ+ discrimination.

THE FRAMEWORKS THAT INFORM THIS RESEARCH

Here, I review some of the major pieces of scholarship that inform the interdisciplinary framework for this book, discussing how they have helped me in answering my research questions. Along with the source materials noted above, this book uses a framework drawn from three specific areas of academic inquiry: feminist scholarship, security studies scholarship, and LGBTQ+ historical scholarship. In the next chapter, I speak to these three elements of the framework in more depth, but briefly noting some preliminary information about these scholarly themes is useful by way of introduction.

The first of these themes, feminist scholarship, assists in framing my work within my own discipline. While I very much consider myself a political scientist, I often feel more at home in the scholarly field of women's, gender, and sexuality studies, given that my work often focuses on issues affecting the LGBTQ+ community. At the same time, this project is very much grounded in my own feminist praxis. It is a product of my own interests, and these interests have been informed by my own lived experience and identities. The second theme, security studies, is critically necessary because of the ways in which the military and intelligence community have conceptualized LGBTQ+ people as threats to national security. Finally, the third theme, LGBTQ+ historical scholarship, deals directly with analyzing not only major moments of American military history but also how the histories of the LGBTQ+ community intersect with them.

FEMINIST SCHOLARSHIP

Unsurprisingly, a great deal of LGBTQ+ scholarship is interdisciplinary and grounded in feminist analysis, since feminist scholarship seeks to understand the importance of gender, sexuality, and other intersectional identities. Feminist scholarship directly influenced the research for this book, as well how I speak about numerous diverse identities within the broader LGBTQ+ community. Given my own personal connection to both the broader LGBTQ+ community and this topic, acknowledging the importance of feminism as a framework is necessary. Below, I very briefly review major pieces of feminist scholarship that underpin the framework of this book.

In her 2006 work, Mary Hawkesworth reviews the trajectory of feminist inquiry, highlighting its impact on a variety of disciplines and their traditional methodological conventions.⁴ This type of feminist inquiry, which seeks to affect the ways in which scholars interact with such conventions, directly supports the framework of this book. Specifically, I seek to understand both sexuality and gender identity beyond the usual bimodal analysis (either "straight" or "not"; either cisgender "man" or cisgender "woman") so often represented in political science and security studies research. Similarly, Brooke Ackerly and Jacqui True's 2010 work illuminates the importance of a feminist praxis in conducting research within the political and social sciences, while also discussing the ways in which feminist research has existed in interdisciplinary forms among multidisciplinary spaces.⁵ This work also influences the framework of this book, since my own lived experiences inform my interest in research related to the broader LGBTQ+ community. Most notably, this feminist praxis—along with the importance of acknowledging its importance—is evident in my research endeavors, given both my investment in this particular history and my own identity as a queer, transgender woman. It is important to note that this book seeks to create space for other LGBTQ+ people to better understand the history of LGBTQ+ exclusion in the American military and intelligence community, while also expanding the scope of future research in queer and transgender histories.

SECURITY STUDIES SCHOLARSHIP

In addition to feminist scholarship, the field of security studies also deeply influences the framework for this book. In political science's subfield of international relations, the area of security studies has been especially thoughtful in considering the importance of LGBTQ+ focused inquiry. Given this book's research questions, it is hardly surprising that it utilizes research produced within the area of security studies, particularly in regard to the analysis of more contemporary policies such as DADT and the evolving debates on open transgender service.

Much of the relevant security studies scholarship within the international relations literature deals with DADT, and a great deal of this research has questioned the necessity of this policy. This body of research, in concert with primary source information related to DADT, proved crucial for the security studies framework used within this book. For instance, Aaron Belkin's article from 2001 specifically questions this policy and states outright that it is not based on military necessity, despite the fact that threats to unit cohesion have often been cited as the impetus for retaining the policy. Belkin directly highlights many of the concerns of the time, while also speaking to the major rationale for retaining the policy.[6] Furthermore, Aaron Belkin and Melissa Embser-Herbert jointly discuss the alternative rationale for this policy: a desire to protect the privacy of other soldiers within the same units as LGBQ service members. More specifically, their collaborative piece highlights a lesser known rationale for DADT. This particular rationale, which ran concurrently with the concern of unit cohesion, suggested (1) we should respect the privacy of straight service members in areas like barracks, shower facilities, etc.; and (2) we can safely assume, albeit tacitly, that LGBQ service members may not be able to restrain their sexual feelings and respect the privacy of their straight colleagues.[7]

In considering other aspects of relevant security studies scholarship, Belkin has been one of the most outspoken scholars about LGBTQ+ inclusion in the U.S. Armed Forces; he has also produced research examining the integration of the Israeli Defense Forces, finding that these concerns by and large did not produce any significant issues.[8] Belkin's research continued to question the rationale for maintaining DADT and banning LGBQ people from the armed forces.[9] In the mid-2000s, Belkin's research demonstrated that lifting this ban would not damage support for the military, though the policy of DADT was not lifted until the summer of 2011 by the "Don't Ask, Don't Tell" Repeal Act of 2010.[10] Certainly, this expansive body of research from Belkin—who was the head of the Palm Center, which researched public policy initiatives regarding sexuality, gender identity, and the military—has been of immense assistance to this project for a variety of reasons. This research directly seeks to understand the rationales of DADT, which aids my project in analyzing the evolving logic of banning LGBTQ+ people from the armed forces in post–Cold War America. This research and the major contributions by Belkin also help to support the security studies framework, which is integrated within and throughout this book.

LGBTQ+ HISTORICAL SCHOLARSHIP

Finally, the framework for this book also utilizes scholarship from the interdisciplinary field of LGBTQ+ studies and related historical scholarship. This diverse field of scholarship helps to conceptualize the numerous ways LGBTQ+ people have historically been treated within the American military and intelligence community.[11] While it may seem obvious, the reader should remember that this particular history is of critical importance, especially since the military's policies have also interacted with other moments of cultural significance in the fight for LGBTQ+ rights over the course of the twentieth century.

Throughout this book, I trace the evolution of various rationales for banning LGBTQ+ people from the American military and intelligence community in each of the aforementioned periods, which requires using interdisciplinary research from LGBTQ+ studies and related historical scholarship. However, a common problem in working with queer and transgender history is that the history of this community has often been erased, "misremembered," destroyed, or simply not recorded at all.[12] While this book cannot address all of the relevant perspectives and individual histories that have been affected by these rationales and policies, it does discuss the ways those rationales and policies have developed since World War I. Still, it remains important to recognize that portions of this history are not available to us, given historical stigma and discrimination against LGBTQ+ people. Although I address these problems as much as possible, there is no perfect solution. Nonetheless, I have been able to use a rich body of literature—underpinned with primary source material—to shape the framework and argument of this book.[13] Following is a brief introduction to some of the major scholarly works that inform our understanding of each period.

Regarding the World War I period, George Chauncey's seminal work, *Gay New York: Gender, Urban Culture, and the Making of the Gay Male World, 1890–1940*, is critical. Chauncey demonstrates how the war effort centralized men into large urban centers, which enabled them to explore their sexual identities and establish the early semblances of a queer community.[14] Other scholars, such as Margot Canaday and Sherry Zane, further demonstrate how the U.S. government became invested in fostering restrictions on queer identities in relation to military service and immigration, while also investigating phenotypes that might "identify" gay men in particular.[15] Chauncey and Zane both provide key insights into the role of vice squads at naval bases in World War I, which led to a government-sponsored sex scandal and embarrassing U.S. Senate hearings.[16] In understanding how these moments shaped the policy of the military, these secondary sources—especially when placed alongside primary source documents like courts-martial transcripts and immigration guidebooks—help to provide a framework for understand anti-LGBTQ+ developments in World War I.[17]

An equally rich body of literature provides a framework for analyzing developments throughout World War II. During this period, more than twenty policy changes attempted to address people of diverse sexualities in the military; these changes are detailed in a study prepared for the Office of the Secretary of Defense in the 1990s.[18] While Canaday also discusses some of the transitioning policies during this period, Allan Berube's *Coming Out Under Fire: The History of Gay Men and Women in World War II* is the most comprehensive work to examine the impact of these policies.[19] In examining the stories of LGBQ people in the armed forces, he importantly lays claim to the idea that mobilization for the war effort placed more LGBQ people in contact with one another, which aided them in coming out. Other secondary source histories also help to conceptualize the framework and evidence during this period, shedding light on why some of these policies were at times applied in a more lackadaisical manner.[20]

For the early and late Cold War periods, there is an even more detailed body of literature regarding the experiences of LGBTQ+ people's interactions with the policies and rationales of the military and intelligence community. In analyzing the early Cold War, David Johnson's *The Lavender Scare: The Cold War Persecution of Gays and Lesbians in the Federal Government* remains the most significant work, detailing how queerness was equated to communism. It demonstrates how a "Lavender Scare" accompanied the more widely known "Red Scare" during the 1950s, a connection that is essential for analyzing this period.[21] Other works showcase how the intelligence community in America became more invested in drawing attention to "un-American" activities like queerness, shaping the framework for analyzing this period. Works that examine the FBI's tracking of LGBTQ+ people and works that explore how cisgender, heterosexual masculinity became a standard contrast to queerness and transness are equally important in understanding the broader social background of the country.[22]

Many of the policies from the late Cold War focus on presumed mental illness and the rise of the HIV/AIDS epidemic; as a result, the framework for this chapter and the works that inform it rely slightly more on primary source documentation. Specifically, this framework and analysis is particularly focused upon actions taken by the CIA, such as those in Director of Central Intelligence Directive (DCID) Number 1/14 of 1987. As I explain in later chapters, this policy directly labeled "homosexual conduct" as incompatible with service to the intelligence community; because it incorrectly presumed that transgender identities were automatically indicative of homosexuality, it also affected gender expansive populations. Other primary source documents, such as those reprinted in *Gays in Uniform: The Pentagon's Secret Reports*, edited by Kate Dyer, show that fears of "the unstable LGBTQ+ psyche" had already been debunked by the military in the late 1950s and early 1960s. However, DoD officials called for the documents to be rewritten to remove "all suggestions that homosexuals could be suitable for service." Thus, these studies were dismissed until the documents were recovered unaltered when congressional action ensured that the reports were released in their full unedited forms in the early 1990s.[23] These primary source documents are only a few key examples of what informs the framework for my analysis of the late Cold War.[24]

When considering the DADT period from the early 1990s to 2011, the framework that I utilize is built largely upon the work of security studies scholars with supplementary information from various primary sources. Other works, including Lillian Faderman's *Gay Revolution*, develop a detailed history of the implementation of the policy and its subsequent repeal.[25] This framework is further bolstered by other sources that also detail the struggle to have this policy repealed.[26] Also important to this portion of the book are primary sources, including documents detailing the actions of organizations like OutServe and Servicemembers Legal Defense Network (SLDN), two of the most prominent organizations fighting for the repeal of DADT. Other nontraditional primary source information—including a comic book from the Department of the Army, made-for-television movies, and YouTube videos featuring Lady Gaga—are important pieces of primary source material that supplement the framework for analyzing the DADT period.

Finally, the book concludes with an analysis of the present period, which explicitly centers on the challenges facing the transgender, nonbinary, and gender expansive community. The framework for this period—not unlike the DADT period—relies largely on primary source information with supplementary secondary source material. Such secondary source material includes research that questioned why transgender people were still not allowed to serve openly with full and unconditional support from their respective branches.[27] Given the limited research that has been conducted by academics at the time of this writing, the framework and analysis of this period's policies and rationales rely on primary source material from the DoD, the White House, and popular media sources like the *Military Times*. Specifically, RAND's 2016 study that assessed the impact that transgender inclusion would have on the military—given that it was commissioned by the Office of the Secretary of Defense—proves useful in framing the discussion about transgender inclusion in the contemporary period.[28] The resulting DoD document, *Transgender Service in the U.S. Military: An Implementation Handbook*, and various executive actions and departmental memoranda from both the Trump and Biden administrations are critical to understanding this period's policies and rationale.[29] This information also provides key insights into future research opportunities for scholars working at the intersections of security studies and LGBTQ+ studies.

WORKING IN A DISCIPLINE THAT IS AVERSE TO LGBTQ+ TOPICS

Within the discipline of political science, LGBTQ+ topics, even through the past decade, have often been underdeveloped and understudied, and somewhat surprisingly, this is especially true of American politics scholarship.[30] Here, I provide a brief overview of the problem, which showcases one element of this project's topical significance to the discipline. Afterward, I draw attention to Richard Valelly's "LGBT Politics and American

Political Development," which frames the methodological significance of this project while also explaining the goals of an American political development or "APD" research framework. My choice of methodological framework—explained later in this chapter—is American political development (APD), and this is also a response to Valelly's article that explains the usefulness of this framework for LGBTQ+ focused research. The discussion of his work then serves as a bridge to discuss my qualitative, methodological approach.[31]

AN ABRIDGED OVERVIEW OF LGBTQ+ STUDIES IN POLITICAL SCIENCE

Scholars working at the intersections of LGBTQ+ studies and political science have widely discussed the production of heteronormative and cisnormative work (work that centers the perspectives of straight, cisgender people) within the broader discipline of political science. This particular problem is one of the primary reasons that I sought to engage in the feminist work of producing research that relates to my own identity and positionality. Previously, I recognized the not-so-well-hidden fact that political science often fails to produce research regarding diverse genders and sexualities, but the impetus to actually take on the research for this book was first spurred by a single article, as noted below. I first provide a brief overview of the state of LGBTQ+ studies in political science more broadly and then briefly discuss both the topical and methodological significance of this particular book.

Julie Novkov and Scott Barclay's "Lesbians, Gays, Bisexuals, and the Transgendered [sic] in Political Science: Report on a Discipline-Wide Survey" highlights numerous problems that the discipline faces regarding support LGBT scholars, teaching, and research.[32] It was this article, first read in the early days of graduate school at the University of Connecticut, that showed me how rampant the problem actually was. Novkov and Barclay's work largely focuses on analyzing key data from a survey of American Political Science Association (APSA) members across the country. Their findings by and large illuminated the problem and led some to question why the discipline was doing so little work with topics centered around the political experiences of people of diverse genders and sexualities. Novkov and Barclay provided an interesting backdrop for understanding how significant even the presence of LGBTQ+ political science scholarship can be, based upon its rarity throughout so much of our discipline.[33] To date, no such study has been conducted, but anecdotal evidence certainly suggests that the problems they describe continue.

To understand the impact of this problem, I reiterate four of the most pertinent findings from the Novkov and Barclay study here. First, Novkov and Barclay present data that demonstrates that the subfield of American politics, which had the highest number of total overall survey respondents, actually appears to have the lowest numbers of representation for LGBT scholars and educators at only 12.9 percent.[34] Second, their research draws attention to the fact that 11 percent of the respondents believed that research on LGBT topics was "not appropriate," while an additional 12 percent reported that they were "not familiar" enough to state an opinion of research on LGBT topics.[35] Third, they show that the number of respondents stating that LGBT topics were within the purview of their own research interests was minimal at best—3 percent of respondents said that LGBT topics were "extensively" represented in their research interests.[36] Fourth and finally, respondents within two subfields, despite their low representation of LGBT scholars, reported favorable reactions to research on LGBT issues. That is, more than 50 percent of respondents in the subfield of American politics reported that LGBT topics in research were "very appropriate," and nearly 50 percent of respondents from the subfield of international relations reported the same.[37]

While Novkov and Barclay's research illuminates some key problems within the discipline of political science, their work also builds upon Timothy Cook's much earlier critique of "political science" being "surprisingly silent" about LGBTQ+ political issues.[38] In his article from 1999, Cook draws attention to three likely reasons for a lack of queer political science research at the time: (1) it may be too "theoretically complex"; (2) it is "methodologically difficult" for a number of reasons; and (3) the field "lacks ready data for analysis."[39] While more work is certainly being undertaken, it would appear that these three problems may still plague the discipline. LGBTQ+ studies are potentially even more complex, thanks to the growth of research on other identities in the broader LGBTQ+ community. Cook's second reason, methodological difficulty, is certainly still present, especially considering that the common use of bimodal analysis often fails to capture data relevant to the LGBTQ+ community.[40] Finally, the lack of data is still pertinent for scholars using both qualitative and quantitative methods; however, thanks to nonprofit-generated data on many topics, this problem has become less prevalent in recent years.

After the Novkov and Barclay article in 2010, *PS: Political Science and Politics* produced a symposium, edited by Paisley Currah, to discuss some of the major issues at the heart of political science's reluctance to discuss research questions related to the LGBTQ+ community. In this symposium, Currah alludes to a number of important political dimensions of sexuality, such as its regulation by political institutions and its fostering of social movements.[41] Contributors to the symposium also speak to some of the problems that lie in the discipline's unabashed acceptance of heteronormativity and cisnormativity. For instance, Joe Rollins claims that the discipline would identify as "straight," if possible, given its refusal to engage queer topics.[42] Other scholars, such as Charles Smith, both criticize the discipline's methodological bimodal assumption of sexuality ("straight" or "not-straight") and hint at the discipline's refusal to seriously engage LGBTQ+ topics as an issue that diminishes methodological innovation.[43] Smith's critique of the discipline tacitly points to an underlying problem: the discipline's refusal to foster LGBTQ+ research might diminish methodological innovation and complexity.[44] To recapitulate, one of Cook's major claims is that queer research is often not undertaken because it might prove too methodologically complex, yet Smith's argument suggests that actively supporting LGBTQ+ research might actually foster more innovation in the discipline, which would solve Cook's stated concern.

Since the publication of this symposium in 2011, there has not been another major published study about the state of LGBTQ+ studies in the discipline of political science. Nonetheless, there has been a notable increase in the publication of new political science research related to the LGBTQ+ community, and this seems to be particularly true in the subfield of international relations. Specifically, scholars of international relations have been actively calling upon the subfield to conduct more research on queer and transgender issues.[45] Furthermore, the APSA established the Kenneth Sherrill Prize in 2015 in order to recognize, celebrate, and fund innovative LGBTQ+ research in the discipline.[46] Still, a great deal of work remains for the discipline of political science, and the discipline certainly will be spending time catching up to other social science fields such as sociology and psychology. At the end of this book, I discuss the question of progress for the discipline, offering insights on future research and noting emerging scholarship focused on LGBTQ+ topics.

THE GREATER SIGNIFICANCE OF THIS BOOK

Given that LGBTQ+ research in political science still lags behind that in many other fields of inquiry, this book is topically unique for the discipline. A great of deal of existing LGBTQ+ research in political science still focuses on how others view this community, rather than the community itself. For instance, there is no shortage of public opinion research related to the topic of marriage equality over the years. Thankfully, this is beginning to change for a number of reasons, including increased disciplinary acceptance in recent years, critiques from scholars who have rightfully questioned the discipline's tacit exclusion of LGBTQ+ topics of inquiry, and scholars who are working at the intersections of LGBTQ+ studies and political science. Moreover, the fact that this book focuses on the LGBTQ+ community and its political rights—instead of the often-belabored topic of whether the general public thinks the LGBTQ+ community *should* have certain rights—speaks to its topical significance.

Beyond its significance within the broader discipline of political science, this book is also unique compared to many of the groundbreaking texts that have analyzed specific periods of LGBTQ+ exclusion in the American military and intelligence community. While works from scholars like Berube, Chauncey, Canaday, Johnson, Zane, and others are crucial to understanding the scope of LGBQ exclusion in specific time periods, this book is uniquely significant and distinct from others for two reasons.[47] First, this is the first major text—barring some quite recent journal articles—that specifically analyzes the history of transgender exclusion in the military within the broader history of LGBQ exclusion in the military. Second, this project is the first that analyzes the specific shifting rationales and policies that allowed for the exclusion of LGBTQ+ people from the American military and intelligence community from World War I to the second Trump administration. Thus, this book, which exists at the intersections of security studies, feminist studies, and LGBTQ+ historical scholarship, is significant both in analyzing the issue of open transgender service and by bridging gaps between discrete secondary source material focused on specific periods.

Finally, this project is methodologically significant in how it approaches these research questions. As discussed in the next section, the book specifically employs a political science methodological framework. Again, this is a direct response to Valelly's research, which called for the discipline to employ this framework in research about the LGBTQ+ community.[48] This book's significance thus extends beyond topical significance within the discipline of political science and topical significance in comparison to similar scholarly works; it is also methodologically significant both to the discipline of political science and to existing LGBTQ+ historical scholarship.

THE METHODOLOGICAL APPROACH

AMERICAN POLITICAL DEVELOPMENT'S (APD'S) GOALS AND LGBTQ+ RESEARCH

While the discipline of political science in general seems to reject many aspects of LGBTQ+ studies, Valelly claims that American political development (APD)—both as a methodological framework and a research subfield of American politics—has, by and large, specifically failed to recognize LGBTQ+ politics as a topic. He claims that this should be remedied given that the two may be quite suited for one another.[49] For the reader who may not be familiar with APD, it is both a methodological framework and a research agenda, while some also claim that it is really an entire subfield within American politics. This framework seeks to understand phenomena that can be categorized into historical periods of durability and the shifts between them. An APD methodological framework generally, though not always, relies on qualitative, historical research; it is often characterized by the sequencing or periodization of portions of American political history, which are separated by some type of shift.[50] Within the discipline of political science, the conceptualization of APD differs quite drastically. Some scholars, like me, consider it both a methodological framework and a research agenda. This conceptualization emphasizes (1) the use of traditional qualitative methods to both describe and explain shifts between periods of durability and (2) the categorization of different periods of American political history based upon those shifts. Others prefer to consider it an entire subfield within the disciplinary subfield of American politics.[51]

Depending on the scholar, different thematic elements of APD become apparent, though elements of historical research that focus on durability, intermittent shifts, and moments of dynamic change are key.[52] For example, Adam Sheingate explains that the APD methodological framework seeks to illuminate "the complex coexistence of institutional dynamism and durability," though some scholars of APD (like me) focus on policy development within politics as well.[53] The framework of APD as both a methodological tool and a research agenda follows the trends set by historical institutionalism in that it looks to history to understand complex phenomena, but both the methodological framework and the research agenda also seek to conceptualize periods of durability and the shifts between them.[54]

Scholars of APD may, at times, disagree on the ways in which they characterize their analysis of durability and shifts throughout American political history. These debates also highlight the discrepancies in how scholars actually understand, explain, and use the APD methodological framework and research agenda. For instance, David Mayhew argues that APD seeks to understand large historical events and their broad impacts on contemporary institutions and policies, while Valelly argues that an APD scholar seeks to understand various historical "outcomes, periods, or eras" in American political history.[55] To the confusion of those unfamiliar with APD as a methodological framework and a research agenda, other scholars have ever so slightly different explanations of their purpose. Notably, Smith labels the goal of APD as understand historical constants, while James Morone focuses on the significance of cyclical moments in political history.[56] Finally, Karen Orren and Stephen Skowronek's argument about the goals of APD, as synthesized by Sheingate, is as follows: to understand "how contemporary features of the political system are the product of an interaction between older and newer institutional forms."[57] Not every APD scholar focuses exclusively on the alteration of institutions, but both the analysis of policy changes, by way of institutional forces, and their historical periodization are fair game for the APD scholar's research interests.[58]

While APD scholars may differ in terms of how they conceive of the focus of their scholarship (i.e., as institutional or policy based, as periods or cycles, etc.) and disagree on the debate of framework versus subfield, they do agree (1) that their work is historical in nature and (2) that it seeks to understand shifts over time. They seek to understand such shifts throughout American political history, and this is largely qualitative in nature. Just as there are levels of difference regarding how APD scholars conceive of their focus, there are more recent shifts in terms of their choice of tools in the broader APD methodological framework as well. Some APD scholars are moving from purely qualitative work to mixed methods work, which further points toward the ability of APD to make more inclusive strides toward fostering a scholarly home for LGBTQ+ politics research. Phil Everson, Rick Valelly, Arjun Vishwanath, and Jim Wiseman's "NOMINATE and American Political Development: A Primer" stands as an example of the ways APD scholarship is demonstrating how it can coexist and complement quantitative methodological tools and a mixed methods research design/agenda.[59] Just as this article demonstrates the flexibility and multipurpose importance of APD scholarship, Valelly argues a similar point in his explanation about the importance of APD scholarship and LGBTQ+ research topics to each other, pointing toward the topical importance of APD's future research agenda too.

In doing so, Valelly explains that "APD has largely neglected ... LGBT politics," despite the fact that such topics would be well-suited to the APD research agenda and methodological framework. He posits that APD scholars might have rejected the topic because "LGBT politics may seem to be evolving" too "rapidly" for their liking. But, he also claims that an APD framework would be quite useful, as "LGBT politics is a[n] ... historically evolving construct" that clearly fits within the parameters of the APD research agenda. Further, Valelly claims that APD might actually prove to be quite useful to the broader discipline, since he says that this particular research framework might help combat the "danger of viewing LGBT politics ahistorically.... within political science."[60]

Valelly's article makes two important claims about the methodological impact of this project. First, it argues that APD has largely failed to take up research pertaining to LGBTQ+ topics, even though the research framework is well-suited for doing so.[61] Thus, I utilize an APD methodological framework to understand both the shifts in rationale for *and* the policies concerning the exclusion of LGBTQ+ people from the American military and intelligence community. In doing so, I demonstrate how (1) LGBTQ+ research can be productively conducted with an APD research framework and (2) scholars can undertake LGBTQ+ topics to produce methodologically innovative research. Second, his article points to potential reasons that APD scholars should be interested in LGBTQ+ topics, as these topics are often historical in nature and evolve over time.[62] This book showcases the historical periodization of discrimination against LGBTQ+ people in the American military and intelligence community. Furthermore, it advances the state of APD research within the discipline; it is, to the author's knowledge, the first piece of LGBTQ+ scholarship to specifically utilize this methodological framework.

Overall, Valelly draws attention to a much broader challenge—for scholars to work at the intersection of an APD methodological framework and LGBTQ+ scholarship. As mentioned, this book is partially an answer to Valelly's tacit challenge, since it specifically seeks to undertake a methodological structure that analyzes the durability of certain periods and the shifts between them. In this context, this book is both methodologically and topically significant because of the historical periods that it connects, but it is also significant in seeking to respond to Valelly's call for scholars to use this APD methodological framework to investigate LGBTQ+ topics that have shifted throughout history. Clearly, this book's topical inquiry fits nicely in line with Valelly's briefly outlined research agenda for political scientists interested in LGBTQ+ topics, and it is also methodologically unique in the fact that it is, again to the author's best knowledge, the first to respond directly to Valelly's stated call to action for the APD methodological framework to answer an explicitly LGBTQ+ themed research question.

APPLYING APD AS A METHODOLOGY

This book is certainly of topical significance to the discipline of political science, given how inhospitable political science has been to LGBTQ+ studies, and its significance extends to the broader body of LGBTQ+ historical scholarship. This book is also of methodological significance, as explained above. Here, I outline the methodology actually used within this book; unsurprisingly, it largely employs the qualitative toolbox so often used by APD scholars. I first discuss the ways an APD methodological framework affects the book and how I conceive of it within the broader APD research agenda. Then I describe its historical qualitative approach, similar to the vast majority of APD scholarship, and discuss the purpose and selection of both primary and secondary source material.

This book is set within a research inquiry of interest to the APD research agenda, which differs widely in terms of topical choice but follows methodologically specific trends—that is, looking for durable periods and the dynamic shifts between them. As previously discussed, APD scholars use this methodological framework in slightly different forms, and many look at various phenomena in distinctly unique ways. Morone's earlier work, for instance, seeks to examine cycles of participatory democracy over nearly two hundred years of American political history, while some of his more recent work examines how religion has created cycles of change and stability in governmental and social issues in the United States.[63] Others, such as Smith, seek to understand the role of constants in American history rather than cycles or shifts.[64] My own conceptualization of the APD methodological framework falls in line with that of Valelly's earlier work, which describes it as a methodological tool to demarcate, analyze, and understand a political phenomenon via distinct periods within American political history.[65] Accordingly, my project examines six periods of discriminatory treatment toward LGBTQ+ people in the military and intelligence community: World War I, World War II, the early Cold War, the late Cold War, the DADT period; and the present period (2011 to the second Trump administration).

I utilize the "traditional" qualitative methodological choices so often employed by APD scholars and described in the previous section.[66] To that end, I have gathered both primary and secondary source material highlighting the discriminatory treatment against LGBTQ+ in the military and intelligence community in each of these six distinct periods. I also draw from courts-martial documentation, particularly for the World War I period, and military documents for all periods, including guidebooks and military codes where applicable. My major goal fits within the APD methodological framework, using historical data to understand the durable periods and the shifts between them as they relate to a particular institutional/policy phenomenon. These data help me to characterize each period's treatment of LGBTQ+ people in the military and intelligence community, and I use both primary and secondary source material to showcase the unique characteristics of each of these six periods. The APD methodological framework thus allows me to examine the shifting rationale for exclusionary policies between periods.

In short, I use this primary and secondary source material both to explore and describe the historical treatment of LGBTQ+ people in the military and intelligence community and to locate the shifts in rationales offered for this discriminatory exclusion in each of the six periods of inquiry. Primary source material is referenced when applicable and possible, with secondary material used to supplement data that (1) may have already been synthesized by another scholar or (2) may be unavailable to me because of logistical constrictions (such as the inability to travel to an inaccessible archival site). The primary source material for this project mostly comes from online electronic archives and the NARA in Washington, DC, but I also use other primary sources, as described earlier. This primary source material is used to discuss the specific codification and implementation of exclusionary policies, while the secondary material helps to describe and analyze each discrete period.

In sum, this book's straightforward methodological tools are organized according to the precepts of an APD framework, as proposed by Valelly.[67] While the discipline of political science is often reluctant to accept LGBTQ+ research as valid, this project stands as a testament to the importance of working at this intersection of political science, security studies, feminist scholarship, and LGBTQ+ studies. The APD framework, borrowed from the American politics literature, provides the best lens to analyze this particular topic, given its explicit focus on qualitative methods and historical data. Its emphasis on the periodization of a certain phenomenon in American political history—in this case, the shifting rationales for banning LGBTQ+ people from the American military and intelligence community—provides a useful methodological framework to both analyze and understand how the treatment of this community has evolved over time.

FORTHCOMING CHAPTERS AND WHAT TO EXPECT NEXT

In analyzing the lavender bans, this book is organized chronologically according to the six periods being analyzed—World War I, World War II, the early Cold War, the late Cold War, the DADT period, and the present period (2011 to the second Trump administration). A short concluding chapter then speaks further to the significance of this book, its implications for future research related to this topic area, and the challenges to continued research on anti-LGBTQ+ discrimination in the American military and intelligence community.

Following this introduction, chapter 1 provides an overview of the interdisciplinary framework that informs and grounds this book. As mentioned earlier, this framework uses research and theoretical frames from three primary areas: feminist scholarship, security studies scholarship from the discipline of political science, and LGBTQ+ historical scholarship. Most notably, feminist scholarship grounds the analysis within this book, while also informing my own sense of feminist praxis.[68] Security studies from the discipline of political science frame my discussion of anti-LGBTQ+ policies in both the DADT and present periods, showcasing the importance of this burgeoning area of research. Most importantly, this chapter discusses the range of LGBTQ+ historical research that informs the project's framework and the resulting analysis. It first explores the history surrounding the development of queer identities in the early twentieth century, as noted by Chauncey, and then seeks to conceptualize some of the broader histories of the LGBTQ+ community's relationship with the military and intelligence community since World War I.[69] This portion of chapter 1 provides a broad overview of

LGBTQ+ military history and also addresses key points regarding language (such as the advent of the terms *heterosexual* and *homosexual*). The chapter builds the framework necessary for understanding my argument regarding the evolution of rationales and policies concerning LGBTQ+ within the military and intelligence community. It concludes with a more detailed discussion about some of the methodological innovation present within this book.

Chapters 2, 3, 4, and 5 are focused on answering the research questions for this book, analyzing the six periods noted above. In these chapters, I demonstrate how the rationales for banning LGBTQ+ people from the American military and intelligence community (the Department of State [DoS] and the CIA in particular) have undergone distinct shifts in these six periods. I also examine the major policy development that accompanied each period, using qualitative data from a variety of primary and secondary source material. Across these chapters, I provide clear evidence of each rationale for the aforementioned periodization and explain the major developments in these rationales and policies from World War I to the present. Specifically, chapter 2 focuses on (1) the ways queer men—as well as those presumed to be queer men—were specifically identified as sexually immoral and unfit for service in World War I and (2) the major shifts to conceptualizing LGBQ people as simultaneously mentally ill and physically unable to serve in World War II. Chapter 3 examines the early Cold War rationale that claimed that LGBQ people might be untrustworthy or susceptible to blackmail by Soviet counteragents. In this chapter, I also show how this governmental policy transitioned to a conceptualization of the broader LGBTQ+ community as mentally unstable in the late Cold War. Following this chronology, chapter 4 examines the DADT period, and chapter 5 focuses on the present period. The rationale during the former period was the claim that LGBQ inclusion in the military, including DoD-adjacent positions in the intelligence community (i.e., active duty positions within the National Security Agency [NSA] and elsewhere), was a threat to both unit cohesion and privacy; in the latter period, the focus is largely on continued restrictions—in a post-DADT military—on transgender service members, as well as others such as non-binary and intersex people. In my discussion of the transgender community in the present period, I analyze the ebb and flow of transgender inclusion in the military and DoD-adjacent positions in the intelligence community across the Obama, Trump, and Biden administrations, though the debate around open transgender military service has continued into the second Trump administration.

The conclusion summarizes my principal argument and underscores this book's significance for a variety of fields, including feminist scholarship, security studies, LGBTQ+ studies, and political science. It also highlights potential areas for future research that may be in conversation with this work, while acknowledging some of the growth within the broader discipline of political science. Finally, the conclusion addresses some of the anticipated future challenges facing transgender people in the armed forces.

1

RESEARCHING WITH INTERDISCIPLINARY FRAMEWORKS

WHO CARES?

This chapter focuses explicitly on the interdisciplinary frameworks that inform the research for this book. As many readers of academic books are aware, it is sometimes the norm for the authors of such books to skip a chapter such as this one. However, I cannot imagine writing this book without a chapter like this. This project—which has been in my life in some way for the past decade—is made possible by the work of so many other scholars who have laid the foundations for this book. Additionally, this book's significance lies partly in that it bridges gaps between existing and currently discrete secondary source material on the topic of anti-LGBTQ+ policies in the American military and intelligence community. With that in mind, this chapter acknowledges these scholars and their work while also building the interdisciplinary framework for the analysis and scholarly gap-bridging within the remainder of this book. The purpose of this chapter is thus twofold. First, it introduces the most important source material that informs the three interdisciplinary frameworks for this book. Second, it showcases where my book fits into existing scholarship related to LGBTQ+ historical research.

Despite my affinity for this chapter, I understand that it might not be of interest to every reader, but I do imagine that it will be of interest to most readers. This is especially true for those interested in history related to the broader LGBTQ+ community, and you likely fall into this category if you are holding this particular book. This chapter establishes the key secondary sources that inform this book and recognizes the important work of scholars, especially queer and transgender ones, who are engaged in the work of historical research related to the broader LGBTQ+ community. As such, I view the content of this chapter as particularly valuable to understanding both the interdisciplinary framework used throughout the book and the broader literature within which this book exists.

THE THREE INTERDISCIPLINARY FRAMEWORKS

As noted in the introduction, this book uses a framework drawn from three specific areas of academic inquiry: (1) feminist scholarship, (2) security studies scholarship, and (3) LGBTQ+ historical scholarship. In this chapter, I explore the contributions of these three areas of inquiry and discuss how they influence this book's framework and analysis. Regarding feminist scholarship, this area of inquiry is especially helpful, since I often feel that my scholarly home is in women's, gender, and sexuality studies, rather than political science. Political science, as previously suggested, has not historically been the most hospitable space for LGBTQ+ focused research, and most of my work explicitly focuses on that community. In terms of security studies, this field helps to frame my question, since it is inherently focused on how queer and transgender people have been presumed to be "security threats" to the American military and intelligence community. Finally, LGBTQ+ historical scholarship is important for obvious reasons, and throughout this chapter, I will discuss the ways in which my work fills gaps in the existing scholarship that sets the broader framework for this book.

FEMINIST SCHOLARSHIP

A major component of this book, especially in relation to its project design, draws upon feminist scholarship. As most readers of this book are likely aware, scholarship that is grounded in feminist analysis seeks to understand the importance of sex, gender identity, gender expression, sexuality, and other intersectional identities; obviously, this book has the same aim in its analysis of anti-LGBTQ+ policy development in the American military and intelligence community. This book is also a piece of feminist scholarship for a reason beyond its topical inquiry, especially since it is directly informed by Mary Hawkesworth's writings about a feminist research ethic.[1] In this discussion of the feminist framework for this book, I note both how my work fits into the large scope of feminist scholarship and how it is informed by such a feminist research ethic.

As a brief overview, Hawkesworth's *Feminist Inquiry: From Political Conviction to Methodological Innovation* traces feminist epistemological development. She also discusses problems historically faced by feminist scholarship and the methodological innovations used to overcome such problems. Of critical importance to this book is Hawkesworth's discussion of "evidence blindness," since some people are reluctant to accept the vibrant history of the broader LGBTQ+ community as valid or factual.[2] Hawkesworth defines evidence blindness as a phenomenon that occurs when, "despite ... compelling evidence to support feminist arguments," people refute "evidence that impugns their own beliefs."[3] Hawkesworth discusses the competing reasons for such evidence blindness, but the overarching point to keep in mind is that many feminist scholars—especially women of color, queer women, and/or transgender women—deal with this reaction to their work, writing, and expertise.[4]

Since this book is focused on analyzing the anti-LGBTQ+ policies of the American military and intelligence community, I expect that such evidence blindness could potentially affect some readers. However, I also imagine that such people are not very likely to reach for this book, especially given current attempts to censor LGBTQ+ focused content from institutions ranging from local libraries to military academies.[5] Though I may not be able to point to what manifestations of evidence blindness might plague any given reader of my work, Hawkesworth points to "sanctioned ignorance" and "invisibility" as two broad symptoms of this phenomenon.[6] She describes the former as "blind spots" that are "constructed by cultural beliefs" and the latter as a form of "social amnesia."[7] According to Hawkesworth, feminist scholarship must remain aware of the phenomenon of evidence blindness, which I recognize may affect my project by way of both sanctioned ignorance and invisibility.[8]

Regarding sanctioned ignorance, many people still report being unsure about the origins of "homosexuality," which may indicate a fair amount of confusion about sexuality and its role throughout history.[9] Only a decade ago, Gallup's Values and Beliefs poll found that 37 percent of Americans still believed that homosexuality was environmental (that is, caused by environmental factors like upbringing).[10] This suggests that a fair number of Americans may lack general knowledge about the community, which may further indicate that they are (1) less inclined to believe that LGBTQ+ people existed in the past and (2) more inclined to believe that LGBTQ+ people are simply a by-product of our contemporary culture.[11] This is a particular concern for my project, given that so many people are unfamiliar with LGBTQ+ history broadly defined. As noted in the introduction, a major issue for those working with LGBTQ+ history is that it is often erased, "misremembered," destroyed, or simply not recorded at all.[12] This lack of knowledge about LGBTQ+ history and the broader LGBTQ+ community is important, because the claim about invisibility by way of social amnesia could manifest as a form of evidence blindness in the mind of the reader. Alongside the censorship issues previously noted, a growing number of states are implementing school curricula that move toward including more LGBTQ+ history.[13] While it is thus possible that evidence blindness may not be as much of a concern for readers in the future, it is something that I heed, as Hawkesworth suggests.

While confronting potential evidence blindness, this book also uses a feminist framework to inform both why and how my project is produced. Earlier scholarship on feminist research, such as Liz Stanley and Sue Wise's *Breaking Out Again: Feminist Ontology and Epistemology*, focuses on feminist research's ability to draw attention to women's experiences, thereby making a "previously untapped store of knowledge" accessible.[14] While my book does not focus on the experiences only of women, it does engage in the act of "feminist consciousness raising"—as Stanley and Wise call it—around the topic of sexuality, gender identity, and history.[15] In addition to raising awareness about the rich history of LGBTQ+ people who have been excluded from the military and intelligence community since World War I, this project also has implications for understanding some of the challenges facing the lived experiences of those excluded by these discriminatory, exclusionary policies. This notion of "lived experience," as noted by Sharlene Hesse-Biber, is a key element of feminist research.[16] International relations scholars, such as Christine Sylvester in *War as Experience: Contributions from International Relations and Feminist Analysis*, note that a focus on war as experience characterizes a growing body of research within both feminist and international relations research.[17] While this book does not directly address the specific lived experiences of individuals, it does lay some important groundwork that can marry historical narratives of individual people's experiences with the broader systemic discrimination that LGBTQ+ people have faced as a result of the policies analyzed throughout this book, and where possible, I attempt to refer the reader to scholarship that does focus on those individualized narratives.

This book contributes to a rich body of literature that seeks to understand the history of discrimination against LGBTQ+ people in the military and intelligence community. Throughout this process, I retain an informed feminist research ethic; as noted by Brooke Ackerly and Jacqui True, "a feminist research ethic is a commitment to inquiry about how we inquire."[18] It is a particular commitment to the goals and practice of the process of inquiry. This commitment and process of ensuring quality research, conducted with a feminist lens of analysis, also affects the act of inquiry. A feminist research ethic requires the researcher to pay particular attention to "the power . . . of epistemology," "boundaries . . . and intersections," "relationships and . . . power differentials," and "your own sociopolitical location."[19] I have taken this into account throughout the process of researching and writing this book, and it is important to remember that the use of a feminist framework requires such an understanding of research practice and ethics. While this is not always at the foreground, each chapter is carefully set within this overarching feminist framework.

Ackerly and True's mention of the researcher's own identity and location within society is also important to address. As shared in the introduction to this book, I am a queer, transgender woman, and my own identity within the broader LGBTQ+ community—along with growing up in a community adjacent to a large military base (Fort Moore, formerly known as Fort Benning)—informs part of my lived experience. Interestingly, the research for this project originally developed during my graduate school days, prior to my coming out as transgender.[20] While many academic books do not spend time acknowledging the identity of the author, this book implements a feminist research ethic and uses a feminist framework throughout. Therefore, it is important to acknowledge that my own identity and lived experience shape a variety of concerns, ranging from why I am interested in the topic to how I approach the research and what I hope readers will gain by reading the book. This feminist research ethic mandates that I acknowledge my own identity, while also considering how it may affect how I undertake my work. In short, my identity and lived experience affect my research and (to some degree) the reader's experience with this book, and I hope that this transparency in recognizing my feminist positionality in relation to this topic and project is beneficial.

Finally, feminist research and scholarship are important to developing the framework used in the book. While this book is very much a work of political science, it is primarily situated in a discipline that—as Helene Silverberg pointed out more than three decades ago—has not seen the impact of feminist scholarship at the same rate as in other disciplines.[21] Political science, while now more attuned to recognizing feminist scholarship, still fails on many accounts to engage meaningful and productive discussions about sexuality and politics, as noted by numerous other scholars.[22] The importance of feminist scholarship to this project ensures that I recognize that it is a piece of interdisciplinary scholarship that (1) remains rooted in other fields of study like security studies and LGBTQ+ studies and (2) grounds itself simultaneously in a feminist research ethic.

SECURITY STUDIES SCHOLARSHIP

A great deal of the relevant security studies scholarship used here stems from the work of Aaron Belkin, as noted in the introduction.[23] Belkin was the head of the Palm Center, one of the leading research groups that investigated public policy issues pertaining to the military and service of people of diverse genders and sexualities. Because of his expansive and long-standing research on "Don't Ask, Don't Tell" (DADT), Belkin's work is critical to informing this project's scope, as well as its addition to the scholarship of the field of security studies.[24] While other pieces of interest are discussed both in this section and in the forthcoming chapters, Belkin's work is an important reminder that a great deal of security studies scholarship has not focused specifically on LGBTQ+ topics, which further emphasizes the importance of this book project for the area of security studies scholarship. Here, I provide an overview of key pieces of scholarship from Belkin as they inform the security studies framework used throughout this book (most notably in my analysis and discussion of both the DADT period and the present period).

Belkin's article "The Pentagon's Gay Ban Is Not Based on Military Necessity" clarifies that DADT, as a policy, was born out of a compromise between President Bill Clinton and the U.S. Congress. In this article, Belkin analyzes many of what he claims are fallacious assumptions pertaining to the policy of forbidding queer people to serve openly. He argues that the policy is not based on necessity, because there is minimal evidence to suggest that inclusion would undermine the military's broader objectives of unit cohesion. Most importantly, Belkin cites four negative costs associated with the policy. First, he argues that the policy is too expensive, citing that (at the time of his writing) the Pentagon spent an estimated "$130 million in lost training." Second, he notes that the military suffers a "brain drain and talent loss" because of the policy's exclusion of people of diverse sexualities. Third, he cites the "psychological scars" on discharged members that create issues for them and the broader society. Finally, he notes some indications that the policy perpetuates or "leads to violence against women" in the ranks.[25] This article is important for understanding the social and political arguments against DADT.

In a subsequent article, Aaron Belkin and Melissa Levitt examined the Israeli Defense Forces (IDF), an early adopter of queer inclusion policies, to understand whether inclusion affected unit cohesion.[26] They chose to specifically analyze the IDF because of the "high-stakes security context" in which it operates.[27] In fact, they found no "data indicating that lifting the ban" had in any way "undermined Israeli military performance, cohesion, readiness, or morale," which are often cited as areas of concern regarding the inclusion of diverse populations in the ranks.[28] In analyzing how integration of the military may have affected preparedness, they found that, despite rhetoric citing a security threat to combat readiness, inclusion may actually "bolster the core Israeli value of common defense."[29] Within security studies scholarship, this article is important in considering LGBTQ+ inclusion in military settings beyond the American context.

Another article, "A Modest Proposal: Privacy as a Flawed Rationale for the Exclusion of Gays and Lesbians from the U.S. Military," examines a secondary vehicle for rationalizing exclusion—privacy.[30] In this article, Belkin and Melissa Embser-Herbert address the claim that the privacy of straight soldiers would be undermined if DADT was lifted. They note that the privacy rationale rests on two assumptions: first, "that service members should have ... partial control over the exposure of their bodies" while serving in the military and, second, that a nude body of the same sex or gender necessarily "arouses sexual desire" in queer service members.[31] Noting that the privacy rationale is primarily rooted in the assumption of the "predatory homosexual," Belkin and Embser-Herbert point out five flaws in this particular rationale: (1) straight service members are already in intimate spaces with queer people; (2) "lifting the ban will not increase sexual disclosures" within the ranks; (3) few straight people "are extremely uncomfortable" around queer people to such an intense degree; (4) using "the analogy to men and women" showering together is an *ad absurdum* argument at best; and (5) "lifting the ban" may actually "enhance heterosexual privacy" to some degree.[32] This article underscores the logical problems with arguing in favor of DADT, and the analysis is helpful in a broader sense within the context of security studies.

After examining many of the rationales for exclusion under DADT, Belkin returns, in an article in *Parameters: U.S. Army War College Quarterly*, to the question of whether the ban is actually based on necessity.[33] Referring to the then-current policy as "an imperfect solution," he reiterates that the major rationale for the policy was unit cohesion.[34] In this study, Belkin expands the argument from the earlier Belkin and Levitt article that the lifting of the military ban in Israel, Australia, Canada, and Britain had "no impact" on unit cohesion.[35] He suggests that an inclusive policy that allows queer service members to serve openly with their straight peers emphasizes "equal standards and an emphasis on conduct." His broader claim is that an inclusive policy may actually ensure that all service members are "held . . . to the same standards," providing anecdotal evidence that it could prove beneficial in a number of other ways too.[36] Overall, this article remains useful for the security studies framework of this project, representing the overarching argument held by many opponents of anti-LGBTQ+ military policies, particularly in the DADT and present periods.

Belkin has produced other pieces of scholarship that are crucial to informing the security studies framework that this book uses, particularly in the chapter focusing on the DADT and present periods. For instance, a 2007 article focuses on the question of whether lifting DADT would undermine the military and its reputation in any way. Based on his previous scholarship, Belkin argues that the policy of excluding queer people from serving openly is what actually harms the reputation of the military. As in other articles from earlier in the 2000s, Belkin provides a laundry list of reasons: (1) the policy of excluding queer people "is inconsistent with public opinion"; (2) it encourages criticism from the media and generates "almost no favorable media coverage" for the armed forces; (3) it "provides a vehicle for antimilitary protesters to portray military culture" in a negative light and in conflict with "widely accepted civilian values" and attitudes; and (4) the policy is largely "inconsistent with the views of junior enlisted service members" who actively defend our country. This article, produced at a time when a larger segment of the American public was beginning to show broader support for LGBTQ+ rights, also tacitly poses the question of whether the military's values should coincide with the values of the American public.[37]

Finally, Belkin's scholarship offers one more major contribution to the scope of this book and the security studies framework that it uses. Belkin's post-DADT book, *How We Won: Progressive Lessons from the Repeal of "Don't Ask, Don't Tell,"* visits the question of what the repeal did for the military, the American public, and the LGBTQ+ community in particular. This text speaks to the strategy that activists and academics undertook in challenging DADT in the late 2000s and early 2010s. Belkin provides a strong overview of the five-pronged strategy to defeat the exclusionary policy: dispelling misinformation that was often perpetuated by conservatives; demanding higher quality research, such as the research produced by RAND in 1993; finding people who could validate the findings and arguments for inclusion; building momentum toward a more inclusive military; and exposing hypocritical comments and opinions that did not actually have the military's well-being in mind.[38] After a rich discussion of what this five-pronged approach looked like in practice, Belkin discusses the moments leading up to the eventual passage of the "Don't Ask, Don't Tell" Repeal Act of 2010.[39] This book clearly supports the security studies framework integrated throughout this text while also providing helpful analysis for the discussion of DADT and its eventual repeal.

While Belkin's work is the most useful in establishing the integrated frame of security studies scholarship, my work, which builds upon his work and that of others within the area of study, is itself a piece of security studies scholarship. Specifically, this book uses this framework—along with feminism and LGBTQ+ historical scholarship—to place itself in conversation with these fields of scholarship. This book reiterates the importance of Belkin's body of work and certainly draws upon it, but it also places itself at a new intersection of security studies and LGBTQ+ studies by incorporating historical scholarship for the broader analysis of the aforementioned periods of analysis. The American political development (APD) methodological framework also brings a fresh approach to studying this topic within the area of security studies. Additionally, this book begins a very timely discussion on the contemporary state of transgender, non-binary, and intersex inclusion and exclusion in the military, which is an area of focus that Belkin's body of research does not generally seek to understand.[40] At the same time, this book certainly acknowledges the work of Belkin, in addition to the activism of the broader LGBTQ+ community, as it seeks to understand both the historical development of the policy of exclusion and the contemporary issues surrounding it. It is important to note how important these elements are in using this security studies framework, especially for the analysis related to the DADT and present periods. As with the feminist framework, the use of this security studies framework is integrated and applied throughout each chapter, though it may seem more or less apparent to the reader at various points throughout the book.

LGBTQ+ STUDIES AND HISTORICAL SCHOLARSHIP

Given my work to bridge gaps between various discrete secondary scholarship related to LGBTQ+ studies and history, this is the largest body of literature integrated into this book's broader framework and related analysis. In discussing LGBTQ+ historical scholarship, I touch on the major pieces of scholarship that help to inform the framework of this research. I mention the significance of each source to this project, while also discussing how this book builds upon the current body of LGBTQ+ historical literature. Though not speaking to every aspect of scholarship pertaining to LGBTQ+ history, I introduce many of the foremost scholars working within the focus area of queer military history. I note these scholars' major contributions to this interdisciplinary area of LGBTQ+ historical scholarship and implicitly highlight how my work situates itself within this unique body of existing scholarship.

Given the chronological nature of this book, the more substantive chapters—those that focus on the analysis of anti-LGBTQ+ policies within the American military and intelligence community—begin with an analysis of such policies during World War I. As described in the next chapter, these early policies largely targeted and affected gay men, including those presumed to be gay men. While the stigmatization of gay men in this period would later be linked to the issue of national security, the formal rise of the "national security state" did not occur until after World War II. However, William Walker's *National Security and Core Values in American History* advances the argument that America underwent a developmental phase of a "proto-national security state" throughout the Gilded Age (the late 1870s to roughly 1900, or between the Reconstruction and Progressive Eras of American history).[41] In making this argument, Walker also claims that President Theodore Roosevelt's "civilization" projects in the late 1890s to early 1900s rapidly became associated with "the preservation and projection of core values" of the nation-state.[42] Throughout this period of settler colonial projects in Puerto Rico, the Philippines, and other island nations, the dominance of the American military, Walker argues, soon began the construction of a national security state, initiated in part by the augmentation of Roosevelt's own presidential power.[43] This period defines key values related to the

American nation-state while setting the stage for the emergence of a national security state in the twentieth century.

Walker further traces the early development of the eventual national security state to the administration of President Woodrow Wilson, focusing on numerous sociopolitical issues as they intersected with concerns of what would now be understood as "national security."[44] Of these, Walker emphasizes the importance of the Espionage Act of 1917, which limited free speech; in doing so, he notes that this particular law was seen as a crucial consolidation of power to support the state's wartime efforts.[45] During this period, the American government also documented several concerns over the possibility of a communist uprising in America, especially following the Bolshevik Revolution in Russia.[46] There was even fear of a domestic communist uprising by people of color. Such concerns caused the officials at the U.S. Army War College to draw up "War Plan White" to prepare for "presumed disloyalty, especially among African Americans and ethnic Americans" who may have been exposed to "communist ideology" and Bolshevism during their time overseas.[47] This example demonstrates how identity—specifically, the intersections of class and race—began to shape concerns around national security.

Walker's contribution provides an important backstory to the beginning of my research and the broader framework for this book, as it demonstrates that national security has long been a concern for the American state. Rather than conceptualizing national security as a phenomenon that simply arose during the aftermath of World War II, Walker's scholarship suggests that it began to develop well before then. This is a useful insight, given that many presume the explicit codification of such policies, via the National Security Act of 1947, occurred only from the mid-twentieth century onward.[48] Other scholars who have explored the early roots of national security policy in American politics reiterate this understanding. For instance, Alan Brinkley examines how states rely on crises to pursue their own interests in the name of national security.[49] Daniel Farber builds upon this scholarship by examining the aforementioned Espionage Act of 1917, as well as the Sedition Act of 1918.[50] The latter of these acts essentially "made it a crime to insult the government . . . or the military," which then had a chilling effect on civil liberties.[51] Other scholars, such as Jan Lewis, date this conception of national security to an earlier period, as similar limitations on civil liberties in the interest of security were undertaken before and during the American Civil War.[52] This discussion, then, allows us to understand that an interest in national security policies was prevalent before and throughout World War I. Thus, the importance of national security—despite the lack of vocal "national security rhetoric" commonly employed in post-9/11 America—before and during World War I underscores this connection to other works relating to LGBTQ+ historical scholarship.

George Chauncey's article "Christian Brotherhood or Sexual Perversion? Homosexual Identities and the Construction of Sexual Boundaries in the World War One Era" provides important insights about how queer sexualities, broadly defined, were understood during the World War I period. According to Chauncey, disagreement existed about who might be labeled queer, even if it was known that two men had engaged in a sexual relationship.[53] The notion of a diverse or "queer" sexuality often relied not on "the extent of" one's "homosexual activity, but" rather on "the gender role he assumed" in a sexual relationship.[54] In other words, being "queer" was largely defined by top and bottom dynamics within the bedroom: "tops" (the person or people doing the penetrating) were not necessarily queer, while "bottoms" (the person or people being penetrated) almost certainly were queer.[55] Chauncey notes that this idea is of critical importance in relation to the military, as many people in the World War I era had "at least heard of 'fairies,'" but "military mobilization" during the era "increased the chances that" people might "encounter gay-identified men and be able to explore new sexual possibilities" and relationships with them.[56] Decades later, Margot Canaday builds upon Chauncey's argument and reiterates that sexuality was "defined . . . in terms of gender" roles in the sex act, rather than "in terms of sexual-object choice."[57]

Margot Canaday, who builds upon and expands Chauncey's arguments from the mid-1980s, mentions that "historians have usually treated World War II" as the point "when the military 'uncovered' sexual perversion" and queer identities in the ranks; however, she notes that this history takes place much earlier, in World War I.[58] Canaday highlights the importance of vice reports during this era of military history and argues that the logic of maintaining morality in the ranks was what "brought the issue of sex perversion," or the taking on of a same-sex sexual relationship, to the forefront.[59] Canaday explores the history of the military, draft boards, and medical boards in shaping who might or might not be fit for military service. She demonstrates that, by March 1918, these boards were provided with revised instructions halting people with a "psychopathic character . . . from the service," and that same guidance also included information on "sex perverts" and "homosexual" people.[60] These instructions were published and disseminated, so that the boards would understand what physical features or phenotypes they might need to look out for; the intent was to be able to identify, based on the presence or absence of such physical features, people who were unfit for service.[61] Canaday, thus, provides a rarely told history demonstrating that the codification of anti-LGBTQ+ policies really began during the period of World War I, one born out of a concern for vice in the ranks.

Building upon the research conducted by both Chauncey and Canaday, Sherry Zane provides an account of the actions of a vice squad at a naval training station in Rhode Island during World War I. Zane's work argues that espionage and sedition laws during World War I were of key importance to furthering anti-LGBTQ+ actions.[62] These laws allowed—and even indirectly encouraged—covert operations to detain and arrest persons suspected of "homosexuality," since sex "'perverts" threatened the Navy's ability to win the war."[63] Canaday demonstrates the importance of vice reports during this period, but Zane goes a step further, demonstrating the actual practice of what vice reporting and the criminalization of queer identities looked like during World War I. In Zane's work, the concept of national security is central to the core argument, since "wartime sedition and espionage laws were still in effect" shortly after the war, which then enabled the Department of Justice (DoJ) to use them "as justification for silencing any opposition to American national security." Policies based on these laws and the designation of a queer identity as incompatible with service would then assist in codifying "consensual 'sodomy'" as a criminal act "under the Articles of War in 1920."[64] Ultimately, the arguments made in these pieces of scholarship help to establish the frame for my analysis of the World War I period, providing important information about the construction of queer identities and enabling me to analyze such identity development concurrently with the evolution of anti-LGBTQ+ national security policy during this period.

While both Canaday and Zane offer important contributions that shape this book and the framework that it employs throughout the coming chapters, their works are also in conversation with an even more seminal text, Chauncey's *Gay New York: Gender, Urban Culture, and the Making of the Gay Male World, 1890–1940*.[65] In this groundbreaking book about the development of queer identities in pre–World War II America, Chauncey seeks to dispel "the myths of isolation, invisibility, and internalization" that are so often placed upon gay male identities.[66] Explaining the affluent gay male subculture that existed prior to the advent of the LGBTQ+ rights movement of the 1960s and today, Chauncey's work demonstrates that gay male identities are not something new; rather, a history of "everyday resistance" and existence was practiced by gay men during the early twentieth century.[67] Zooming out for a larger picture, Chauncey's book demonstrates that gay male life was not actually invisible but merely "less visible" and often disappeared from history simply because "nobody looked for it" in the historical record.[68] His work begins with an explanation of the etymology of words like *gay* and *queer*, which I discuss in more detail in the next chapter. More importantly, Chauncey seeks to understand the ways that urbanization throughout this period of time and mobilization, particularly during World War I, helped to shape the gay male identity, even though this history has often undergone a process of misremembrance and erasure.[69]

All of the aforementioned authors provide important insights into understanding the construction of anti-LGBTQ+ military policies during World War I, and all have assisted in shaping the historical framework for this project, especially in terms of understanding national security policy as something that developed well before World War II. Canaday and Zane demonstrate the investment that the military had in screening potential recruits for problematic behavior and sexual vices, such as "homosexuality."[70] Their research helps to further advance arguments made by Chauncey, whose research demonstrates the ways in which the gay male identity was constructed during World War I. His earlier work allows us to understand who might be conceived of as a "sex pervert" unfit for service during this period, and his later research demonstrates the ways in which the gay male identity was constructed in post–World War I America, particularly through urbanization and the increased likelihood of men's bodies being in closer quarters. Chauncey's broader work on the construction of the gay male identity throughout this period remains integral to the framework of this book, especially considering the military's codification of anti-LGBTQ+ policies in the Articles of War in 1920.[71]

Each of these scholars contributed an important element to the discussion about what discrimination against members of the LGBTQ+ community, particularly queer men, looked like during World War I. They also set the stage for key developments that shaped the ways in which the military codified exclusionary, discriminatory policies throughout World War II. While my work builds upon the work of these scholars, I also connect their scholarship to the broader tracing of such anti-LGBTQ+ policies into the twenty-first century. Following World War I, some historical events of the interwar period, though not of direct interest to this book's analysis of anti-LGBTQ+ military and intelligence community policy, are worth mentioning. Notably, Robert Beachy's *Gay Berlin: Birthplace of a Modern Identity* argues that the conceptualization of a "fixed sexual orientation" was a particularly Berlin-based phenomenon, for a number of reasons. Beachy provides evidence to suggest that the construction of "homosexual" and "transsexual" identities as a category occurred from the late nineteenth century through the fall of Germany's Weimar Republic in the 1930s.[72] Using a trove of historical data, Beachy argues that the advent of such identity labels was actually a product of (1) the Berlin medical/scientific community and (2) a Berlin activist community that consisted of people of diverse genders and sexualities.[73]

Clearly responding to Chauncey's work, Beachy argues that certain words, such as *homosexual* and *transsexual*, were most widely used in Germany, where they were actually coined. He then traces the intersections of the medical/scientific community in Berlin, which, in coordination with a number of proto-LGBTQ+ activist groups, managed to create socially progressive spaces in Berlin, despite the formal codification of anti-LGBTQ+ policies. Beachy's work, while not in the context of the American military, provides a rich history of relevant terminology, which is of interest to the scope of this project and the period of time being analyzed. Similarly, Beachy's claim that a 1907 sex scandal in the court of Kaiser Wilhelm II injected the idea of diverse sexualities into the public discourse also parallels the public dialogues following the American sex scandal discussed in Zane's work. Beachy's scholarship adds nuance to the broader discussion of language and identity throughout early-twentieth-century history, which is of direct significance to this book's discussion of the World War I period in particular. For that reason, Beachy's work, in addition to helping provide the framework for this book's analysis of the World War I period, also has a place in the following chapter.

Regarding LGBTQ+ historical scholarship about the World War II period, this book's framework is most directly informed by Allan Berube's *Coming Out Under Fire: The History of Gay Men and Women in World War II*. Berube's work is the product of both archival research and primary data via in-person interviews; in it, he argues that World War II marks the moment where the military began its active discrimination against queer people. Berube uses in-person interviews to explore the human experience of these anti-LGBTQ+ policies, a method this book does not employ, yet such work is crucial to understanding the real-world impact of these policies on service members and veterans. Berube also seeks to understand how the military institutionalized its exclusionary policies, which is more closely akin to the work undertaken in this book.[74] Throughout this process, Berube explores the importance of the military's increasingly common use of psychiatry as a way to reinforce formal policies that excluded queer men in particular.[75] Berube also notes a shift in the conceptualization of "homosexuality" as an act; during this period, it was viewed more specifically as a mental illness rather than simply a criminal activity. Arthur Dong's documentary adaptation of *Coming Out Under Fire*, which was cowritten by Berube, speaks to this change and further reiterates its impact on the human experience, particularly in the lives of the queer veterans interviewed.[76] Both the original book and the companion film demonstrate the invasive and dehumanizing nature of the screening process, which Canaday also discusses; this process included looking for phenotypes or physical traits to "identify" queer men in particular.[77]

Building on a framework that is informed by Berube's book, the framework used here is also partially informed by Lillian Faderman's *Odd Girls and Twilight Lovers: A History of Lesbian Life in Twentieth-Century*

America, which is the most comprehensive historical text about lesbian American history.[78] While Faderman's research seeks to understand the broader history of the lesbian experience throughout the entire twentieth century, her discussion of World War II offers some specific points about the impact of anti-LGBTQ+ military policies and their impacts on lesbian women specifically. In fact, Faderman makes a similar argument to Chauncey's in her analysis of World War II, noting that the military—particularly through the development of the Women's Army Corp (WAC; originally named the Women's Army Auxiliary Corps, or WAAC)—brought more women into the military, put them in closer contact with one another, and actually may have encouraged connections between lesbian women.[79] Further, Faderman's book explores how the military's policies affected lesbian subculture, especially the "formation and development of a distinctive lesbian 'style'" and aesthetic both during and after the war.[80] While the development of a "butch" lesbian style is not of direct interest to the research goals of this book, this is useful to note, given the broader impact of these policies on the queer community. Moreover, this is a compelling history that exists at the intersections of queer studies, American history, American studies, and fashion studies, among other areas of inquiry.

As a reminder, the overarching goal of this book is to analyze the development of anti-LGBTQ+ policies in the American military and intelligence community over time; in line with this goal, this book's framework is also informed by other portions of Faderman's book, such as her discussion of lesbian women's experiences during the early Cold War. Faderman, in her analysis of this period, discusses the concerns that many government officials had with "homosexual" people, who were often viewed as threats to American society and its values. This would later be linked to communism and other types of "un-American" activities, and Faderman briefly traces the development of a key executive order, Executive Order 10450, signed by President Dwight D. Eisenhower in 1953.[81] This portion of her book helps to inform my early discussion of this period. As noted by other scholars, Executive Order 10450 was meant to root out another "domestic enemy...—homosexuals."[82] While others have discussed portions of the history of Executive Order 10450, my book's framework for this discussion is more directly informed by David Johnson's *The Lavender Scare: The Cold War Persecution of*

Gays and Lesbians in the Federal Government.[83] With regard to the early Cold War period, I utilize a variety of other primary and secondary sources to frame my understanding, analysis, and discussion of this period, along with its indirect influence on presumptions of gender and LGBTQ+ identities.[84] Even so, this book's framework and discussion of this period is most actively informed by Johnson's scholarship on the exclusion of LGBTQ+ people from the intelligence community during the early Cold War.

Johnson's work focuses on the so-called Lavender Scare of the early 1950s, which was when "homosexuality first became a national political issue," noting that "members of Congress were calling for investigations" by spring 1950.[85] While a great deal of the language throughout the initial hearings was coded and implied, it would soon become evident that the hearings on the Lavender Scare were intended to root out whatever un-American persons were supposedly working for the Department of State (DoS). Johnson suggests that the hearings were actually political theater, initially aimed at embarrassing the DoS and, by extension, the entire Truman administration, though the impact of these hearings would extend into the Eisenhower administration as well.[86] At the start of the Lavender Scare, ninety-one "homosexual" people were fired from the DoS, leading to a greater politicization of anti-queer rhetoric and a "heightened concern about internal security."[87] Johnson focuses on the developments leading up to and during the Lavender Scare, from its roots in 1947 to its implications in the 1950s, such as Eisenhower's signing of Executive Order 10450 in 1953. Johnson's research is crucial for this book's framework and analysis because of (1) how it traces the development of the Lavender Scare and (2) how it describes the development of anti-LGBTQ+ paranoia as moving "beyond partisan rhetoric to ... part of standard, government-wide policy."[88] Johnson, thus, provides a key piece of scholarship for those interested in examining the intersections of security studies, historical scholarship, and LGBTQ+ studies. His work helps to develop this book's framework for analyzing anti-LGBTQ+ military and intelligence community policy during the early Cold War period; it also helps to inform the subsequent discussion of late Cold War policy, which was ultimately affected by the events of the Lavender Scare in the 1950s.[89]

In addition to Johnson's scholarship, other texts that help to inform the framework used in my analysis of both the early and late Cold War periods include Douglas Charles's *Hoover's War on Gays: Exposing the FBI's "Sex Deviates" Program*. Charles examines the ways in which the Federal Bureau of Investigation (FBI) and DoJ were involved with anti-LGBTQ+ policies and monitoring from World War II to the Nixon administration; this work is especially useful in better understanding what policy shifts were occurring in the intelligence community during this time.[90] While I do not directly analyze the internal policies of domestic intelligence monitoring agencies like the FBI (as compared to foreign intelligence monitoring agencies like the Central Intelligence Agency [CIA]), Charles's historical tracing of the FBI's investment in anti-LGBTQ+ tracking, surveillance, and monitoring is useful, particularly since it demonstrates the pervasiveness of national security concerns targeting the broader LGBTQ+ community. Charles also contributes a unique perspective to my project in that he directly examines the involvement of the FBI during the Lavender Scare, something with which Johnson does not engage as deeply; as such, his work is beneficial to my framework and research, even though it is not as actively engaged as that of other scholars.[91] Charles also offers unique insights into some of the broader themes of the early Cold War in particular. Other texts, such as Walter Frank's *Law and the Gay Rights Story: The Long Search for Equal Justice in a Divided Democracy*, also mention the FBI's role in anti-LGBTQ+ activities, and such works are also employed by this book.[92] However, Charles's research on the intertwined histories of the FBI and the broader LGBTQ+ community provides some of the most useful supplementary information to help inform this book's framework and analysis of such policies during the early Cold War period.

In crafting my framework of analysis for the late Cold War, I largely draw upon primary source documents from governmental offices and agencies, since there is not a large body of scholarship related to this period. But as noted earlier, I also utilize secondary source material when relevant and possible. While there are not as many major scholarly works dealing with LGBTQ+ exclusion from the military and intelligence community during the late Cold War period, Randy Shilts's *Conduct Unbecoming: Gays and Lesbians in the U.S. Military* does prove helpful in informing my analysis and discussion of this period and the succeeding DADT period.[93] Many people of a certain age within the broader LGBTQ+ community are familiar with Shilts and his various works, but for those who are not, Shilts discusses the personal narratives of queer service members, while also highlighting key aspects of military history in relation to the exclusion of queer people in the armed forces. Though these personal narratives do not fall within the broader scope of this book, they offer helpful insight to the reader, especially given the lack of other relevant scholarship to the late Cold War period. Ultimately, my discussion of this period relies on primary source material more than the other periods, because of the lack of secondary source research.

Unsurprisingly, LGBTQ+ historical scholarship is an important part of this book's analytical framework, but unlike the feminist and security studies components, this is much more obviously on display to the reader. While this book does significant work to bridge gaps between existing and currently discrete secondary source material, there are some periods for which I more actively rely upon primary source documents in addition to or in lieu of such secondary source scholarship. This is especially true for the DADT period and the present period, with some minor exceptions. For the World War I period, I examine naval courts-martial transcripts and other relevant military documents, which have also informed the work of Canady, Chauncey, and Zane.[94] In my discussion of the World War II period, I utilize documents that show the codification of exclusionary policies in the Uniform Code of Military Justice (UCMJ) by 1950.[95] Additionally, I tacitly reference and draw upon interview data from queer veterans who served during World War II.[96] While not a source of data for this book, narratives in the form of letters to *ONE* magazine, which was the nation's first openly gay publication, do inform my feminist praxis at times.[97] This portion of my project also incorporates primary source material when discussing Executive Order 10450, and it draws from congressional documents and transcripts from the height of the Lavender Scare.[98] In analyzing these exclusionary policies in the early Cold War period, I refer to other relevant documents like the so-called Crittenden Report, which was the Navy's hidden report detailing the nonimportance of sexuality to military service.[99]

Again, the use of such primary source material is especially vital to my analysis of later periods because of the lack of major scholarly publications about exclusionary anti-LGBTQ+ policies from the late Cold War onward. For instance, I analyze the importance of reports issued by the Department of Defense's (DoD's) Personnel Security Research Center (PERSEREC).[100] Other primary source materials include the Director of Central Intelligence Directive (DCID) Number 1/14 in 1987, federal court documents pertaining to *Dubbs v. Central Intelligence Agency*, and more.[101] This book's transition from the late Cold War period to the DADT and present periods places further emphasis on RAND's *Sexual Orientation and U.S. Military Personnel Policy: Options and Assessment*, which was a precursor study to understand what the integration of gay and lesbian service members under "Don't Ask, Don't Tell" might look like.[102] Other relevant primary source materials that guide the discussion of these periods include (1) RAND's *Sexual Orientation and U.S. Military Personnel Policy: An Update of RAND's 1993 Study*, (2) RAND's *Assessing the Implications of Allowing Transgender Personnel to Serve Openly*, and (3) the DoD's *Transgender Service in the U.S. Military: An Implementation Handbook*.[103]

WHAT'S NEXT?

Utilizing the multidisciplinary framework of feminist scholarship, security studies scholarship, and LGBTQ+ historical scholarship described in this chapter, the coming pages offer the reader a clearer and more complete picture of what anti-LGBTQ+ exclusion in the American military and intelligence community has looked like from World War I to present. Moreover, this project also initiates an importance conversation on how the historical exclusion of queer people relates to contemporary discussions about transgender, non-binary, and intersex inclusion in the military. While clear answers to these contemporary discussions will not likely present themselves at the time of publication, my hope is that this book will expand interest in the issue of the lavender bans among the broader public and within academic fields, including political science.

The next chapter focuses on the exclusion of LGBTQ+ people from the American military during the World War I and World War II periods. In this and subsequent chapters, I discuss the rationales for banning

LGBTQ+ people from the American military and intelligence community, while also tracing the relevant and specific policy developments that codified this exclusion. At the beginning of the next chapter, I introduce some relevant historical information pertaining to the development of what we understand to be queer identities; this important discussion helps to frame my discussion of identities within the World War I period and throughout the remainder of the book. I then discuss how the rationale and policies of the World War I period affected the exclusion of queer men in particular, while also having inadvertent effects on other portions of the broader LGBTQ+ community, including intersex people in particular. I continue to discuss this history within the context of the World War II period, offering the same analysis related to policy development during this period. Importantly, this chapter sets the stage for anti-LGBTQ+ policy development throughout the remainder of the twentieth century.

2

THE EARLY YEARS OF ANTI-LGBTQ+ MILITARY POLICY

World Wars I and II

In this chapter, I examine the anti-LGBTQ+ policies that developed during the World War I and World War II periods, while also focusing on the rationales that promoted such policies in the first place. Prior to this, discussing the importance of culturally specific language, as used in queer communities during this time, is crucial, particularly for those interested in referring to the primary source documents used within this chapter. Following this brief discussion, the focus shifts to an analysis of the policy developments and associated rationales during the World War I period. Next, I focus on the analysis and discussion of these topics during the World War II period. Finally, I offer some concluding thoughts about the legacies of these two periods, their anti-LGBTQ+ policies, and the impact on our broader understanding of national security, which becomes a more prominent topic of discussion during the Cold War.

FRIENDS OF DOROTHY AND THE IMPORTANCE OF QUEER LEXICONS

Before discussing the anti-LGBTQ+ policy developments of the World War I and World War II periods, this subsection explains relevant language, as used during the 1910s to 1930s. Because so much of this language differs from our current understanding, providing these insights is helpful to the reader, particularly when working with primary source documents such as court-martial transcripts. Here, I first define some of the key terms that arose throughout my research on this time period, which helps to contextualize the often-fluid identity labels that described people with diverse sexualities during this time (such as, for example, the euphemistic "friends of Dorothy").[1] The terms discussed here are represented in many of the primary source documents that informed my research for these periods; however, many other terms within broader queer lexicons of the time are not discussed here. Although terms like *butch*, *dyke*, and others rose in prominence from the late 1930s onward, I focus on the key words most often referenced in the primary source documents that have informed my analysis of these periods, their anti-LGBTQ+ policies, and their related rationales. With that in mind, I provide a brief but important clarification of historical connotations and denotations for the following terms: *queer, homosexual, transsexual, trade,* and *fairy*.

In this book, I use the word *queer* at various times and in many contexts.[2] This should be understood as an umbrella term that refers to people of diverse sexualities, including lesbian, gay, and bisexual people and regardless of historical or geographic considerations; it encompasses people who have a diverse sexuality but use another term not described here. I specifically chose to use this word throughout my discussion of the World War I period, because it best reflects the fluid nature of sexualities during this time. From an historical perspective, early conceptualizations of "queerness had more to do with gender roles than with who was sleeping with whom," though this differential may be absent in modern understandings of the word.[3] During the early to mid-twentieth century, the term *queer* often referenced a unifying principle of diversity related to someone's sexuality; interestingly, this term could also reference one's gender expression, which might signal some element of diverse sexual identity too. Among people who claimed and used this word to describe their own lived experiences, the use of this and other terms led to more self-identification within the queer community from the 1910s into the 1930s.[4]

Eventually, such self-identification—along with other factors to be discussed in my analysis of the World War I period—helped in the formation of gay and lesbian subcultures during the socioeconomic hardships of the Great Depression of the 1930s. During this time, the use of "queer" as a label also indicated clear ties to a person's class status.[5] More specifically, this term often denoted an association with a middle-class lifestyle, emphasizing a certain amount of privilege held by many of those identifying with this particular label.[6] Over time, the use of this term filtered into mainstream, straight society, and its meaning eventually shifted from a label that described a middle-class person of a diverse sexuality "to an epithet of derision, a word with which no one wanted to be associated," as noted by David Shneer and Caryn Aviv.[7] I use the term particularly in discussing the World War I period; its use in this specific context is historical, given that words like *homosexual* and *gay* did not emerge into popular use until later.

Just as *queer* has shifted in its meaning, so has the word *homosexual*. As one might guess, based on the clinical connotations of the word, this term originally evolved from the medical discourse. Richard von Krafft-Ebbing, a German sexologist, coined the word *homosexuality* in the early 1890s; as noted by Shneer and Aviv, the purpose was to create terminology to describe "a person who had a 'great diminution or complete absence of sexual feeling from the opposite sex, with substitution of sexual feeling and instinct for the same sex.'"[8] Similar to *queer*, *homosexual*, along with its counterpart *heterosexual*, largely failed to enter popular culture or mainstream discourse until the 1930s. Before the 1930s, there was also a rather vague conception of who might be considered someone of a diverse sexuality (i.e., queer, homosexual, or the like). Before these terms were used more regularly by the broader society, a certain ambiguity often accompanied non-straight sexual relationships. For instance, "even when witnesses agreed that two men had engaged in homosexual relations with each other," disagreement still existed as to "whether both men or only the one playing the 'woman's' part" (i.e., the person who was penetrated, or who "bottomed") "should be labelled as 'queer' or 'homosexual.'"[9]

This ambiguous understanding of non-straight sexual behaviors and identities did not begin to shift radically until the late 1930s to early

1940s. During that time, society became less reliant on factors such as someone's sexual position (i.e., "top," "bottom," or "switch") and gender expression (i.e., masculine, feminine, androgynous, or something else) to define queerness or "homosexual" behaviors. Instead, society began to understand non-straight identities as being determined mostly by sexual desires and behaviors.[10] Corresponding with this societal shift in understanding, some people who had not previously been labeled as non-straight because of their role in a particular sex act (as a "top" and not a "bottom," for instance) could now be labeled as such.[11] In this chapter, I discuss a series of military sex scandals that occurred toward the end of World War I; these incidents, along with the series of embarrassing and quite public U.S. Senate hearings, helped to shift the American public's consciousness and understanding of who might be non-straight.[12] This shift in the conceptualization of who was non-straight also corresponded with an increased realization that effeminacy in dress, mannerisms, and other forms of gender expression was not the only indicator that a man might have sexual interests in people of the same sex or gender.[13]

More recent scholarship on this topic and the evolution of LGBTQ+ communities during the 1920s and 1930s notes that the prevalence of certain terms also depended, at least in part, upon one's geographic location.[14] In *Gay Berlin: Birthplace of a Modern Identity*, Robert Beachy claims that the term *homosexual* was a uniquely German innovation, fostered by the connections between the medical and sexologist community and the open culture of sexual and gender minorities of Berlin under the Weimar Republic from the late 1910s to 1933.[15] Beachy argues that Berlin's medical community and its relationship with activists—whom we would today understand as being within the broader LGBTQ+ community—spurred further research about diverse genders and sexualities.[16] The activism of this community also ensured that Berlin was one of the most progressive cities for people of diverse genders and sexualities in the early 1930s.[17] This cultural openness and the medical community's connections to people of diverse genders and sexualities, Beachy argues, augmented the use of terms like *homosexual* in texts, both in Germany and beyond.[18] From the late nineteenth century into the 1930s, some medical providers also subscribed to the theory of "sexual inversion," labeling queer people as "inverts." As noted by Jack Halberstam in *Female Masculinity*, this "theory of homosexuality folded gender variance and sexual preference into one economical package" that attempted to explain sexuality via an inversion of gendered traits.[19] Returning to Beachy, his argument does not refute the reasons previously presented for the shift in conceptualizing non-straight identities; rather, it emphasizes one of the key reasons that we see this shift in the cultural understanding of who was someone of a diverse sexuality. Beachy's contribution shows that a wider conceptualization of "homosexual" came to include people who were sexually interested in people of the same sex or gender, instead of just a man who had a more effeminate gender expression.[20]

This same medical community also maintained deep connections to people of diverse genders, and because of these connections, words to describe people of different gender identities and expressions also emerged during this time. One such example is the German word *transsexualismus*, coined by the renowned sexologist Magnus Hirschfeld in the early 1920s.[21] Though this word would not immediately percolate into non-German medical literature, it is still a significant development in our understanding of gender diversity and early terminology within the broader LGBTQ+ community.[22] When it eventually did appear outside of the German medical literature in the late 1940s and early 1950s, this word was translated into English as *transsexual* and then eventually replaced in many contemporary spaces by the term *transgender*.[23] These meaningful connections between leading medical providers and sexologists, like Hirschfeld and colleagues from his Institute for Sexual Science, and everyday people of diverse genders and sexualities helped to foster a sense of community and collaboration. Ultimately, this intentional collaboration led to a greater scientific understanding of gender diversity, sexuality, and related topics, while also producing an early lexicon to describe LGBTQ+ experiences and identities more clearly.[24]

While discussing such common terms as *queer*, *homosexual*, and *transsexual*, I should also mention some other key terms that I encountered during my research for the World War I and World War II periods. Importantly, the "history of homosexuality and transsexuality," as noted by Halberstam, "was a shared history . . . and only diverged in the 1940s, when surgery and hormonal treatments became [more readily] available."[25] While these terms often appear only in an anachronistic way in today's culture, they were terms that people used to describe their own unique, lived experiences, highlighting the greater fluidity of sexual identities under the broader queer umbrella of the early twentieth century. Their relatively niche use in different subcultures, rather than in mainstream society, further underscores how and why a term like *homosexual* came into more common use in the mainstream culture.[26] A variety of other terms are no doubt lost to history; as people began to congregate into more densely packed urban centers throughout the twentieth century, these terms, their connotations, and the communities that used them continued to evolve.[27] Here I discuss two specific terms that I encountered in my research: *trade* and *fairy*.

Trade, a term more commonly used during the World War I period and the Great Depression, referred to a man who purposefully entered into a non-straight sexual and/or romantic relationship with another man because of the potential financial benefits. As Shneer and Aviv explain, this term "said as much about a man's class status as about his gender presentation or sexual orientation."[28] Self-identifying as "trade" also implied a certain aggression in combination with one's masculinity.[29] It emphasized that the man was not actually queer, was not "effeminate," but would engage in sex with other men for financial benefit.[30] Given the economic uncertainties and class struggles during this time, *trade* was a term more commonly encountered from the late 1910s through the mid-1930s. As the Great Depression was ending, this term fell rapidly out of regular use, and terms like *homosexual* entered more popular usage during the 1930s and into the World War II period.[31]

Similar to *trade*, the word *fairy* was a relatively more common term in particular subcultures; it referred to a man who had an overtly feminine gender expression. Unlike some other terms that circulated during this time, *fairy* carried meaning both within subcultures and in the dominant mainstream culture. However, this term did not have the same class connotations across these different communities. For instance, the LGBTQ+ community understood *fairy* to emphasize that a man was working or middle class, rather than lower class or in an economically difficult situation (as with *trade*), but no significant class connotations extended to the dominant mainstream culture's understanding of the term.[32] The term *fairy* extended into more common usage beyond the 1930s, used largely as a slur and insult by those in the dominant mainstream culture. Both of these terms demonstrate some of the nuanced difficulties of working with the histories of LGBTQ+ communities in the early to mid-twentieth century. Their meanings can be difficult to describe, generally centering around one's own self-identification, though the labels are sometimes ascribed by others. More importantly, these labels changed and evolved over time.[33]

Again, the primary purpose of this introduction to language is to clarify some of the common language used to describe people of diverse genders and sexualities in the early to mid-twentieth century. While I have focused only on a few specific terms most often referenced in the primary source documents that have informed this book, other terms, such as *butch, dyke,* and other identity labels also evolved from the late 1930s onward. Though these words were not encountered with the same frequency as those I have described, they are still important to acknowledge.[34] As for the terms discussed here, many have fallen out of usage both within subcultures and in the mainstream popular discourse. Our understanding of these words shifts and evolves: *gay* or *lesbian* replaces *homosexual, transgender* replaces *transsexual,* and so on. As our understanding of genders and sexualities increases, additional terms come to prominence, and this cultural production still continues today. These are important considerations for moving through the remainder of this chapter and book.

Later in this chapter, I discuss the impact of discriminatory military policies. Because of historical realities (i.e., a fighting force of people presumed to be all "men" or "males"), most of these policies affected queer men. Yet, policies during this period almost certainly also affected others, such as non-queer people presumed to be not straight, intersex people, transgender people, and others. Some of these historical figures may not have been equipped with the language to describe their lived experience accurately in today's terms. Thus, my analysis and discussion centers on policies that specifically targeted "homosexual" men, but bear in mind that these same policies also inadvertently affected others.

THE WORLD WAR I PERIOD (1917-1921): SEXUAL IMMORALITY DURING A TIME OF WAR

You need not be bashful in using the blunt language before this Court. Just exactly what do you mean by a man entering another man?

—LIEUTENANT LESTER W. COOCH, USNRF, JUDGE ADVOCATE, EXAMINING HARRISON ALLEN RIDEOUT[35]

I begin by exploring how the U.S. military first constructed the idea of queer service members as a security threat during the World War I period, defined as roughly from 1917 to 1921. The beginning date is when the United States formally entered World War I, while the end corresponds to the end of hearings related to a government-funded gay sex scandal that defined the period. As noted earlier, being identified as "homosexual" or "queer" during this period was defined not by "sexual-object choice but rather in terms of gender" roles and one's assumed sexual position(s) within a sexual act.[36] This conceptualization of queerness involved a great deal of disagreement about who might be classified as a "sexual deviant," which was the stigmatizing language of this period; in broader society, people almost universally agreed that the person who was "bottoming" (i.e., the person who was penetrated) would be labeled as some form of "sexual deviant."[37] In other words, queerness and "homosexual" identity were defined not by engaging in non-straight sexual activities but, rather, by *how* one engaged in those activities.[38] While the notion of queerness remained malleable during the World War I period, this time frame is particularly significant because the notion of queerness as a security threat to the United States and its military first arose during World War I and the succeeding years.

Before the government-funded gay sex scandal mentioned earlier, the U.S. military began a reformation crusade aimed at the moral and physical health of service members.[39] The idea of this reform campaign was to bring the morality politics of the day—harking back to Victorian Era ideas of "virtue"—into the military.[40] At this point in American history, it was common practice for vice squads, especially in larger urban areas, to investigate a variety of morally dubious issues within society; within the military, morally corrupt behaviors that were targeted included drug use, sex work, and other presumed immoral sexual behaviors.[41] These vice squads were focused on bringing "the issue of sex perversion" and queerness to the forefront of this institutional shift toward creating a more moral fighting force.[42] These operations occurred in both military and military-adjacent/off-base locations. This led to the creation and dissemination of so-called vice reports warning "of female impersonators in . . . cabaret shows that soldiers attended," among other immoral activities.[43] Such reports indicated issues that needed to be addressed by key military officials, the broader rationale being to ensure that the enlisted ranks could be kept morally clean and fit for war.

As a product of this ongoing morality crusade both across the country and within the military, local draft and medical advisory boards were provided with new guidance in 1918. Early that year, these administrative bodies of the military, as noted by Canaday, were given instructions that would prohibit anyone with a "psychopathic character including the homosexual" from joining the armed forces.[44] While the broader rationale for banning LGBTQ+ people from military service during the World War I period was sexual immorality in a time of war, these guidelines about queerness and psychopathic illness relied on a presumption of sexual immorality, rather than medical diagnostic criteria.[45] Following this initial guidance, the government produced more detailed guidebooks and manuals that would list "defects" that had been identified in drafted men. The idea was to help draft boards pre-identify so-called defected men, excluding them from the quickly expanding military.[46] One such manual was Albert Love and Charles Davenport's *Defects Found in Drafted Men: Statistical Information Compiled from the Draft Records* (1919). Some of the "defects" mentioned in this document included venereal diseases, obesity, alcoholism, epilepsy, defective speech, constitutional psychopathic states, myopia, cardiac disorders, and asthma. In addition to noting such physical "defects," Love and Davenport further noted that men with "mental disease and pathological mental states . . . , such as hysterical stigmata, phobias, morbid doubts and fears, anxiety attacks, hypochondriasis; also, psychopathic character, including the homosexual, grotesque liars, and vagabonds" should be denied entry into the military.[47]

This early codification of an exclusionary policy against LGBTQ+ people specifically framed queerness as sexually immoral and psychopathic.[48] This definition is significant because it laid foundational reasons for broader concerns of immorality within the military, which largely mirrored the moral panic throughout American society at that time.[49] While the broader rationale for anti-LGBTQ+ policies during the World War I period was sexual immorality in a time of war, the seeds for a future argument about pathology and mental illness were also sown. In fact, this early reference point would prove crucial to further developing such pathologized notions of queerness, which the military would use as a rational for these policies during World War II.[50] Some draft boards during the World War I period also looked for potential physical signs of immorality by stripping and examining the bodies of recruits. While this would become common practice during World War II, some draft boards were doing this in an effort to identify people who presented themselves as men but had what might appear to be feminine primary and/or secondary sex characteristics. Such characteristics included wider hips, the presence of breast tissue, smaller testicles, or a smaller phallus; the presumption was that these might indicate that someone was a "homosexual."[51] While it is important not to ascribe labels to historical figures, some of these people, presumed to be men with feminine-coded primary and secondary sex characteristics, were likely intersex people who had been assigned male at birth.[52] While several thousand women also served in the Army and Navy in World War I, documented use of such procedures largely focused on "overly feminine" men.[53] And despite documented instances of examining physical morphology or phenotypes to identify "defects" in recruits, the military relied much more heavily on the notion of sexual immorality, which was later presumed to be a manifestation or indication of pathology or mental illness.[54]

This specific presumption of queerness as a manifestation of sexual immorality and a character flaw was represented in the Articles of War of 1916, the first codified policy that identified LGBTQ+ people as a security threat to the military.[55] This document actually specified that "homosexuality" was the act of "assault with the intent to commit sodomy." As noted by Rhonda Evans in a report for the Center for the Study of Sexual Minorities in the Military in the early 2000s, the revised Articles of War of 1920, following the war, represented a shift in understanding, now labeling "homosexuality" as any form of "consensual sodomy" with someone of the same sex or gender "as criminal behavior."[56] However, the previous understanding during World War I technically relied upon the presumption of a nonconsensual assault only. As demonstrated by George Chauncey and Sherry Zane, such issues—even under the Articles of War of 1916, when the country was at war—were not treated lightly by any means.[57] In the context of the naval case study at the core of both Chauncey's and Zane's work on World War I, a variety of punitive measures could be imposed if a man was found guilty of sodomy with another man. Such sanctions could include a court-martial, dishonorable discharge, and/or imprisonment.[58] For instance, in one Navy court-martial in 1919—as noted in the official documentation of the event—the accused, Harold J. Trubshaw, was found guilty of "commit[ting] sodomy in and upon" his body with "the United States then being in a state of war."[59] Following his court-martial, Trubshaw was dishonorably discharged and subsequently sentenced to twenty years in prison. Though Trubshaw's sentence would later be reduced to ten years by the Judge Advocate General (JAG), the impact of these policies was bleak. The creation of this formal anti-LGBTQ+ policy in the Articles of War of 1916 had a drastic impact on the lived experiences of individuals serving in the military during World War I, and it set the stage for anti-LGBTQ+ policies to expand and develop in the future. The use of policy to perpetrate harm on queer people, along with its accompanying rationale, is quite obviously on display in one of the most infamous sex scandals in military history.[60]

Along with the use of vice squads in both American society and the military, the events of this sex scandal originated with a decision by Assistant Secretary of the Navy Franklin D. Roosevelt. Following reports of vice at naval bases and port cities, Roosevelt, via an odd circumstance of events, authorized the creation of a clandestine team to undertake a covert operation to gather evidence against all manners of vice (i.e., drug use, sex work, and immoral sexual behaviors like "homosexuality").[61] The group, dubbed Section A, was directed to root out vice—specifically including "cocksuckers" and "rectum receivers"—at the naval station in Newport, Rhode Island.[62] Funded with nearly $50,000 (or nearly $1.1 million in 2025 dollars, adjusted for inflation) from Roosevelt's office, Section A's members were to identify, seek out, and seduce service members who might be "engaging in homosexuality" and to collect proof that could be brought into courts-martial proceedings.[63] As a consequence of this instruction, the members of Section A—as documented by the Committee on Naval Affairs of the

U.S. Senate—arrived in Newport with the goal of allowing "immoral acts to be performed upon them" if it proved necessary for the identification of "alleged sexual perverts" like queer people.[64] While this may seem rather shocking, these commands were actually authorized by emergency wartime laws, made possible because of the historic scale of World War I. Specifically, the Espionage Act of 1917 and the Sedition Act of 1918 helped to authorize the use of such tactics in pursuit of the national interest and security.[65] Several of the officers who oversaw the actions of Section A, which operated under the purview of the Office of Naval Intelligence of the Navy, perceived queer people as sexually immoral threats to the military and the nation-state; they considered the actions of Section A as integral to the arrest of "sex perverts," who they believed posed a direct threat to the military and its success in the war.[66]

The sexual encounters of Section A's members were documented in richly detailed journals, enabling the entrapment and courts-martial of seventeen sailors in Newport. The entrapped men identified with a variety of labels such as queer, trade, etc.; while awaiting their courts-martial, they underwent a lengthy detainment of nearly six months under the aforementioned national security laws.[67] In the courts-martial proceedings for these men, Chauncey notes, "many witnesses indicated that they had at least heard of 'fairies' before joining the service"; this term was understood to indicate a more flamboyant "homosexual" male. Additionally, it was not uncommon for some men to join the military to explore potential sexual relationships that were not available outside of this almost exclusively all-male environment.[68] However, the notion of a queer sexuality was still largely presumed to be based on one's sexual position (i.e., whether someone was a "top" who penetrated another man or a "bottom" who was penetrated by another man).[69] While the men who were "tops" or "switches" (i.e., someone who might "top" or "bottom," switching between positions) would use this argument in an attempt to protect themselves, the men who were "bottoms" could face an even more dire situation. Although this book focuses on policy instead of individual histories, it is helpful to look at a specific case to better understand how this disparity functioned. In the "Case of Harold J. Trubshaw" from 1919, Trubshaw was charged with both "scandalous conduct tending to the destruction of good morals" and sodomy.[70] He was found guilty of these charges and the four specifications listed: three counts of providing oral sex to another man and one count of providing anal sex to another man. The testimony against Trubshaw was more damning because he had "bottomed" for another man.[71] As explained previously, courts-martial for men who were "tops" or "switches" did not generally result in the same punitive measures, because society at this time had a more flexible and fluid view of who was a "homosexual."[72]

The actions of Section A and the resulting courts-martial would eventually result in a series of investigative hearings by both the Navy and the U.S. Senate's Committee on Naval Affairs in the years following World War I. The court-marital proceedings—including the detailed sexual encounter journals that members of Section A kept as evidence against the men whom they were entrapping—proved shocking to both of these governmental bodies. Both the Navy and this senatorial committee found the use of same-gender sexual acts as a method of entrapment to be morally reprehensible, but Roosevelt, who testified in defense of his actions, claimed that it was necessary because of wartime conditions.[73] Following these hearings, the senatorial committee made its proceedings public, while also agreeing that the members of Section A should not be punished for their actions. The logic was that these sailors had acted on orders given by a superior officer, which compelled them to engage in these same-gender sexual acts with other men in and around Newport.[74] In addition to other cultural touchstones throughout the 1920s, the resulting outrage over the Navy's decision to command sailors to perform these sexual acts with other men helped to shape public consciousness about who and why someone might be considered "homosexual." The notion that this label would be applied only to the person who was "bottoming" was beginning to change.[75] The idea of who was defined as "queer" or "homosexual" would culturally solidify more fully by the early 1940s.[76] And while the military would no longer create clandestine operations to lure men into same-gender sexual activity, the idea of banning queer people from military service was more readily discussed in the lead-up to World War II, with such recruits being viewed as a threat to the nation and its successful military operations.[77] The result was an increase both in the military's attempt to screen and dismiss queer people from the service and in the number of administrative discharges of queer service members.[78]

The early codification of anti-LGBTQ+ exclusionary policies in the American military specifically framed queerness as both sexually immoral and psychopathic, and the government's actions during World War I largely mirrored the moral panic throughout American society at that time.[79] Even so, the codification of this anti-LGBTQ+ policy, as seen in the Articles of War for 1916 and 1920, and the rationale for this policy would undergo a distinct shift both during and following World War II. In this new period, the military made two major administrative shifts that jointly affected both the codified policy and the corresponding rationale. First, military courts began to establish the concept that both parties were equally guilty in acts of sodomy and should be punished accordingly.[80] Second, they moved toward a model of court-martialing only people accused of violent sexual offenses, while pursuing an administrative discharge for people who were either involved in consensual acts of a sexual nature with a person of the same sex or gender or found to have expressed or held same-gender sexual desires.[81] These punitive measures and the process for pursuing them would fundamentally shift alongside the changes in the military's anti-LGBTQ+ policies and rationales in the coming decades.

THE WORLD WAR II PERIOD (1939-1945): PSYCHOLOGICAL ILLNESS AND PHYSICAL INCAPABILITY FOR MILITARY SERVICE

> *We just lined up, and they looked at us. You know, it was very unnerving, and I kept thinking—my God, are they going to see something? Is there some kind of a telltale thing, you know, that a doctor can look at you and say, 'Ah ha! There's one!'*
>
> —ANONYMOUS VETERAN, AS INTERVIEWED IN *COMING OUT UNDER FIRE*[82]

As in World War I, specific anti-LGBTQ+ policies were developed during World War II, and while the formal language around national security would not become commonplace until after the war, rationales that viewed queer service members as threats to the nation were even more pervasive during this period. This period, which began nearly twenty years after the conclusion of World War I, was also marked by a number of linguistic changes. Terms like *sexual deviant*, *sex pervert*, and *invert* that were common at the beginning of the twentieth century had largely fallen out of fashion. In their place, pathologized words like *homosexual* and *transsexual*—along with laypeople's terms like *gay* and *lesbian*—were becoming increasingly common. These changes were due in part to the widespread use of such language in the medical community of Weimar Germany, but they were also the product of a growing urban queer community in metro centers across America throughout the Roaring Twenties.[83] While these linguistic shifts were happening between the wars, the military also considered adopting a new set of policies that would move away from court-martialing service members for engaging in sodomy to simply issuing an administrative discharge, known as a "blue discharge."[84] Yet, this change would not become a reality until America's involvement in World War II.[85] This shift in punitive measures was presumably spurred by the blunders made by the Navy in World War I, the indirect impact of the public hearings of the U.S. Senate's Committee on Naval Affairs, and the critical need for bodies to serve in the war effort following the attack on Pearl Harbor in 1941.[86] These changes in punitive measures, along with new anti-LGBTQ+ policies and associated rationales, also fit within the larger backdrop of overt militarization, related industrialization, and the rapid growth of military enlistment throughout World War II.

During the four-year period of American involvement in World War II, anti-LGBTQ+ policies in the Army underwent twenty-four different revisions related to anti-"homosexual" regulations.[87] Like the changes in discharge preferences, the numerous policy revisions were largely the result of a rapidly growing fighting force, which included roughly twelve million enlistments via the new selective service process from 1941 to 1945.[88] During the war, these discharge policies resulted in nine thousand documented cases of expulsion from the military; following the conclusion of World War II, the newly created Department of Defense (DoD) integrated the intent of these anti-LGBTQ+ policies into the Uniform Code of Military Justice (UCMJ) in 1950.[89] Of course, the actual number of those who might have been excluded from joining the ranks will never be known, since some people were administratively discharged under other premises too. Despite changes in the policy location for the Army's anti-LGBTQ+ policies, the rationale that deemed LGBTQ+ people a security threat to the military and the state differed only slightly from the rationale in World War I. The principal change in the World War II period was an increased focus on psychological readiness and physical ability, rather than notions of morality. This presumption of LGBTQ+ people's psychological illness and physical inability was also marked with a more formalized process of prescreening bodies ahead of enlistment, and part of this screening process was evaluating potential recruits for queerness.[90] Such notions would eventually enter a discourse of discrimination that facilitated a renewed medicalization of "homosexuality" both during the war and, notably, throughout the 1950s.[91] This model of "diagnosing" queer tendencies as a regular process was initiated in part during World War I, but a clear change began in World War II, when it became more standardized. This change resulted in men who were suspected of "homosexuality" being more regularly examined for physical traits that appeared feminine, which was presumed to indicate a problem or weakness. Such traits included wider hips, the presence of breast tissue, smaller testicles, a smaller phallus, less muscle mass, and other stereotypical "female-like" characteristics.[92] Less frequently, women's bodies, too, could come under scrutiny, particularly if they exhibited masculinized characteristics like an enlarged clitoris.[93] As with the irregular and infrequent use of this practice during World War I, it is almost certain that this practice erroneously identified intersex people as "homosexual" during World War II as well.[94]

These twenty-four separate revisions to anti-LGBTQ+ policies began appearing just before the Japanese attack on Pearl Harbor in 1941, and with the new model of regularly screening for queerness and presumed physical traits, the military developed an innovative new way to standardize discrimination throughout the Department of War (DoW).[95] As noted by Douglass Stuart in *Creating the National Security State: A History of the Law That Transformed America*, "the proponents of national security were vindicated by Pearl Harbor" and the tragic events of that day.[96] In essence, the attack on Pearl Harbor triggered a rise in militarization and in the associated policies related to a rapid entry into another global conflict. Ahead of America's involvement in World War II, the U.S. Congress approved an augmented defense budget of roughly $17 billion, nine times the previous year's budget.[97] While the seeds of national security policy were planted during the World War I period, more visible manifestations began growing ahead of the attack on Pearl Harbor in other ways too. For instance, President Franklin D. Roosevelt—who had escaped largely unharmed from the Newport sex scandal of World War I and found his way to the White House—had already instructed the DoW to engage in intelligence-sharing activities in 1939. Specifically, Roosevelt instructed the DoW to coordinate its efforts and share intelligence with the Federal Bureau of Investigation (FBI).[98] Roosevelt's preparation for war, which began quietly ahead of the attack on Pearl Harbor, was also viewed as judicious following the Japanese attack on the American naval fleet. Both Roosevelt's intelligence-sharing instructions and the advance security preparedness would have impacts on anti-LGBTQ+ policy development and execution in World War II and throughout the early Cold War period.[99]

While these anti-LGBTQ+ policies were certainly part of a larger agenda for military preparedness and national security, the military's first codified and explicitly anti-LGBTQ+ policy also included an interesting exemption, allowing the military to temporarily permit non-straight people to remain in the service if doing so would serve the broader war effort.[100] Similarly, the Women's Army Auxiliary Corps (WAAC), created in 1942 and later renamed the Women's Army Corps (WAC), had specific policies that discouraged officers from exposing or punishing lesbianism. As noted by Lillian Faderman in *Odd Girls and Twilight Lovers: A History of Lesbian Life in the twentieth Century*, officers were instructed to be tolerant of potential lesbian friendships and relationships, since such womanpower was an important supplement to the war effort.[101] In fact, some WAAC/WAC officers argued that lesbianism posed no serious threat to the military because there was no risk of pregnancy and a lower risk of venereal disease for women having lesbian sex.[102] Overall, the immediate concern of securing the European and Pacific theaters, while avoiding another front on American soil, superseded discharging queer people, and while less common, this tolerance sometimes even applied to gay and queer men.[103] Even so, serious criminal charges and administrative discharges could still happen, particularly for sex involving two or more men.[104] Despite some leniency, the military still discharged thousands of men and a lesser number of women throughout the war, particularly when their sexualities were seen as a direct threat to military operations.[105] The need for personnel to aid the war effort led to other changes too. For example, this reality largely stymied rhetoric about how work might masculinize women, as women were also called to do patriotic work that would aid the country.[106] While the military now screened outright for "homosexual" inclinations, women in the WAAC/WAC were generally disqualified only for flagrant and inflammatory answers.[107]

The decision to overlook queer behaviors was left largely up to the person's commanding officer, and thousands of people were still discharged under these policies.[108] This looming threat of discharge or refused enlistment relied on the presumption that queerness was a threat to the state's success in the war; to reiterate, these anti-LGBTQ+ policies were based on LGBTQ+ people's presumed psychological illness and physical inability, rather than morality.[109] Just as the degree of flexibility under these anti-LGBTQ+ policies often differed between men and women, so did the presumed rationales, particularly related to physical abilities and traits. The WAAC/WAC screening process rarely focused on examining the physical traits of women, who might even be praised for having a "butch" aesthetic; such examinations for physical concerns were far more common during the draft boards' examinations of men's bodies.[110] These rationales also complemented shifting ideas about queerness in American society and culture. Though often applied less stringently, these anti-LGBTQ+ policies—including Roosevelt's orders that the military share intelligence with the FBI—indirectly encouraged broader national security state projects, such as the FBI's nationwide surveillance of queer bars in the 1950s.[111] While the military was no longer discharging LGBTQ+ service members because of concerns about morality, the national security state, as evidenced by these emerging actions of the FBI, did presume that LGBTQ+ people were subversive elements against the "American ideal."[112] While this began with the creation of a list of "known homosexuals," the FBI, after World War II, folded it into a larger domestic surveillance project under the direction of J. Edgar Hoover.[113] This manner of surveillance would be a key feature of the early Cold War period, but it is important to acknowledge that it had roots in the security concerns and procedures of World War II.

Despite the constant threat of these anti-LGBTQ+ policies, World War II facilitated opportunities for queer people to connect with one another. For queer service members who passed the draft screenings and avoided being put on an FBI list of "known homosexuals," opportunities arose to flirt with queerness, particularly when stationed in more remote locales overseas. For instance, some found solace in the so-called solider shows, in which male GIs dressed in women's clothing and performed in drag for their fellow troops.[114] In fact, the prospect of a male service member performing in drag was not solely an American phenomenon. Service members in the Canadian military, which also had an anti-LGBTQ+ policy during this time, undertook similar endeavors in an effort to "find their niche" and, at times, to subtlety advertise their sexual preferences from within the ranks.[115] Interestingly, some of the men who participated in these drag shows went on to continue working as "female impersonators" and drag queens following the end of the war, because of the praise that they received during their solider shows.[116] Women, too, were able to experiment with gender expression in new ways. For instance, a redesign of uniforms for the Army Nurses Corps—spearheaded by Dorothy Shaver, of fashion giant Lord & Taylor, during her stint as a consultant to the Army's Office of the Quartermaster General—led to white, starched skirts and stockings being replaced with practical, more masculine field gear-like pants.[117] In essence, there were some positive experiences, and some queer people found community while in the service, but the threat of an administrative discharge still loomed in the background.[118]

Similar community building occurred for lesbian and queer women during the World War II period. As noted by Faderman, communities of lesbian and queer women were, in a sense, accidentally established by the military.[119] Specifically, Faderman argues that the military fostered some level of tolerance among straight women toward their lesbian peers, which then established certain social views among women who had served.[120] The masculinity of women in the armed forces allowed some women to explore gender expressions both during and after the war, which later influenced "butch" lesbian subculture throughout the 1950s.[121] Lesbian subculture was partially fostered by the military and government because of the particularly lenient measures that were taken against lesbian and queer women.[122] The military's policy of discharging queer people to the nearest U.S. port, Faderman also suggests, may have inadvertently helped to develop those communities in larger urban areas.[123] Interestingly, this argument of queer community building during and after World War II builds upon a similar argument that

Chauncey makes; specifically, he notes that the urbanization following World War I had a significant impact on the creation of queer communities, and gay male subcultures in particular.[124]

The anti-LGBTQ+ policies of the American military—while damaging to the lives of individual queer people who were affected by them—and the associated effects on urbanization had the unintended effect of supporting the development of LGBTQ+ communities and subcultures, which would continue growing throughout the 1950s and into the 1960s.[125] Despite the ways in which the military inadvertently aided in the development of queer communities, the anti-LGBTQ+ policies of the World War II period still caused harm in a number of ways. As noted earlier in this chapter, the locations of these codified policies shifted several times throughout and immediately following World War II, and the military, due to the need for bodies to occupy positions crucial to the war effort, did not enforce these anti-LGBTQ+ policies in every situation. Rather, the military invoked these policies selectively, despite the rationale that suggested LGBTQ+ people were too psychologically ill or physically incapable for military service.[126]

LEGACIES OF POLICY DEVELOPMENT DURING THESE PERIODS

While the further development of queer communities and subcultures in urban areas represented some positive by-products in the World War I and World War II periods, the events of these periods also influenced other issues at the intersections of LGBTQ+ identities and security. Both the attack on Pearl Harbor and World War II more generally provided key security lessons to public policy personnel moving forward; as noted by Stuart, one of these lessons was that "Washington needed to provide military leaders with a permanent and influential role in the formulation of peacetime foreign and security policy."[127] Following the American victory in World War II, the nearly immediate start of the Cold War coincided with the enactment of the National Security Act of 1947, which created a "policy home" for broader national security issues and concerns. In addition to formally creating the DoD and the CIA, this new policy and its subsequent amendments would result in a dramatic shift in the rationales used against LGBTQ+ people, both in the military and in the growing national security apparatus.[128] In short, the National Security Act of 1947 helped to create both new policy homes and new rationales for excluding LGBTQ+ people from the military and the growing intelligence community in post–World War II America.

3

THE COLD WAR, COMMUNISTS, AND QUEER BOOGEYMEN

Scholars of American foreign policy often point to the advent of "national security" and related rhetoric as being a post–World War II phenomenon, but this is an overly simplistic view, particularly as it relates to LGBTQ+ people in the American military and intelligence community. As mentioned previously, LGBTQ+ people were considered threats both to America's war efforts and to society as early as World War I and throughout World War II. While the rationales and associated policies varied, the presumption of being a security threat remained. Although the language of "national security" did not emerge in more easily recognizable ways until the early Cold War period, the history of anti-LGBTQ+ exclusion from the American military in World War I and World War II is undeniable. The national security apparatus and related rhetoric grew throughout the Cold War and beyond. Signed into law by President Harry Truman, the National Security Act of 1947 made the following structural changes to the American military and intelligence agencies: (1) replacing the secretary of war with a secretary of defense; (2) merging the Departments of War and Navy into the National Military Establishment (NME), which became the Department of Defense (DoD) after a 1949 amendment; and (3) creating the Central Intelligence Agency (CIA), which is largely focused on foreign intelligence gathering.[1]

In this chapter, I examine the anti-LGBTQ+ policies that developed throughout the Cold War, broadly defined as the period from the signing of the National Security Act in 1947 to the fall of the Berlin Wall in 1989. In contrast to the World War I and World War II periods, the Cold War represents more than four decades of history. During this time, policies excluding LGBTQ+ people from the American military and intelligence community—along with the related rationales for such policies—shifted multiple times, but with durable shifts falling into two distinct periods: (1) the early Cold War (1947 through the 1970s) and (2) the late Cold War (the 1980s). Despite some element of flexibility with this chronological boundary, a rather distinct shift occurs in the final decade of the Cold War, meriting its treatment as a separate period. Here, I begin by discussing the early Cold War period, which includes both the Red and "Lavender" Scares in relation to potential blackmail by Soviet spies. I then shift focus to the late Cold War period, with its rationales related to mental stability and trustworthiness. Finally, I offer some concluding thoughts on the impact of HIV/AIDS activism, which sets the stage for the "Don't Ask, Don't Tell" (DADT) period from the early 1990s to 2011.

THE EARLY COLD WAR PERIOD (1947-1970s): SUSCEPTIBLE TO SOVIET BLACKMAIL

I sometimes wonder how many of these homosexuals have had a part in shaping our foreign policy. How many have been in sensitive positions and subject to blackmail. . . . The Russians are strong believers in homosexuality. . . . Perhaps if all the facts were known, these same homosexuals have been used by the Communists.

—REPRESENTATIVE ARTHUR L. MILLER, NEBRASKA'S 4TH DISTRICT[2]

While LGBTQ+ people were already being constructed as threats to the nation and its security from World War I through World War II, the rhetoric around national security as a rationale for banning LGBTQ+ people from the American military and intelligence community intensified during the early Cold War period. The earliest policies in this period automatically denied a security or intelligence clearance to anyone who was presumed to be queer, and in general, this trend continued throughout the Cold War.³ Replacing the hodgepodge of World War II era policies, this blanket denial largely stemmed from the fear that LGBTQ+ people, including those in the military and intelligence community, were at increased risk of blackmail by counterintelligence operatives from the USSR.⁴ During this time, leaders in the military and the newly created CIA reasoned that "gays are easy targets for blackmail by enemy agents" because they might wish to keep their sexuality as discreet and secret as possible.⁵ To federal officials, the presumption that Soviet espionage efforts could successfully blackmail LGBTQ+ people justified the policies of the early Cold War period, since this could directly affect America's military, government, and society as a whole.⁶ However, the history of anti-LGBTQ+ policies during the early Cold War was more complex than simply denying security clearances.

By the time of the National Security Act of 1947, concerns for national security were readily apparent, spurring America's centralization of national security efforts in the newly created DoD and CIA. Concerns about national security, along with anti-communist sentiment, became commonplace by the 1950s. While the fear of communism, McCarthyism, and the associated Red Scare are common knowledge, the fear of "homosexuality" and LGBTQ+ people more broadly, culminating in the so-called Lavender Scare throughout the early years of the Cold War, is less generally known.⁷ Interestingly, the Cold War's Lavender Scare was rooted, at least in part, in a sort of mythologized event from the final days of World War II. According to Neil Miller's *Out of the Past: Gay and Lesbian History from 1869 to Present*, an unverified rumor, publicized by anti-LGBTQ+ members of the tabloid press, helped to further a conspiracy theory. According to their telling, despite the Nazis' contempt for and active persecution of people of diverse genders and sexualities throughout the Holocaust, Adolf Hitler had a secret plan for using queer people. The story, as told by the tabloids, was that Hitler had a Nazi-generated list of queer people from across the world, people who were particularly susceptible to blackmail and could be used for espionage enlistment on behalf of the Nazis. This infamous—almost laughably false and certainly unverified—list or "little black book" was supposedly obtained by the Soviets, who reached the *Führerbunker* ahead of American and British units; as the story goes, it was then given to Joseph Stalin, who now had a global network of queer spies ready for recruitment by the Soviets.⁸ The presumption was that LGBTQ+ people would spy for any regime because they wanted to conceal their sexuality from disclosure and therefore were a prime target for blackmail by the Soviets. This story clearly captures the prevailing anti-LGBTQ+ sentiments and imagination of the early Cold War period.⁹

With anti-LGBTQ+ anxieties stoked by the media, these anxieties grew rapidly after World War II, and by 1946 the U.S. Senate's Committee on Appropriations began to show early concerns related to potentially security risks in the Department of State (DoS).¹⁰ In 1948, Alfred Kinsey published *Sexual Behavior in the Human Male*, which made claims about the commonality of queer sexual behavior within the broader population.¹¹ These early anxieties, growing media pressure, and the publication of this groundbreaking text helped to set the stage for the Lavender Scare.¹² Just a year after Kinsey's publication, the DoD, which had already adopted policies of automatic security clearance denials for non-straight people, formulated a more unified definition of military policy related to "homosexual" behavior. A DoD memo later that year stated: "Homosexual personnel, irrespective of sex, should not be permitted to serve in any branch of the Armed Services in any capacity, and prompt separation of known homosexuals from the Armed Forces be made mandatory."¹³ Building through the end of the 1940s, these events serves as anti-LGBTQ+ kindling, which was then ignited a by a little-known U.S. senator from Wisconsin. In February 1950, Senator Joseph McCarthy gave his infamous speech claiming that there were communists throughout the DoS. Citing a variety of supposed cases, McCarthy specifically mentioned "homosexual" behavior in two cases, most notably linking the idea of communism directly to "homosexuality" in his discussion of "Case 62." Consequently, McCarthy inadvertently lent some element of assumed credibility to the anti-LGBTQ+ tabloid press's telling of World War II and the growing anxieties of the Cold War.¹⁴ Given the rumors that Stalin might have Hitler's list of "homosexual" spies, McCarthy's actions were significant in that they asserted a link between "homosexual identity" and communist ideology and gave indirect credibility to those rumors.¹⁵

Within a week of McCarthy's speech, John Peurifoy, then the deputy undersecretary of management for the DoS, denied that the department employed any communists. At the same time, he admitted "that a number of persons considered to be security risks had been forced out" and that this group contained ninety-one "homosexuals."[16] Following this seemingly inconsequential statement of fact, a national debate soon emerged among government officials and members of the tabloid press.[17] Over the forthcoming months, the issue of queer people in positions at the DoS and other federal agencies—particularly those focused on intelligence and foreign policy issues—became highly politicized.[18] In March 1950, a bipartisan, two-person subcommittee was created as an offshoot of the U.S. Senate Subcommittee on Appropriations for the District of Columbia. This subcommittee of a subcommittee, whose work was dubbed the Wherry-Hill investigation in reference to its two members, heard testimony from Capitol police, who testified that they believed roughly 3,700 of the city's 5,000 estimated queer residents were employed by the federal government. With newfound speculation and circumstantial "evidence," the two-person subcommittee soon became concerned about this alarming estimate; the concerns increased after realizing that some of the ninety-one queer people purged from the DoS had been rehired in other parts of the federal government bureaucracy.[19]

Dubbed the Lavender Scare by historians, this fear of a "homosexual" invasion of the DoS and the federal government more broadly grew throughout the remainder of 1950.[20] Peurifoy's comment about ninety-one "homosexuals" having been removed from their posts in the DoS created additional concerns about internal security in the agency, and this spread well beyond the DoS into other areas of the federal government.[21] About a month after the launching of the Wherry-Hill investigation, discussions on the floor of the U.S. House of Representatives echoed concerns over queer people in the intelligence community. Representative Arthur Miller of Nebraska, directly referencing Peurifoy's statement, declared that that "homosexuals" were "like birds of a feather, they flock together. Where did they go?"[22] In his lengthy speech on the House floor, he also suggested that some "homosexuals" should be "pitied" rather "than condemned" because, he said, they have similar urges to kleptomaniacs, pyromaniacs, and other persons with a "pathological condition" that could not be easily controlled.[23] Here Miller was echoing concerns about mental illness that were common in the psychological community shortly after World War II.[24] Finally, his direct linking of communist ideology to "homosexual" identity underscores the broader shifts that were occurring during the early days of the Lavender Scare.[25]

In underscoring the apparent problem of queer people serving in the federal government's bureaucracy, Miller questioned where the "disgraced" federal employees from the DoS had gone. He further stated: "The Government has the right, nay the obligation, to set up standards for performance of duty not only for prospective employees but for those already on the rolls. This sacred obligation to the taxpayer implies the summary removal of any employee who does not measure up to these standards."[26] At the end of this floor speech, Miller expressed his disbelief that only the DoS had an issue with the employment of queer people, concluding with a critique of the Truman administration for its presumed unwillingness to expunge queer people from the intelligence community and the federal government more broadly.[27] However, the Truman administration was no friend to queer people, and its actions actively fueled both the Red and Lavender Scares throughout the early Cold War period. In 1947, Truman signed Executive Order 9835, which established the Federal Employees Loyalty Program.[28] Nonetheless, many Republicans still criticized the Democrats for being "soft on communism." Miller's critique and others like it stemmed from the fact that Executive Order 9835 allowed only for an initial investigation of new federal employees by the Federal Bureau of Investigation (FBI).[29]

Amid the increasingly politicized rhetoric about queer people in the federal government, the official policy did not immediately change for federal employees in the intelligence sector. However, the two-person senatorial subcommittee began pointing to "successes." For instance, circumstantial evidence and testimony from the Capitol police's vice squads made it appear as if efforts to remove "homosexuals" from the federal government were yielding results. This semblance of traction was intensified after some officials from governmental agencies reported employees for suspected "homosexual" activity.[30] In spring 1950, Governor Thomas Dewey of New York—similar to Miller in the U.S. House of Representatives—publicly accused both Truman and the Democratic congressional leadership of being soft on communists and "sexual perverts."[31] Later that summer, the U.S. Senate, in an effort to further investigate allegations of "homosexuality" in the federal government, formed a new administrative body—the Hoey Committee. Unlike the previous two-person Wherry-Hill investigation, the Hoey Committee was a senatorial subcommittee directly under the Committee on Expenditures in the Executive Department; in 1952, it was officially renamed the Committee on Government Operations. The Hoey Committee's primary purpose was to cast a wider net in an attempt to determine the pervasiveness of queerness within the federal government.[32] McCarthy, whose name is synonymous with anti-communist sentiment, served only briefly on this committee, but his platform ensured that he influenced the broader goals of the Hoey Committee's investigation throughout the so-called Lavender Scare.[33] The Hoey Committee was tasked with creating a database of known or suspected "homosexuals" so that the federal government could conduct risk assessments of these presumed blackmail targets.[34] Before the end of 1950, dubious connections were actively being made between communist ideology and "homosexual" identity, bound together by the assumption that both groups constituted un-American subcultures.[35]

Led by Senator Clyde Hoey of North Carolina, the Hoey Committee's formal investigation would evolve rapidly from 1952 to 1954; during this time, the committee investigated anecdotal instances of potential blackmail in an effort to "ensure security" across federal governmental agencies. In the earliest days of the committee, members consulted with Capitol police, members of the judiciary in Washington, DC, medical and psychiatric providers, and eventually even agents from the FBI.[36] Many medical professionals suggested that "homosexuality" was difficult to detect and that non-straight people could present themselves in a "well-adjusted manner."[37] While the Hoey Committee did not receive the desired support from the medical community, they did begin to include the FBI in their efforts to identify queer people serving in the federal government and intelligence community.[38] In the early 1950s, there was a simultaneous increase in independent efforts within the FBI. Expressing similar concerns throughout the Lavender Scare and beyond, J. Edgar Hoover, the long-serving director of the FBI from the Roosevelt to Nixon administrations, directed the agency to collect intelligence on "known homosexuals" and others who were affiliated with queer spaces and groups. Known as the Sex Deviates Program, this burgeoning intelligence-gathering effort would culminate in roughly 350,000 pages of material before its destruction in the early 1970s.[39]

While the Hoey Committee's investigation resulted in negligible evidence to substantiate this presumption, they nonetheless issued a report, titled *Employment of Homosexuals and Other Sex Perverts in Government*, stating that "homosexuals" in the government posed a clear security risk to the country.[40] For much of the Cold War, this report, with its unfounded claims of queerness posing a security risk, continued to shape policy decisions and presumptions barring queer people from the intelligence community.[41] The report affirmed that "homosexuality" was incompatible with governmental service and directly discussed the rationale for banning queer people from the intelligence community: "The social stigma attached to sex perversion is so great that many perverts go to great lengths to conceal their perverted tendencies. This situation is evidenced by the fact that perverts are frequently victimized by blackmailers who threaten to expose their sexual deviations."[42] Unlike the roundabout presumptions and frequently shifting policies of the World War I and World War II periods, the early Cold War period was unabashedly defined by making a (presumably) clear connection as to how and why "homosexuality" posed a threat to national security. In addition, the report furthered the notion that queer people would seek one another out, form communities, and desire to "be with" their "own kind."[43] Recall that both George Chauncey and Lillian Faderman have argued that the discriminatory actions of the military and the societal stigma generated by a discharge from the military actually helped to establish early queer communities in major cities across America.[44] In all probability, the irony was almost certainly lost on the members of the Hoey Committee.

The Hoey Committee's report also focused on how the issue of security and sexuality was being addressed in the military and more broadly within the federal government, noting that gay men and lesbian women were being "found out" and removed from these institutions.[45] Curiously, the Hoey Committee paid special attention to bisexual people, specifically mentioning that bisexual people were also a security threat because of the presumed potential for blackmail. They warned that bisexual people "are often married and have children, and except for their perverted activities they appear to lead normal lives."[46] Though transgender and gender expansive people were not mentioned in the report, stigma and presumptions about sexuality often caused such people to be punished with policies that specifically (and theoretically only) targeted gay men, lesbian women, bisexual people, and queer people more broadly. As in previous periods, it is also quite likely that these policies and practices also negatively affected some intersex people—particularly those whose physical traits may have been understood as queer in some way—who were presumed to be "homosexual" by a commanding officer. At the time of their report, the Hoey Committee noted that nearly five thousand people had been discharged from the military, and they also mentioned the transition from the use of courts-martial to blue and other administrative discharges.[47]

Most importantly, the Hoey Committee's report officially articulates the developing rationale for banning LGBTQ+ people from the military and intelligence community: the presumed threat of blackmail by the Soviets. The historical impact of this report is not a dramatic calling of names and demands to appear before a congressional committee, as with the Un-American Activities Committee of the U.S. House of Representatives during the height of the Red Scare. Rather, the Hoey Committee's significance extends beyond that, often in more subtle ways.[48] With tacit congressional authority and the veneer of presenting factual information, the actions of the Hoey Committee helped to further institutionalize the anti-LGBTQ+, pro-security sentiment rooted as far back as the World War I period, while also laying the groundwork for the forthcoming actions of the Eisenhower administration.[49] In an effort to concurrently substantiate the Hoey Committee's claims and this newly emerging rationale, the fledgling CIA conducted an initial study in 1950, later revisited in a Navy investigative report in 1957.[50] Although the Truman administration had established a loyalty review program for federal employees in the late 1940s, President Dwight D. Eisenhower would take these actions a step further—in part because the Hoey Committee's report failed to make any specific legislative recommendations.[51] In an attempt to address the presumed problem of blackmail risks against LGBTQ+ people in the military and intelligence community, Eisenhower, in 1953, signed Executive Order 10450, which codified "sexual perversion" and homosexuality as grounds for dismissal from any federal position, relying on the same rationale advanced by the Hoey Committee at the height of the early Cold War period's Lavender Scare.[52] Four years later, the Navy Board of Inquiry further examined some of the claims stemming from the Hoey Committee report.[53] In a likely effort to bolster the claims of the Hoey Committee, the CIA, and the Eisenhower administration, the Navy produced the so-called Crittenden Report, named for board chair Captain S. H. Crittenden, Jr., which examined the validity of the claims equating "homosexuality" to security risks.[54]

As noted by David Johnson in *The Lavender Scare: The Cold War Persecution of Gays and Lesbians in the Federal Government*, the Crittenden Report actually found the claims of the Hoey Committee's report to be both negligible and erroneous.[55] In fact, the Crittenden Report stated that there was absolutely no data to indicate the supposed linkage between "homosexuality" and susceptibility to blackmail.[56] In addition, the Crittenden Report speculated that there was a significantly higher number of LGBTQ+ people in the country than previously assumed. While the political actors of the day continued to propagate the presumed connection between "homosexuality" and susceptibility to blackmail by the Soviets, the Crittenden Report unabashedly refuted this claim and the resulting rationale used to exclude LGBTQ+ people from the military and intelligence community.[57] The Crittenden Report's claims were controversial; unsurprisingly, even the Navy Board of Inquiry seemed suspicious of these findings.[58] In fact, the report and its findings remained secret until the early 1980s, when a declassified version was finally retrieved via a highly contested Freedom of Information Act request. Until then, the Navy denied that it possessed any data specifically demonstrating that LGBTQ+ people were not security risks to the military, the intelligence community, and the nation more broadly.[59] Since the national security state must seek to retain its power structures around a "secure state," the Navy likely refused to release the report because of the nature of its findings; this certainly seems to be the case, given that it remained hidden until its court-ordered release it more than twenty years later.[60]

The refusal to release, or even to acknowledge, this report to the intelligence community and other branches of the military implicitly condoned the developing rationale and continuance of anti-LGBTQ+ policies. More specifically, it tacitly enabled the DoD, in coordination with Navy leadership, to issue DoD Directive 1332.14 in 1959.[61] Despite clear evidence indicating that "homosexuality" was not a risk factor for blackmail by the Soviets, DoD Directive 1332.14 went into effect, specifying that any form of homosexual behavior would render someone fully unfit for military service. Moreover, it clearly stated that "sexual perversion" was not in line with military values; this had an even broader impact on LGBTQ+ people, particularly given that transgender and gender expansive people were often presumed to be egregiously mentally ill and/or sexually perverse.[62] Thus, the presumed threat of blackmail from the Soviets, the ongoing political rhetoric, the Hoey Committee's investigative report, and the advent of Executive Order 10450 all led to continued concerns about security risks being inherently linked to LGBTQ+ people, which then culminated in a much more direct and harmful DoD policy, in the form of DoD Directive 1332.14, by the end of the 1950s.

In many ways, this new DoD policy was an extension of earlier iterations of anti-LGBTQ+ policy from the DoD's predecessor administrative bodies. Like the policies of the World War II period, this new policy would uphold the notion of avoiding courts-martial and potentially damning public hearings like those from the World War I period; however, this new policy would be far more centralized, consistently applied, and clear than the numerous policy shifts that occurred during the World War II period. The DoD allowed this new and more centralized policy to go into effect, despite the fact that the Navy had produced evidence that directly contradicted it.[63] The rationale for this policy is a more formalized and consolidated notion of the national security state, as outlined by the National Security Act of 1947 and related legislation. Less than fifteen years after Congress passed that landmark legislation, anti-LGBTQ+ policies for the military and intelligence community had become more formalized, centralized, and strengthened by way of both an executive order and the new DoD policy, which officially claimed that "homosexuality" was a national security risk because of susceptibility to blackmail by the Soviets.[64]

By burying the Crittenden Report and keeping it out of public view, the government's investment in anti-LGBTQ+ policies and the backdrop of the Cold War together ensured that anti-LGBTQ+ discrimination would become more pervasive throughout the military and intelligence community in the coming decades. These actions and this discriminatory practice echoed throughout the whole of the Cold War and even into the eventual policy changes of the 1990s. When the military's move to an all-volunteer force eliminated the draft in the early 1970s, the policies excluding LGBTQ+ people from the military and intelligence community remained.[65] In 1975, the language of DoD Directive 1332.14 shifted from "sex perversion" to "homosexuality" and "homosexual acts," but despite a change in political rhetoric, the rationale for this policy did not alter much at all.

While the rhetoric used against LGBTQ+ people experienced a broad shift in American society, only slight revisions were made to anti-LGBTQ+ military and intelligence community policy during President John F. Kennedy's truncated tenure and for the remainder of the early Cold War period. The DoD made only one major revision to its anti-LGBTQ+ policy in 1965, enabling service members who were accused of being "homosexuals" and who faced less than honorable discharges to plead their case to an administrative discharge board and be represented by counsel. Permitting service members to have their own counsel during these proceedings was seen as a liberalization of some broader policies during this era of student protest and anti-war sentiment.[66] At the same time, the visibility of the broader LGBTQ+ community increased significantly throughout the 1960s, and major transitions and developments for the community occurred throughout this significant decade.[67] During this time, the LGBTQ+ community won numerous legal battles that were crucial to their civil liberties and rights, such as the right to receive gay publications through the mail in *One, Inc. v. Olesen* and *Manual Enterprises, Inc. v. Day*.[68] Through cases like *Stoumen v. Reilly* and *Vallegra v. Dept. of Alcoholic Beverage Control* in the 1950s, the community won the legal right to congregate at a queer bar.[69] Most notably, the LGBTQ+ community undertook the earliest known examples of organized queer activism and physical resistance during this decade. Examples included the picketing of President Lyndon B. Johnson's White House for workplace rights in 1965, resisting police harassment during the Compton's Cafeteria Riot in 1966 in San Francisco, and most notably in the Stonewall Riots in 1969 in New York City.[70] This more formalized queer resistance continued through the 1970s and 1980s, having both direct and indirect impacts on anti-LGBTQ+ policies in the military and intelligence community in the coming periods.

As in the 1960s, there were only minor changes to anti-LGBTQ+ policies in the DoD throughout the 1970s. As noted earlier, one of the most significant DoD policy shifts during this decade was the move to an all-volunteer force and the elimination of the draft. Signed into law in 1971 by President Richard Nixon, the policy became effective in early 1973, when the U.S. Selective Service System was placed on "standby."[71] While this policy decision from the Nixon administration did not directly affect anti-LGBTQ+ policies in the military, it meant that LGBTQ+ people could now avoid such policies and military service, unlike the nearly two million people who had been conscripted to fight in the Vietnam War from 1964 to 1973. During this time, the LGBTQ+ rights movement—learning from the civil rights movement of the 1960s and occurring alongside student protests against the Vietnam War, a rise in environmental activism, and the fight for women's liberation—grew in significant ways, with added visibility throughout the 1970s.[72] Protests against the anti-LGBTQ+ policies of the military and intelligence community were also beginning. The most famous of these was when Sergeant Leonard Matlovich of the Air Force took to the cover of *Time* magazine in 1975, saying "The Air Force pinned a medal on me for killing a man and discharged me for making love to one."[73] The same year, President Gerald Ford oversaw an executive branch that made some progress on LGBTQ+ rights. Most significantly, the U.S. Civil Service Commission announced, in 1975, that it would "end its policy forbidding employment of gay people in federal jobs"; this halted the Eisenhower administration's anti-LGBTQ+ civilian-focused policies across federal bodies, including some within the intelligence community such as the DoS, the Department of Transportation (the agency with oversight of the Coast Guard during peacetime from 1967 to 2003), the Department of the Treasury, the White House, and others.[74] The Ford administration, also in 1975, revised DoD Directive 1332.14 from 1959, changing archaic terms like "sex perversion" to "homosexuality," which was a significant move away from the stigmatizing language of the 1950s.[75]

Following the Arab oil embargo of the early 1970s, the Carter administration, in 1977, oversaw the creation of the Department of Energy, which housed the first intelligence community element free of a blanket anti-LGBTQ+ policy.[76] Despite that sense of progress, there were effectively no significant changes to the DoD's related policies during the 1970s. In 1981, Deputy Secretary of Defense W. Graham Claytor, Jr., who served under President Jimmy Carter, commented on the Ford administration's revisions to DoD Directive 1332.14. Recalling that the Carter administration had left these revisions intact, Claytor reiterated that these revisions made clear that any form of engagement in a "homosexual" act or any "homosexual" behaviors were incompatible with military service and would result in a discharge.[77] The Ford administration's policy revisions, which this member of the Carter administration referenced, included the first official use of the phrase "homosexuality is incompatible with military service."[78] This consequential sentence was repeated by many presidential administrations, military officials, and others through the 1990s and 2000s. While the language had moved to a less stigmatizing place, DoD policy still clearly stated that LGBTQ+ people were a security risk to the military, the intelligence community, and the nation-state more broadly.

THE LATE COLD WAR PERIOD (1980s): MENTAL INSTABILITY TO HANDLE SECURE INFORMATION

You have acknowledged that you have been an active homosexual since your teenage years and that you have had relationships with various women lasting from four months to two years. However, this information does not appear to have been volunteered or in any way acknowledged by yourself, or your partner, during the course of your initial security investigation . . . The initial silence . . . indicates . . . a willingness to engage in deceptive behavior.

—WILLIAM KOPATISH, DIRECTOR OF SECURITY FOR THE CIA,
IN A LETTER DENYING A SECURITY CLEARANCE TO JULIE DUBBS,
SENIOR TECHNICAL ILLUSTRATOR FOR A DEFENSE CONTRACTOR[79]

While the presumption that LGBTQ+ people were security threats to the nation-state persisted throughout the Cold War, the rationale shifted in the 1980s, away from the notion that LGBTQ+ people were uniquely susceptible to Soviet blackmail. Instead, the late Cold War rationale emphasized a presumed mental instability to handle secure information, which could result in security vulnerabilities and concerns related to trust; ultimately, this rationale would bar LGBTQ+ people from both military and intelligence community positions that required security clearances. This new rationale emphasized some of the already debunked presumptions of anti-LGBTQ+ psychology from the World War II period. At the same time, the fear of HIV/AIDS arose as a supplementary quasi-rationale to ban LGBTQ+ from military service. Here, I examine these rationales and discuss how the federal government, the military, and other security-related institutions such as the CIA interpreted LGBTQ+ people as security threats in the late Cold War period. Important developments during this period include two reports funded and supported by the DoD's Defense Personnel Security Research Center (PERSEREC); the Director of Central Intelligence Directive (DCID) Number 1/14; the case of *Dubbs v. Central Intelligence Agency*; and the outbreak of the HIV/AIDS epidemic in the mid-1980s.[80] Though the language used to discuss LGBTQ+ people in the military began to shift by the end of the Carter administration, the new rationale emphasizing mental instability, along with the quasi-rationale of fear of HIV/AIDS, principally characterized the tenure of President Ronald Reagan from 1981 to 1989.

In 1986, PERSEREC was established within the DoD with the goal of improving DoD personnel security through research and education.[81] Among the various types of security-related research produced by the institution, PERSEREC investigated whether queer people were actually less mentally stable than their straight peers, and hence whether an adequate and logical reason existed for maintaining the military's anti-LGBTQ+ ban.[82] Ironically, this research project relied on outdated presumptions advanced by the American Psychiatric Association's (APA's) *Diagnostic and Statistical Manual of Mental Disorders* published in 1968 (*DMS-II*), but the APA had in 1980 released a new edition (*DSM-III*) that removed claims about a potential link between "homosexuality" and a higher occurrence of mental instability, noting that there was "no diagnostic category for homosexuality."[83] In other words, one of PERSEREC's early objectives was to fund and produce research related to claims that had already been discounted nearly a decade earlier. This demonstrates how dated the military's ideas of human sexuality were, even by the professional standards of the psychological community in the 1980s. Even so, the DoD's newly formed research and education group sought an answer to this question, and eventually they obtained one, similar to that of the Navy's Crittenden Report of 1957.[84]

Ultimately, the research funded by PERSEREC resulted in two reports—Theodore Sarbin and Kenneth Karols's *Nonconforming Sexual Orientations and Military Suitability* in December 1988 and Michael

McDaniel's *Preserve Adjustment of Homosexual and Heterosexual Military Accessions: Implications for Security Clearance Suitability* in January 1989—both of which investigated claims about LGBTQ+ people's presumed mental instability, which was the emerging rationale of the late Cold War, and related untrustworthiness.[85] Framing the question of mental stability as an issue of vulnerability assessment and trustworthiness, the primary objective was to produce reports that examined an exclusionary rationale, which stemmed from the APA's already outdated *DSM-II* and "from the fact that lesbian and gay male applicants for security clearances do not always volunteer the information that they are gay."[86] In the first report, Sarbin and Karols found no specific sexuality-related security risks in the handling of secure information in the intelligence community; in fact, they found that non-straight people "are every bit as suitable for service as heterosexuals" in the same position and "are not different from heterosexual men and women in regard to adjustment criteria or job performance" within the DoD or related intelligence community.[87] Interestingly, McDaniel, in authoring the second of these reports, suggested that non-straight service members and intelligence officers—given their personal discretion in reference to disclosing their sexual identities—might actually be *more* trustworthy in handling secure information related to the government's military operations and intelligence community.[88] As the reader might imagine, these reports and their findings were deemed unacceptable to Pentagon officials. PERSEREC was directed to essentially rewrite the report, redacting any suggestion that "homosexuals" might be suitable for service in the military or intelligence community.[89] However, congressional action, by way of Representatives Gerry Studds of Massachusetts and Patricia Schroeder of Colorado in 1990, resulted in enough media attention to force release of the report in its original, unaltered form, which is the only reason we know of its contents today.[90]

While PERSEREC and the DoD were facing this attempt to redact and rewrite their findings, the intelligence community, by way of the CIA, was also implementing a new rationale in the late Cold War period. DCID Number 1/14, issued by the CIA originally in 1984, with amendments in 1987, stated that "to be eligible for SCI [security clearance information] access, individuals must be stable" and that "homosexual conduct . . . is to be considered as a factor in determining an individual's... stability" of the mind, related trustworthiness, and ability to handle secure information.[91] The CIA's newly instituted policy thus shifted from a rationale concerning blackmail to a much broader concern about the mental stability and related trustworthiness of LGBTQ+ people more generally. Like the DoD, the CIA also relied on an erroneous and outdated understanding of LGBTQ+ people, as represented in the APA's *DSM-II* instead of the *DSM-III*. In practice, the CIA's newly instituted policy would use discriminatory tactics to reject nearly all security clearance applications by LGBTQ+ people on the basis of false claims about mental stability, related trustworthiness, and the capability to handle secure information. But with an increasingly visible and boisterous LGBTQ+ rights movement building throughout the 1980s, the policy was ultimately challenged in federal court.[92]

Because of their close association with the DoD, many elements of the intelligence community apparatus largely mirrored the exclusionary policies and rationales of the military, which were rooted in the already outdated notions about LGBTQ+ people. In many ways, this is counterintuitive, and while I could not identify a definitive reason, it may have been due in part to the influence of the Reagan-era "Moral Majority"—a Christian Right sociopolitical movement led by Baptist preacher Jerry Falwell, Sr. during the 1980s. Acting as thought leaders who helped support a new Christian Right coalition, Falwell and other prominent members of the Moral Majority actively shaped Republican politics and, consequently, the Republican Party platform throughout the 1980s.[93] Despite the Moral Majority's declining influence at the end of the decade, libertarian ideas about queer people in the military still began to shift to greater alignment with those of more traditionalist peers, which further demonstrates the impact of this coalition on the Republican Party and the federal government.[94]

Despite the common rationales between the military and intelligence community, the CIA's DCID 1/14 from 1984 and 1987 marks a slight break regarding the language of the policy. Unlike its DoD policy counterpart, DCID 1/14 directly states the rationale for LGBTQ+ exclusion—the supposed mental instability and related untrustworthiness of LGBTQ+ people—within the text of its policy. This policy was challenged in federal court, culminating in *Dubbs v. Central Intelligence Agency* in 1989. The plaintiff in the case, a lesbian woman working for a defense contractor, had been actively denied a security clearance on the basis of her sexuality. Ultimately, the federal judge ruled in favor of the CIA. While Dubbs's legal team argued that the anti-LGBTQ+ policy was arbitrary and capricious, the judge (1) affirmed the district court's decision "not to review CIA security clearance determinations under the arbitrary and capricious standard of the APA" [Administrative Procedure Act] and (2) affirmed the ability of the agency's director to apply the standards as directed by the president of the United States via executive order.[95] Though this attempt to rescind the policy failed, DCID 1/14 was ultimately amended in 1994, following the passage of DADT. The revised version stated: "the individual must be stable; trustworthy; reliable; of excellent character, judgment, and discretion; and of unquestioned loyalty to the United States," marking a clear turning away from the explicitly homophobic language of earlier iterations of the directive.[96] Following that revision, sexuality would no longer determine the ability of an intelligence agency to deny queer people access to security clearance information.

Between the late Cold War period of the 1980s and the DADT period in the early 1990s, the HIV/AIDS epidemic created a supplementary quasi-rationale for banning LGBTQ+ people from the military in particular. While the overarching rationale of the late Cold War period remained a broader claim about the mental stability and trustworthiness of LGBTQ+ people, the stigma and fear of the newly emerging virus—along with its disproportionate impact on queer men and transgender women—hovered in the background, bolstering the existing ban. Following its emergence in the mid-1980s, the HIV/AIDS epidemic also fostered a new wave of LGBTQ+ activism and media attention. In the early 1980s, Lester Kinsolving became the first White House correspondent to ask a question about HIV/AIDS, originally known as Gay-Related Immune Deficiency Syndrome (GRIDS). In 1984, Kinsolving asked whether the president had expressed concerns about protecting the military from HIV, and for years to come he continued to ask questions about the Reagan administration's inaction and reluctance to publicly acknowledge the growing HIV/AIDS epidemic. Deputy Press Secretary Larry Speakes consistently responded in an exaggerated and sarcastic manner, questioning why Kinsolving was *so interested* in a "gay topic."[97] By the late 1980s, in the face of unprecedented deaths and government inaction, HIV/

AIDS activists, guided by the AIDS Coalition to Unleash Power! (ACT UP!) and other organizations, were building a new advocacy strategy. Eventually, ACT UP! framed the failure of the Reagan administration to adequately address the public health issue as "AIDS-Gate." During this period, large protests and demonstrations were organized on a number of fronts, including major pharmaceutical companies and industry associations, the Catholic Church and other religious institutions, the Food and Drug Administration (FDA), and the National Institutes of Health (NIH), among others.[98] Upon realizing that HIV could be transmitted to non-LGBTQ+ people, the Reagan administration ultimately did—under the direction of Secretary of Defense Caspar Weinberger—test virtually the entire military for the virus in 1987, and following increased attention from the FDA, NIH, and public health apparatus, such screening protocols became more common as the HIV/AIDS epidemic continued into the 1990s.[99]

THE IMPACT OF HIV/AIDS ACTIVISM ON THE CAMPAIGN TRAIL

With the HIV/AIDS epidemic at its height in the early 1990s, increased activist pressure was continuing to mount on government officials, including President George H. W. Bush and others in the White House.[100] During this transition from the late Cold War period to the DADT period, ACT UP! initiated a number of actions, including ones targeting the H. W. Bush administration and the presidential campaign of Governor Bill Clinton. As noted by David France, these activists, at a campaign stop, directly and very cleverly pressured Clinton to make an off-the-cuff remark about HIV/AIDS, thus ensuring that it became an issue in the 1992 presidential election. Even more notably, activists pressured the H. W. Bush administration, in 1992, by exhibiting the newly assembling AIDS Memorial Quilt in Washington, DC, and then leading a march across the National Mall; the action culminated in scattering the ashes of people who died from AIDS-related causes onto the South Lawn of the White House.[101] Such highly publicized actions garnered significant media attention and helped to ensure that the HIV/AIDS epidemic would be more readily addressed by the FDA, NIH, and future administrations.

At yet another campaign stop during the 1992 presidential election, Clinton was nudged into pledging to allow queer people into the military if they wished to join and met the required qualifications. Following his election, President Bill Clinton, via Secretary of Defense Les Aspin, commissioned the RAND Corporation—a nonprofit public policy think tank developed with support from the military following World War II—to undertake a study on the ability of queer people to serve in the armed forces.[102] The resulting report, *Sexual Orientation and U.S. Military Personnel Policy: Options and Assessment*, analyzed the question of allowing queer people to serve and addressed two major concerns that were quickly being brought to the national forefront: the potential for antigay violence and the spread of HIV/AIDS throughout the military.[103] The report also focused on the question of "unit cohesion," which developed into the primary rationale for the soon-to-be-introduced policy of DADT. The introduction of DADT, which was originally intended as a legislative compromise, and the Clinton administration's attention to the issue can be credited to the work of (1) LGBTQ+ activists who pressured Clinton on the campaign trail and (2) ACT UP! and HIV/AIDS activists who used more direct and aggressive tactics in the burgeoning national fight for LGBTQ+ rights.[104] This activism helped to spur a shift in the anti-LGBTQ+ policies of the military and intelligence community, as well as in the rationale behind them, that would persist through the DADT period of the 1990s and 2000s.

4

IT'S MILITARY READINESS AND UNIT COHESION, *NOT* DISCRIMINATION

Following the 1992 presidential election, the RAND Corporation, as mentioned earlier, undertook a study about the ability of queer people to serve in the U.S. Armed Forces. The result of their study was a report, *Sexual Orientation and U.S. Military Personnel Policy: Options and Assessment*, that addressed two major concerns that had entered into the national dialogue: (1) the potential for antigay violence and (2) the spread of HIV/AIDS through the military.[1] In addition to these major concerns, the RAND Corporation explored the question of "unit cohesion"—whether the presence of queer service members would dramatically impede military readiness and effective communication within the unit. The election of President Bill Clinton, the work of LGBTQ+ activists, and a changing social climate in the early 1990s helped to spur a shift away from the Reagan-era policies of the late Cold War period—the presumed mental instability and related untrustworthiness of LGBTQ+ people—to an entirely new policy: "Don't Ask, Don't Tell" (DADT).[2] Originally intended as a "compromise," DADT represented the next major shift in anti-LGBTQ+ policies within the Department of Defense (DoD) and DoD-adjacent positions in the intelligence community. DADT, which extended well beyond the early 1990s, had a broad impact on popular culture as well as on future policies in the armed forces.

In this chapter, I examine the anti-LGBTQ+ policies that developed throughout the DADT period from the early 1990s to 2011. The burgeoning queer activism of the HIV/AIDS epidemic laid the groundwork for an even more politically active LGBTQ+ community in the early 1990s and beyond; as explained in the previous chapter, this was clearly seen on the campaign trail during the 1992 presidential election. With this new activism came a new rationale for banning LGBTQ+ people from the military and intelligence community. While the RAND Corporation study focused primarily on the issues of potential antigay violence and the spread of HIV/AIDS, the rationale that ultimately emerged focused on unit cohesion, along with related concerns such as "privacy." I begin by analyzing these initial concerns and the eventual rationale of unit cohesion. Later, I discuss the eventual repeal of DADT in 2011, leading into a discussion of transgender-specific policies throughout the 2010s and into the 2020s.

THE "DON'T ASK, DON'T TELL" (DADT) PERIOD (EARLY 1990s TO 2011): UNIT COHESION AND RELATED CONCERNS

As a soldier, I had to swear an oath to uphold the Constitution; written into that noble document are the words 'all men are created equal.' I believe in that document and those words, and so I don't believe that I should be made to feel unequal under a discriminatory policy like "Don't Ask, Don't Tell."

—LIEUTENANT DAN CHOI[3]

Originally drafted and implemented as a compromise to allow queer people to serve more honorably in the military, the policy of "Don't Ask, Don't Tell," or DADT, was that queer people should be "left alone as long as they did not reveal their sexual orientation" or attempt to engage in any "homosexual conduct."[4] Regarding the provision about "homosexual conduct," the Army and the broader DoD took the position that being lesbian, gay, bisexual, queer, or any other label was not the issue of concern to the military; the concern was about the conduct, *not* the identity, of service members. While many service members and veterans from the DADT period would likely argue that the policy was not implemented in such a manner, the Army, specifically, released detailed information about the types of situations that might trigger or initiate separation procedures for a solider under DADT: (1) if a soldier demonstrated that they had or intended to engage in a "homosexual act"; (2) if a soldier solicited another person to engage in a "homosexual act"; (3) if a soldier married someone of the same sex or gender, or tried to do so; or (4) if a soldier admitted to being gay, lesbian, bisexual, or queer and there was credible intent/proof to believe this statement was true and accurate.[5] While DADT was supposedly focused only on the conduct of service members, the reality was that it would have a much broader reach across the DoD and its service branches during this twenty-year period.

The policy was originally intended to allow all people to serve without questions related to their sexuality, presuming they could meet the military's standards of service and adhere to the restrictions on conduct. In reality, DADT failed to bring greater tolerance of queer service members, and the widespread discussion of queer people in the military caused direct harm to many who enlisted during this period.[6] Intended to nullify the significance of sexual identities in the military, DADT actually reinforced their importance, further encouraging the heterosexism and homophobia that had spread across the military and intelligence community in the previous century. Reiterating the status quo, DADT led to vigilante-style investigations aimed at rooting out people presumed to be queer.[7] It also facilitated a shift in the rationale for banning LGBTQ+ people from the military and active duty positions in the intelligence community, ultimately conceptualizing queer people—when engaged in "homosexual conduct" or simply disclosing their identities—as a "hard" security threat affecting unit cohesion and, thus, military performance and readiness.[8] However, this rationale emerged only later; initial concerns were focused on antigay violence and fears about HIV/AIDS. I begin by discussing these early concerns, with reference to the RAND Corporation's 1993 report, and then turn to examining the eventual rationale of unit cohesion and related concerns like privacy.

THE EARLY CONCERNS: ANTIGAY VIOLENCE AND THE SPREAD OF HIV/AIDS

In response to the secretary of defense's request for a feasibility study about allowing queer people to serve in the military, the National Defense

Research Institute produced *Sexual Orientation and U.S. Military Personnel Policy: Options and Assessment.* This 1993 RAND report provided a brief overview of major policy developments related to the treatment of queer people in the military from World War I to the early 1990s, along with relevant analysis to help Pentagon officials in making a formal policy recommendation to Clinton regarding service for queer people. The report covered a wide variety of topics, ranging from generalized discussions of human sexuality to public opinion about queer inclusion in the armed forces. Major sections explored topics such as analogous experiences in foreign military forces and domestic police and fire departments, historical data pertaining to the racial integration of the military, public opinion regarding the military more generally, and various legal issues to be considered. Other topics included statistics on the rates of engagement in oral and anal sex by straight and queer people, the integration of women into the military, and an overview of "military culture." For policy purposes, the most important portions were the sections that debunked the decade's early arguments against queer inclusion in the military—namely, the potential for antigay violence and the spread of HIV/AIDS within the military. The report explicitly debunked these two early concerns, thereby creating room for a new rationale for the policy of DADT.[9]

An early concern about allowing queer people to enlist was the fear that it would increase the occurrence of antigay violence throughout the military. The concern was that straight service members would react to the news of queer inclusion with acts of homophobic violence because they would be expected to serve alongside non-straight colleagues. Early in their report, the RAND Corporation explicitly refuted this concern, citing evidence from limited data sources that studied such inclusion within the civilian population.[10] They returned to this issue later in the report, where they pointed out that such occurrences are partially a reflection of leadership, noting that effective leadership from a commanding officer and a zero-tolerance policy toward violence likely offered key solutions in curbing such incidents.[11] Thus, the researchers explicitly debunked the concern over a significant rise in antigay violence as a result of this policy change, noting that a clear policy paired with effective leadership would help to minimize any such increase.[12]

The 1993 report also debunked the concern that queer inclusion in the military would cause an increase in the prevalence of HIV/AIDS within the armed forces. Perpetuating homophobia and stigma about HIV, the presumption was that queer inclusion would affect the health of the military, compromising the ability of service members to engage in combat situations. The recent history of the HIV/AIDS epidemic had been marked by years of practical inaction by the Reagan administration, a more conservative social climate, a lack of medically accurate information about HIV, and stigma about testing positive for HIV. Unfortunately, these realities made this argument seem logical to some people in the early 1990s. However, the RAND Corporation's report laid out numerous reasons why this concern was likely not a problem for the military of the early 1990s.[13] While the researchers noted that there was no way to predict the magnitude of the HIV epidemic's impact on enlisted service members, they debunked the notion that the accession of queer people into the armed forces would directly correspond to a marked, significant increase of new HIV diagnoses within the military. They pointed to the military's standing practice of screening for HIV before deployment, which was a preexisting policy rooted in stigma from the early days of the HIV/AIDS epidemic. They reiterated that (1) "all military personnel whose health is seriously affected by HIV are discharged" and (2) "the military blood supply would remain safe," given the current status of HIV testing procedures within the military.[14] By describing the military's screening method for HIV in detail, they explained why the military blood supply would remain safe, even with the accession of queer service members. Such methods included regularly scheduled sexual health screenings and testing before accession, routine testing through enlistment, and testing before deployment.[15]

While the RAND Corporation actively debunked the early concerns about rising rates of antigay violence and the spread of HIV/AIDS within the military, they also examined another potential concern—unit cohesion. Following their report, this would become the primary rationale for implementing DADT in the early 1990s, and throughout the 2000s the phrase *unit cohesion* would become one of the prevailing buzzwords in political debates about allowing queer people to serve openly.

THE EVENTUAL RATIONALE FOR DADT: UNIT COHESION AND THE RELATED CONCERN OF PRIVACY

While the RAND Corporation's 1993 report helped to mitigate concerns over antigay violence and the spread of HIV/AIDS, another concern still lingered. Critics of LGBTQ+ inclusion in the armed forces in the early to mid-1990s repeatedly cited concerns relating to the broad idea of unit cohesion, which soon became the leading rationale of the DADT period. Though the RAND researchers did discuss this concern, their report left enough room for it to persist and to become the emerging rationale for limiting the ability of queer people to serve more openly. Unlike the earlier concerns, the concept of unit cohesion remained one of the most discussed issues leading up to the eventual creation and implementation of DADT in early 1994.[16] Here, I discuss the rationale of unit cohesion, along with the related concern about privacy, particularly in relation to straight service members who might soon be serving alongside queer people. In analyzing and discussing these concerns, I highlight the erroneous logic associated with each of them before pivoting to a discussion of the eventual demise of DADT in the early 2010s.

The concern with unit cohesion, which eventually emerged as the primary rationale for DADT, was that queer people could undermine other service members' ability to function efficiently and effectively within their unit. The argument was that permitting queer people into a service branch would create a cultural climate issue within their unit and consequently disrupt the unit's cohesion, which would in turn affect its combat readiness. The unit cohesion problem, thus, presented a real-world concern that combat readiness might suffer from the inclusion of queer people. This hyperbolic concern was clearly a reach at best, but this key assumption underpinned the rationale, while also blaming queer people for any type of possible incongruity within a unit. Rather than framing this as an issue of homophobia within a unit, this rationale presented a slippery slope in which queer service members could ultimately undermine units across service branches and hence the overall effectiveness of the country's armed forces. This fear of queer people serving openly in the military also reinforced traditional notions of hegemonic masculinity and the notion that the military was a place for masculine dominance;

the prevailing notions of queer identities challenged, subverted, and disrupted that ideal of masculinity. Allowing queer people into the military would directly challenge that idea, along with the heteronormativity that the military had been intentionally cultivating since World War II.[17] In sum, the emerging unit cohesion rationale argued that queer people would—by their very nature—disrupt a unit's cohesion, the military's culture, related posts within the intelligence community, and the country's effectiveness in combat.

Eventually, unit cohesion would emerge as the primary and official rationale of DADT, and the mere idea of allowing queer people to serve openly in the military was halted by a concern about military effectiveness and performance.[18] Scholars, particularly in the early to mid-2000s, criticized the policy by analyzing other militaries that had integrated queer and straight service members into various units. For example, Aaron Belkin and Melissa Levitt, writing a decade before the repeal of DADT, utilized a detailed empirical analysis to determine that there was no "data indicating that lifting the gay ban undermined" the "performance, cohesion, readiness, or morale" of the Israeli Defense Forces (IDF).[19] They specifically chose to critique the unit cohesion rationale by discussing the IDF, given the numerous security concerns within the context of Middle Eastern geopolitics. The rationale of unit cohesion as a security concern for the federal government, as noted by the RAND report, arose from anecdotal evidence that straight service members did not like queer people.[20] Yet, the organizational and leadership structures within the military, along with findings from military theory literature, demonstrate that there is no correlation between liking peers within a unit and the ultimate performance of that unit.[21] The rationale of unit cohesion reimagines the idea of banning queer people from serving openly as being rooted in "logic," but that argument is simply fallacious.

A secondary and related rationale for DADT, which sometimes arose alongside or in place of unit cohesion, was privacy—specifically for straight service members. Rooted in the idea that queer inclusion meant infringing upon the privacy rights of straight service members who lodged, showered, communed, and served with queer service members, the supplementary rationale of privacy again presumed that all of this would lead to a reduction in unit cohesion. This circuitous notion of queer inclusion affecting privacy and unit cohesion was also premised upon the idea that queer people would be attracted to their straight peers, which would lead them to propositioning them for some type of sexual interaction or relationship. This secondary rationale incorrectly and salaciously presumed that queer people were predators who would seduce, coerce, and manipulate straight peers into having sex with them.[22] Assuming that same sex/gender nude bodies in shared quarters would immediately cause arousal for queer service members perpetuates this idea, while also fueling myths about the hypersexualization of queer men.[23] The supplementary rationale of privacy thus relied heavily upon the myth of the gay male predator, which assumed that queer men would be unable to control their sexual appetite and might seek out nonconsensual physical or sexual encounters with straight men.[24] While this rationale of privacy may seem like a nonconcern in today's world, the debate around the issue remained present at various points throughout the DADT period.[25] At any rate, several flaws quite obviously existed in relation to the privacy rationale, which simply relied upon these outdated and disproven historically rooted myths about queerness and, in particular, queer men.[26] This specific rationale also demonstrates how DADT fit neatly within and relied upon the anti-LGBTQ+ policies and norms of the American military, government, and security-related bodies throughout the previous century.

THE DEMISE AND EVENTUAL REPEAL OF DADT

While the concerns affecting the question of queer inclusion the military largely evolved into a discussion of privacy and unit cohesion, the fight against DADT was an effort on multiple fronts, led by congressional leaders, queer activists, service members, and veterans. This multifront effort was bolstered by several other realities, including the misguided implementation of DADT throughout the early 2000s, the extraordinarily high financial cost of the policy, evolving discussions about the policy's ineffectiveness, and continued resistance against DADT in the late 2000s. In this section, I discuss these factors in relation to the demise of DADT and its corresponding rationale. I also map how DADT evolved throughout the tenure of President George W. Bush from 2001 to 2009;

this evolution is of particular interest, because it later affects the actions of congressional leaders and queer activists during President Barack Obama's first term from 2009 to 2013. The concluding portions of this section focus on the history of DADT's demise and repeal by detailing the activism that occurred from the end of the Clinton administration to the first term of the Obama administration.

DADT, as negotiated by Congress and the Clinton administration, was initially intended to be a compromise; Clinton considered himself to be doing work akin to Truman's efforts to desegregate the military in the 1950s.[27] The original intent was that DADT would allow LGBTQ+ people to serve in the military so long as they were not in any way open about their identity. The presumption was that this would simply render sexuality a nonissue, thereby ending the long history of witch hunts against LGBTQ+ people in the military and intelligence community. Several factors accounted for the failure of this policy and its original intent, despite the hope that it would ensure that people could serve without any questions about their LGBTQ+ status. Some the earliest critiques of the military's application of the policy actually came from President Clinton and then First Lady Hillary Clinton, following the brutal murder of Private First Class Barry Winchell in July 1999. Winchell, while asleep in his Army barracks, was beaten to death by fellow soldiers; their motive was that they believed Winchell was not straight, since he was dating a transgender woman.[28] Following this horrific murder, President Clinton, in December 1999, said the policy was "out of whack" with the intent of the 1993 law. Hillary Clinton, who was then running as a candidate for the U.S. Senate, was even more deeply critical of the military's application of DADT; some people observed that the president's opinions appeared be nudged left by the first lady turned senatorial candidate, particularly since she had been so outspoken about the policy and other measures like health care reform. Toward the end of his administration, Clinton stated that he had hoped to do more for LGBTQ+ inclusion in the armed forces but that DADT was the best he could do at the time.[29]

A number of factors, including the brutal murder of Winchell and the sharp response from the White House, prompted the Pentagon to commission a review of the policy and the associated climate of the armed forces.[30] Amid some early public critiques of the policy, the Pentagon began to review the climate at major military bases and installations across the country. The White House said that Clinton would not push for a more inclusive measure to replace DADT, citing his limited time remaining in office, but Clinton did state that he hoped the military would "live up to its end of the bargain and obey the ... spirit of the compromise" that had sparked the development of DADT in the early 1990s.[31] Concurrently, the personnel and related financial costs of implementing DADT were beginning to mount, and the number of annual discharges under the policy began to rise by the end of the decade. This increase was driven, at least in part, by the policy's misapplication and increases in internal vigilante pseudo-investigations against fellow service members who were presumed to be queer. By that time, the DoD was averaging just over a thousand annual discharges for "homosexual conduct."[32] Less than two months after the Clintons' critique of DADT, the Pentagon announced that, because of the disturbing events surrounding Winchell's murder, every member of the armed forces would receive anti-harassment training.[33] While these new trainings were occurring within the military, the country was rapidly moving into the 2000 presidential campaign between Governor George W. Bush and Vice President Al Gore. Many remember the election for "hanging chads" in Florida and the involvement of the Supreme Court; each of the candidates made timely remarks about DADT, given the increased national attention on the military after the brutal murder of Winchell and the launch of a training campaign across all service branches.[34]

Following his electoral victory, President-Elect Bush, who had vocalized his support for DADT during the 2000 election, set about selecting his nominee for secretary of defense. Republican leaders noted that Bush appeared to be taking his time and weighing the decision carefully, given their critique of the three different secretaries who had served during the Clinton administration. Republican congressional leaders also suggested that the forthcoming Bush administration likely wanted to avoid what they considered missteps during the early days of the Clinton administration—specifically, the rollout of DADT, which the DoD began implementing in the early years of Clinton's presidency.[35] Initial speculation suggested that Bush might nominate a former senator, Daniel Coats of Indiana, but some Republican groups, including the Log Cabin Republicans, urged him to select another nominee.[36] Their concern stemmed largely from Coats's socially conservative views and his opposition to allowing queer people to serve, even if they did not disclose their sexuality.[37] Given these concerns and other political forces, Bush ultimately nominated Donald Rumsfeld, who had previously served as secretary of defense and chief of staff during portions of the Ford administration, and the Senate confirmed him in January 2001.[38]

Following the mandated anti-harassment training across all service branches, the Army—during the first year of the Bush administration—was also working to better explain elements of DADT, such as "homosexual conduct," anti-harassment policies, and separation proceedings, to soldiers. To that end, the Army produced a training manual in the form of a comic book, titled *Dignity & Respect: A Training Guide on Homosexual Conduct Policy*, in 2001.[39] Through this comic book, soldiers were expected to learn the intended application of DADT; it also included conversations about dealing with antigay harassment. Confusion around the application and implementation of DADT was a key reason behind the decision to develop this training tool as a comic book. While *Dignity & Respect* was intended to clarify the policy in a more engaging and accessible way for younger enlistees, it has become infamous for numerous reasons. It begins innocuously, informing the reader of the Army's policy on homosexual conduct, which it defines as "an act or statement by a soldier that demonstrates a propensity or intent to engage in homosexual acts, the solicitation of another to engage in a homosexual act or acts, or a homosexual marriage or attempted marriage."[40] The comic book then allows readers to engage with a number of hypothetical scenarios to understand how the policy should be implemented. In the first portion of *Dignity & Respect*, soldiers learn about credible information pertaining to a discharge on the basis of homosexual conduct; the text reiterates that credible information must stem from "a statement by a reliable person" that they had witnessed a homosexual act or discussion of a homosexual act by another soldier. This definition also encompassed "a statement by a reliable person" who "had observed or discovered a soldier . . . acknowledging a homosexual act or the intent to engage" in one.[41] As noted in Fenton Bailey and Randy Barbato's *The Strange History of Don't Ask, Don't Tell*, this created a number of serious issues regarding respect and privacy for queer service members, who served without disclosing their sexuality. Fellow service members sometimes attempted to "discover" something about their colleagues' sexuality via vigilante-style "investigations" that often involved invasions of privacy, lies, and even threats.[42] While *Dignity & Respect* was intended to clarify the supposed non-harassing elements of the policy, it showcased several issues with DADT and its day-to-day application; moreover, it invited the military to examine the life of anyone who was simply accused by someone deemed a "reliable person."[43]

There were clear issues of implementation around the policy during the late Clinton administration and early Bush administration, and criticisms were lodged against DADT in the early 2000s, particularly after the terrorist attacks of September 11, 2001. Just one day before the attack on the World Trade Center and the Pentagon, the federal government intercepted two phone calls foreshadowing these events. In these intercepted communication, the callers, who were speaking in Arabic, said that "tomorrow is zero hour" and that "the match is about to begin."[44] As noted in Nathaniel Frank's *Unfriendly Fire: How the Gay Ban Undermines the Military and Weakens America,* the National Security Agency (NSA) initially marked these intercepted conversations as high priority, and the calls were sent to an Arabic translator. They were translated two days after the coordinated terrorist attack by Al-Qaeda.[45] According to the *9/11 Commission Report*, the Federal Bureau of Investigation (FBI) "lacked sufficient translators proficient in Arabic and other key languages," which resulted "in a significant backlog of untranslated intercepts."[46] While many questions remain about DADT's impact on the intelligence community and its contribution to this security failure, a Freedom of Information Act request from the Center for the Study of Sexual Minorities in the Military found that, between 1998 and 2004 (important years leading up to and immediately following 9/11), the military discharged twenty Arabic speakers and six Farsi speakers. Even more alarming, discharges of queer linguists in the military grew throughout America's military operations in Afghanistan, Iraq, and the War on Terror.[47] Years later, the Government Accountability Office (GAO) released a report showing that the military had used DADT to discharge 757 service members who held critical positions in the military; 322 of these service members had skills relating to foreign languages, including 54 Arabic speakers.[48] Again, we will never know the impact that DADT had on the military and intelligence community's inability to prevent the tragic events of 9/11, just as we will never know of the policy's impact on the troops deployed to the Middle East in the following decades. But, we do know that DADT removed hundreds of service members with critically necessary linguistic skills during a time when these skills were in short supply at the NSA, and data from the GAO demonstrates the potential impact of these discharges and dismissals on national security.[49]

Following the continued critiques of DADT by LGBTQ+ activist groups like Servicemembers Legal Defense Network (SLDN) and OutServe throughout the 2000s, serious efforts to dismantle and repeal the policy eventually came during Obama's first term, following a campaign that had promised "change we can believe in." Though reluctant to cede ground on some areas of LGBTQ+ rights (specifically marriage equality), Obama, while attending a fundraiser for the Human Rights Campaign in 2009, announced his recommitment to ending DADT and some other Clinton-era policies that negatively affected LGBTQ+ Americans.[50] As noted in Aaron Belkin's *How We Won: Progressive Lessons from the Repeal of "Don't Ask, Don't Tell,"* the path to victory often felt like a troubled road, particularly since many White House officials were still looking for pro-repeal guidance from the Pentagon.[51] By February 2010, Secretary of Defense Robert Gates and Chairman of the Joint Chiefs of Staff Admiral Michael Mullen established a working group with the Pentagon—the Comprehensive Review of the Issues Associated with a Repeal of "Don't Ask, Don't Tell"—to review the policy and any potential impacts that repeal might have on military effectiveness and, particularly, on unit cohesion.[52] As the Pentagon's working group began to analyze the policy and the impact of its potential repeal, the Senate Armed Services Committee was scheduled to vote on attaching a DADT repeal amendment to the National Defense Authorization Act (NDAA) in the spring of that year, and by May 2010, the U.S. House of Representatives voted 324–194 to proceed with the so-called Murphy Amendment to do just that.[53] The rapidly evolving discourse about "change" and the potential repeal of DADT then shifted to the U.S. Senate, which now had to decide what action (if any) would be taken on the NDAA and its accompanying amendment. However, the movement stalled, and no significant action came until after summer 2010.[54]

Amid these extended discussions about the possible repeal of DADT, Gates announced that the office of the secretary of defense, at the request of the chair of the Senate Armed Services Committee, had commissioned

RAND to update to its 1993 report.[55] The new report, which was completed in 2010, provided an overview of the history of DADT, a review of the unit cohesion rationale, a discussion of social changes and public opinions regarding queer people since the early 1990s, and an analysis of the potential impacts of the current policy on recruiting and retention in the military.[56] Researchers for the updated report conducted focus groups to gauge opinions on queer inclusion within the military, as well as surveys aimed at intentionally capturing insights from closeted queer service members.[57] The results of the updated report were telling. For instance, the researchers found that 46 percent of respondents simply avoided talking about sexual orientation, which was the initial goal of DADT (that service members not discuss their sexuality and simply be able to serve). Among the rest, 22 percent of respondents across all service branches reported that they pretended to be heterosexual (rather than opting to simply not discuss sexuality), another 29 percent said that they were sometimes open about their diverse sexuality, and 3 percent said they were already openly queer within their units.[58] The researchers also asked respondents how the repeal of DADT might affect their openness within their units. When faced with this possibility, only 4 percent of respondents reported they would pretend to be heterosexual, and 21 percent suggested they would still avoid talking about sexuality. Potentially of more interest, 15 percent of respondents said that they would come out openly as queer within their unit, and another 59 percent reported that they would sometimes be open about their sexuality. The updated RAND report showed that queer service members would feel more secure in their units, and the researchers unabashedly concluded there would be "little reason to expect that ending DADT would produce any notable deterioration in unit performance."[59]

Following the release of RAND's 2010 report and the successful repeal vote in the U.S. House of Representatives from spring 2010, the U.S. Senate took up the issue of DADT repeal in fall 2010, but a number of challenges remained in that chamber. In September 2010, Senator John McCain of Arizona led a successful filibuster against debating the NDAA, the Murphy Amendment, and the repeal of DADT. Fifty-six senators voted to end McCain's filibuster, but this was four procedural votes short of moving forward.[60] Activists organized and vocalized their critique against the filibuster, calling for an end to the Clinton-era policy of open queer exclusion in the armed forces. Most notably, Lady Gaga, then a relatively recent pop culture sensation, organized a rally against DADT; she also reached out to her YouTube subscribers with a plea to contact their elected representatives, while showing them how to do that.[61] During her nearly eight-minute video, Lady Gaga began by specifically addressing McCain, along with Senators Mitch McConnell of Kentucky and Jefferson Sessions of Alabama, among others. In the video, she referenced the long-standing work of the SLDN, which had advocated for changing the policy since 1993. The video continued by recounting the experiences of queer service members who had been targeted by DADT, and she concluded by calling her senator's office and then asking her viewers to call the Capitol switchboard to contact their elected officials in Congress too.[62]

Following this national call to action and the ongoing activism from advocacy groups like the Human Rights Campaign, the SLDN, and OutServe, pressure continued to mount on the Pentagon, the Obama administration, and Congress, particularly as LGBTQ+ service members continued to share their stories even more publicly.[63] This pressure intensified following some high-profile service members beginning to come out and subsequently facing administrative discharge under DADT. With that in mind, the Pentagon's working group released its findings concerning the potential repeal of DADT in November 2010, stating that there were few risks in repealing the policy and that these could be mitigated through effective leadership from commanding officers across service branches. While acknowledging that there might be some short-run issues around culture, they confirmed that DADT was outdated and based upon stereotypical misperceptions about queer people.[64] Following the breaking news concerning the Pentagon's findings and RAND's 2010 report, Gates—who served under both the Bush and Obama administrations—publicly urged Congress to forge ahead with repeal. Gates reminded congressional members that the federal courts might strike down DADT by "judicial fiat" if Congress failed to act on the repeal.[65] Gates's argument was that Congress—if they acted promptly enough to pass a repeal of DADT—could set an implementation timeline, allowing the DoD and its service branches time to prepare for queer people to serve openly. His concern was that the federal courts, if given the opportunity, might simply strike down DADT as unconstitutional and require open service effective immediately, giving the DoD little to no preparation time.[66]

However, the Senate, in early December 2010, failed to advance a key procedural vote to allow amendments, such as the Murphy Amendment from the U.S. House of Representatives, to the NDAA, the larger defense bill.[67] As a response to this inaction, Senators Joe Lieberman of Connecticut and Susan Collins of Maine—rather than trying to amend the existing legislative text—introduced a bipartisan, stand-alone bill that contained some adjustments to the larger NDAA including, notably, a repeal measure for DADT.[68] Following this introduction of the "Don't Ask, Don't Tell" Repeal Act of 2010 in the Senate, Representative Patrick Murphy of Pennsylvania cosponsored it in the House of Representatives, where it passed by a largely partisan vote of 250–175.[69] Just a few days later, the Senate closed debate on the bill, and it proceeded to a vote on December 18, 2010. Although McCain raised arguments against the bill once more, the Senate—likely heeding the warning from the secretary of defense—ultimately voted in favor of the bipartisan bill by a margin of 65–31, with four senators not voting.[70] Obama signed the "Don't Ask, Don't Tell" Repeal Act of 2010 into law on December 22, 2010; Lieutenant Dan Choi, who had been discharged under the policy, along with other leading advocates, stood around Obama during the signing ceremony.[71]

With the stroke of that pen, the Obama administration delivered on its promise to repeal DADT, and as Gates had hoped, Congress gave several months as an on-ramp for full implementation of the new law. In a press release following the vote in the Senate, Gates stated:

> The legislation provides that repeal will take effect once the President, the Secretary of Defense and the Chairman of the Joint Chiefs of Staff certify that implementation of the new policies and regulations written by the Department is consistent with the standards of military readiness, military effectiveness, unit cohesion, and recruiting and retention of the Armed Forces. As I have stated before, I will approach this process deliberately and will make such certification only after careful consultation with the military service chiefs and our combatant commanders and when I am satisfied that those conditions have been met for all the Services, commands and units. . . . In the meantime, the current law and policy will remain in effect.[72]

As required by the new law, the Pentagon needed to report that they had met various statutory requirements outlined by Congress prior to allowing full open service for queer people in the military and active duty positions in the intelligence community. While some worried about how long it would take for DADT to become null, the DoD made these preparations in less than a year. The new law went into full effect, and the DADT era ended, on September 20, 2011.

THE UNFINISHED BUSINESS OF TRANSGENDER INCLUSION

While DADT began as a compromise between Congress and the Clinton administration in the early 1990s, its implementation had a detrimental effect on both the lives of queer service members and the readiness of the armed forces. Tragic events, such as the brutal murder of Barry Winchell in 1999 and the shortage of Arabic linguists in the intelligence community in pre-9/11 America, are a testament to the devastating impact that this policy and its predecessors had on America. And while the repeal of DADT in 2011 marked a new chapter for the military and intelligence community, the question of transgender inclusion—within an organizational culture that maintained both conservative ideas about gender and gender-specific policies—remained as unfinished business. Discriminatory policies, including those before DADT, were often applied to transgender and gender expansive people, who were sometimes presumed to be of a diverse sexuality or who were not equipped with the language to accurately describe their experience in today's terms. It is important to remember that transgender and gender expansive people—along with other groups like intersex people—were already being negatively affected by anti-LGBTQ+ policies, gender-specific policies and regulations, and rigidly binary medical policies within the American military and intelligence community. Open transgender service—allowing transgender people to serve, while providing them with the necessary resources for success in their service branch—was still disallowed even after DADT's repeal in 2011. The growing acceptance of LGBTQ+ people more broadly, which grew alongside the increasing visibility of transgender people in the 2010s, led to renewed advocacy on the question of transgender rights and open transgender service in the American military and active duty positions in the intelligence community. This issue, which is still undergoing vigorous debate in America, is addressed in the next chapter.

5

A MEANDERING PATH TOWARD TRANS INCLUSION

Transgender, gender expansive, and intersex people were negatively, though often inadvertently, affected by discriminatory policies targeting queer people throughout the periods from World War I to "Don't Ask, Don't Tell" (DADT), as discussed throughout the earlier chapters of this book. Gender-specific policies and regulations essentially rendered the question of transgender inclusion moot, and anti-trans and anti-intersex medical policies—which presumed illness, medical inferiority, and incapacity for military service—ensured that transgender, gender expansive, and intersex people were excluded from the American military and intelligence community. The question of intersex inclusion remains relatively unclear; I discuss this in greater detail in the conclusion. Here, I examine the meandering path of open transgender service during the present period (2011 to the second Trump administration). As defined earlier, open transgender service means allowing transgender people to serve, while providing them with the necessary resources for success in their service branch. The repeal of DADT left this question completely unanswered until the later years of the Obama administration. During the present period, the issue of open transgender service has ebbed and flowed with the actions of Presidents Donald Trump and Joe Biden during their respective terms. This chapter focuses on the shifting policies and related rationales that banned, allowed, banned again, and again allowed transgender people in the

American military and active duty positions in the intelligence community during the present period.

THE PRESENT PERIOD (2011 TO THE SECOND TRUMP ADMINISTRATION): CHANGING REGULATIONS, RESURRECTING THE UNIT COHESION RATIONALE, AND SHIFTING GROUND

> *I'm here today to announce some changes in the Defense Department's policies regarding transgender servicemembers. Before I announce what changes we're making, I want to explain why. And there are three main reasons—having to do with our future force, our current force, and matters of principle.*
>
> —SECRETARY OF DEFENSE ASH CARTER[1]

The present period is marked by constantly shifting ground, as the question of open transgender service has been affected by the prevailing political winds across multiple presidential administrations. In this sense, this chapter may feel incomplete because the fate of open transgender service may continue to be affected by forthcoming presidential administrations and continued political discourse about transgender rights. Despite that uncertainty, this chapter explores the policies and associated rationales that have repeatedly banned and allowed transgender people in the military and DoD-adjacent positions in the intelligence community, such as active duty positions with the National Security Agency (NSA) and the Office of the Director of National Intelligence. Restrictions on transgender people remained largely unchallenged until the later years of the Obama administration. Following this, open transgender service was again restricted during the Trump administration and subsequently allowed once more during the Biden administration. Unsurprisingly, open transgender service was disallowed yet again during the second Trump administration. We may experience continued ripple effects on the broader discourse about transgender inclusion in the armed forces in the coming years and throughout subsequent administrations.

CHANGING REGULATIONS DURING THE OBAMA ADMINISTRATION

While the repeal of DADT allowed queer people to serve openly, the question of transgender inclusion was left unanswered, and the status of transgender inclusion in the armed forces remained precarious at best. A year after the repeal of DADT, Bernard Rostker, who was one of the researchers for RAND's 1993 and 2010 reports, wrote a short piece for the organization's blog in which he discussed the major changes from the previous year. Rostker noted that no significant negative events had happened following DADT's repeal. Some smaller incidents did occur in the ranks, but they were handled locally and with the watchful monitoring of advocacy groups like the Servicemembers Legal Defense Network (SLDN).[2] Later in the Obama administration, queer inclusion in the armed forces saw key advances in other areas. For instance, Eric Fanning was confirmed, in May 2016, as secretary of the army, making him the highest-ranking LGBTQ+ official in the history of the country's military.[3] Fanning's confirmation in the U.S. Senate encountered little controversy and only a slight delay.[4] The queer community largely seemed to view Fanning's confirmation as a de facto signal that the military was continuing to move in more progressive directions. But potentially even more notable was Secretary of Defense Carter's announcement the previous summer of a transgender-related policy shift for the military.[5]

At a televised press conference in July 2015, Carter described the DoD as a "learning organization," reiterating that this extended to institutional policies. He noted that "current regulations regarding transgender service members are outdated and are causing uncertainty that distracts commanders from our core missions." Citing the concepts of equality, dignity, and respect, the secretary then announced that a new working group would assess any barriers to transgender inclusion in the armed forces, beginning with the presumption that transgender inclusion would *not* have "adverse impact on military effectiveness and readiness."[6] Soon after that, he mandated that the DoD would not involuntarily separate from the military any transgender personnel—who were currently serving but not yet out—on the basis of their gender identity, effective immediately.[7]

As with the implementation of DADT in the 1990s and its reassessment in 2010, the DoD commissioned the RAND Corporation to undertake the study, and in 2016, RAND published *Assessing the Implications of Allowing Transgender Personnel to Serve Openly*.[8] This report outlined research on a number of relevant issues that could face transgender people in the military and active duty positions within the intelligence community; topics included transition-related health care needs, potential issues with military readiness, accession into and retention within the ranks, and various policy barriers currently in place. Most notably, the researchers found that "a change in policy" to allow transgender people to serve openly would "likely have a marginal impact on health care costs and the readiness of the force," noting that private health-care costs "for transgender employees increased premiums by less than 1 percent."[9] In sum, RAND's 2016 report found that no significant barriers existed for transgender inclusion in the armed forces. In June 2016, the Pentagon announced that all transgender military personnel could serve openly in the armed forces.[10]

In his military-wide memo, Carter included an attachment, DTM-16-005, which noted major changes to several pertinent areas of military policy, including separation and retention, accession into the military, in-service transitions, the military's medical policy, equal opportunity within the ranks, education and training around transgender issues, and an implementation timeline.[11] Within this document, Carter mandated that the military, no later than October 1, 2016, issue a training manual for commanding officers, which would further ensure their compliance with the new guidance for transgender inclusion in the armed forces.[12] He noted that "DoD Instruction 1300.28: In-Service Transition for Transgender Service Members" would go into effect simultaneously on October 1, 2016.[13] In building out the new policy for transgender inclusion, that document established transition guidelines for transgender military personnel, listed the personnel requirements for that process, and specified the medical requirements for a service member's transition. Under this new guidance, a transgender person—due to circumstances related to their gender identity—would be disqualified from accession into the military only in specific scenarios: (1) having a history of gender dysphoria, *unless* a medical provider states that person is stable with no significant distress or impairment in multiple areas for at least eighteen months;

(2) undergoing a medical treatment associated with transitioning, *unless* that person has completed that medical portion of their transition, been "stable" in their gender identity for eighteen months, and/or been on their hormones for eighteen months; and/or (3) undergoing a gender affirming surgery, *unless* a medical provider states that it has been at least eighteen months since that time and that no limitations exist/persist from the surgery.[14] Some short-term, specific restrictions to accession still existed for transgender people, but most of them expired at an eighteen-month threshold; the DoD noted that this new guidance on accession should remain flexible to any recruit's unique health care situation, meaning that it could be waived/lowered in individual cases.[15]

The Pentagon, as mandated, released a transgender inclusion training manual for military commanders before the October 2016 deadline. Released on September 30, 2016, *Transgender Service in the U.S. Military: An Implementation Handbook* was intended to serve as a resource guide for transgender service members, their peers, and their commanding officers.[16] It provided detailed information related to a number of key issue areas such as periods of adjustment, harassment/bullying, respect, and medical concerns. The manual outlined nineteen different scenarios, ranging from inability to meet standards during transition to the use of shower facilities, attire during swim tests, and assignment to living quarters. The roles of all parties involved with an in-service transition—the transgender service member, their military medical provider(s), their commanding officer(s), and the branch of the military in which they served—were also made clear and direct. In combination with the previously mentioned policy guidance, it represented a new shift toward more inclusive open service for transgender personnel, who had previously been disallowed from such service in the military and active duty positions in the intelligence community.

Following the publication of this manual, Donald Trump, then the Republican candidate for president, criticized the Pentagon's new policy allowing transgender people in the military as "political correctness" run amok.[17] The Democratic candidate, Hillary Clinton—given her record of removing transition-related barriers to U.S. passport updates during her time as secretary of state from 2009 to 2013—was expected to be a strong advocate for the transgender community, retaining and expanding the Obama-era policies related to transgender inclusion in the military.

Trump's victory, however, caused advocates to fear that he might be planning to reverse these recently established Obama-era policies. Days before Trump took the presidential oath of office, Obama formally rescinded Eisenhower's Executive Order 10450—which had been halted in application (though not actually rescinded) under the Ford administration—from the earliest days of the Lavender Scare.[18]

RESURRECTING AND SUPPLEMENTING THE UNIT COHESION RATIONALE DURING THE TRUMP ADMINISTRATION

Following his inauguration in January 2017, President Trump and his originally piecemeal administration began to cause alarm within a number of progressive constituencies across the country. Within the first month of the Trump administration, the level of alarm continued to rise, especially among transgender military personnel, who feared what this meant for their ability to serve in the military and in related posts within the intelligence community. In February 2017, Trump rescinded some Title IX protections for transgender students, citing state and local autonomy in school bathroom regulations as the rationale for doing so.[19] Military families with transgender children were left wondering what this meant for their children in DoD-funded schools on military bases across the country.[20] Within less than a week, it became clear that schools funded through the DoD were to stop enforcing the Obama-era directive concerning Title IX and transgender student rights.[21] As other concerns continued to develop for the broader LGBTQ+ community, queer, and specifically transgender, military personnel and their advocates waited for the potential change in policy, as hinted at during the 2016 presidential campaign. While no official news about a policy change in the DoD had yet occurred, other concerns began to emerge. Trump's second nominee for secretary of the army, State Senator Mark Green of Tennessee, faced public outrage in May 2017 following the release of a radio interview in which he offered provocative commentary on transgender people and Muslims.[22] Following allegations of transphobia and Islamophobia, Green quickly withdrew his name from consideration, which had also been the fate of Trump's first nominee for the post.[23]

Amid the growing concerns for the broader LGBTQ+ community during the early months of the Trump administration, other revelations developed throughout 2017. These ranged from erasing LGBTQ+ related content from the White House website to concerns with other political appointees in key cabinet and judiciary appointments.[24] But the first few months of the Trump administration left the question of transgender inclusion in the military unanswered until July 1, 2017, which was the eve of the Obama-era deadline for allowing the accession of new transgender recruits into the military. Ahead of this date, Secretary of Defense James Mattis—a retired Marine Corps four-star general who served as Trump's first appointee to the post—issued a statement announcing the delay of the Pentagon's anticipated new policy to allow transgender people to newly enlist.[25] Then, at the end of July, with little to no forewarning and seemingly no coordination with senior officials in the DoD, Trump issued a series of tweets about the state of transgender inclusion in the armed forces:

> After consultation with my Generals and military experts, please be advised that the United States Government will not accept or allow . . . transgender individuals to serve in any capacity in the U.S. Military. Our military must be focused on decisive and overwhelming . . . victory and cannot be burdened with the tremendous medical costs and disruption that transgender [sic] in the military would entail. Thank you.[26]

While the American public largely appeared to be taken aback by this sudden announcement, some advocates were likely less than surprised. In addition to Mattis's implementation delay earlier that month, Lieutenant Colonel Myles Caggins, spokesman for the Army, had previously refused to comment on whether the DoD was reassessing the military's Obama-era policies related to transgender inclusion.[27] Even so, heated discussions about the topic began immediately. The White House press secretary Sarah Huckabee Sanders dismissed questions about what might happen to transgender people who were currently serving; instead, she invoked the rationale of "unit cohesion," which had previously been used to justify DADT for nearly twenty years.[28] While the unit cohesion rationale was being resurrected in the White House briefing room, the irony was that the attempted removal of transgender service members and colleagues was more likely have a negative impact on unit cohesion. Despite the claims from Sanders, the national media largely focused on Trump's supplementary claim about the presumed high financial cost of transition-related medical care. The RAND Corporation had already offered insights on this during the Obama administration. Many publications, including ones with readership primarily in the armed forces, focused on the small relative cost compared to other military-covered expenses. For instance, the *Military Times*, on the day that President Trump tweeted his decision, produced an article showing that the military actually spent more than ten times as much ($84 million per year) on erectile dysfunction medication than it would spend on transgender health care ($8 million per year, according to the DoD). At the same time, a study by the Palm Center estimated that discharging and replacing all the military's transgender service members would cost roughly $960 million.[29] Moreover, any transgender military personnel seeking transition-related health care services would first need to gain the approval of their commanding officer and a military medical provider, following the clear process established within DoD 1300.28 and *Transgender Service in the U.S. Military: An Implementation Handbook*. Despite all of this, the announcement initiated the steps to retract and replace the Obama-era policy with one that, once again, viewed transgender people as unfit for service in the military and related posts within the intelligence community.

Following the announcement to stop the accession of new transgender people into the military, questions still remained about the state of transgender personnel who were currently serving. Meanwhile, further actions to disallow new transgender enlistees were taken. In the months following Trump's Twitter announcement, numerous organizations, including the American Civil Liberties Union and Lambda Legal, challenged the proposed transgender ban in the federal courts, halting its implementation in 2017.[30] Following months of litigation and court rulings that consistently affirmed the right of transgender people to enlist in the military, the Pentagon began to prepare for the newly prescribed implementation deadline of January 1, 2018, as set by the judiciary.[31] On that date, transgender accession would formally begin, as promised during the Obama administration, yet uncertainty around the status of this policy remained.[32] While transgender people were thus allowed to serve in early 2018, a court document in one of the federal cases petitioning against the Trump administration's transgender ban revealed, in February 2018, that the administration was preparing a new policy proposal, which transgender rights advocates dubbed "Trans Ban 2.0." Following this breaking news, Mara Keisling, the executive director of the National Center for Transgender Equality, responded:

> President Trump's transgender ban is senseless, unconstitutional, and bad for the country. Trans Ban 2.0 is sure to also be senseless, unconstitutional, and bad for the country. No matter how the administration re-brands, any policy that singles people out because they are transgender cannot pass the smell test. Professional associations like the American Medical Association have rejected the notion that anything about being transgender makes one unfit to serve, and the Department of Defense's own studies have confirmed this. Thousands of trained, capable transgender troops in every branch of service prove every day that they are fit to serve, and firing even a fraction of them just because of who they are would be a pointless and heartless waste of resources. Congress must act now to stop this ban—and all of its iterations—once and for all.[33]

"Trans Ban 2.0" was a result of the Trump administration's anticipated loss in the federal courts. This new policy proposal sought to replace a blanket transgender ban with a more insidious and targeted approach. Previously, the Trump administration had made two claims to rationalize the transgender ban: (1) unit cohesion, resurrected from the DADT period; and (2) the high financial costs of medical care. This time the Trump administration laid claim to a new rationale: physical fitness and combat readiness. In March 2019, the DoD released a memorandum that no one would be separated or denied accession into the military "solely on the basis of his or her gender identity."[34] The document stated that all service members should be held to the same standards, which some transgender people might not meet. It was evident that the intended target was anyone who had been diagnosed with gender dysphoria, which was a requirement for service members to access transition-related medical care and an in-service transition.[35] In short, the policy would target the people who had actually taken steps to medically and socially transition under the military's existing policies. There was a great deal of confusion, as many advocates noted, about whether transgender people with diagnoses of gender dysphoria would be immediately deemed unfit for service under these alleged physical fitness standards and claims about combat readiness. The full policy went into effect in April 2019. As the Palm Center noted, the new policy was a parallel to DADT: transgender people were allowed to serve, so long as they did not pursue a medical transition or the necessary diagnosis of gender dysphoria. Transgender people who were currently serving and who had already initiated their in-service transition were able to continue serving, so long as they met the physical fitness criteria. However, future in-service transitions were essentially inaccessible.[36]

While the legal battles against "Trans Ban 2.0" continued into 2020, the COVID-19 pandemic set a new backdrop for the upcoming presidential election. Biden's electoral victory in 2020 set the stage for ending the Trump administration's policies, which were still being actively contested and challenged in federal courts.

RETURNING TO INCLUSION DURING THE BIDEN ADMINISTRATION

With the ongoing COVID-19 pandemic and the country moving in and out of lockdowns, Trump—whose administration had been embattled by a lengthy special counsel investigation and repeated turnover of high-ranking staffers—lost his 2020 re-election bid. Many advocates expected the forthcoming Biden administration to make numerous, substantial changes to several key areas of policy, including those at the DoD and other executive branch agencies. Interestingly, this is also a unique point where my own research intertwines with this policy history. Earlier that year, the Modern Military Association of America (MMAA), which was formed as a merger of the SLDN, OutServe, and other LGBTQ+ focused military nonprofit organizations in the mid-2010s, invited me to draft the third edition of the country's largest LGBTQ+ service member and veteran resource guidebook, *Freedom to Serve*.[37] By fall 2020, the final draft was complete, and following the 2020 presidential election, the Biden presidential transition team reached out to MMAA to secure an advance copy. They were interested in using that as a road map to understand and dismantle the Trump administration's "Trans Ban 2.0," while also reversing course on other key DoD and intelligence community policies that Trump and his cabinet had enacted.[38] Provided to the Biden transition team by MMAA's leadership, the document subsequently helped with the reversal of numerous Trump administration policies and directives.

Ahead of Biden's inauguration in January 2021, advocates and military leaders generally expected him to rescind the Trump administration's regulations, reinstating those from the final years of the Obama administration.[39] And on January 25, 2021, Biden signed an executive order that rescinded the Trump administration's previous executive guidance on transgender service members.[40] Later in March, the White House issued the institution's first-ever presidential proclamation in recognition of Transgender Day of Visibility, which is a day to recognize the contributions made by transgender people.[41] That same day, the Pentagon released the Biden administration's updated DoD guidance, which formally replaced the remaining Trump-era directives and officially allowed for open transgender service and accession to begin in one month on April 30, 2021.[42]

The Biden administration, in taking these actions, refuted the Trump's administration's shifting rationale for banning transgender service members from the armed forces. Open transgender service was now in effect across all service branches, including the newly formed Space Force. In comparison to the previous administration, the Biden administration proved far more hospitable to open transgender service, and in his first year, Biden appointed Dr. Rachel Levine to the U.S. Public Health Service Commissioned Corps in the Department of Health and Human Services (HHS), which made her the first-ever transgender four-star officer in American history.[43] Transgender service members shared powerful and positive stories about their ability to serve openly in the armed forces throughout the Biden administration.[44] Despite these moments of progress, transgender people, including service members and veterans, still faced numerous challenges. Throughout the Biden administration, there was a significant rise in anti-trans legislation with hundreds of bills emerging in state legislatures across the country.[45] In 2022, the Supreme Court, in *Dobbs v. Jackson Women's Health Organization*, also reversed course on the constitutional right to abortion, and as noted by researchers at the RAND Corporation, this could have unintended impacts on national security and military personnel across service branches.[46]

ON TENTATIVE GROUND

Given the influence of executive actions like executive orders, DoD directives, and related agency rulemaking in deciding matters related to open transgender service, uncertainty remains. Obama, Trump, and Biden each shifted the military's stance on transgender inclusion via the use of executive actions and presidential authority, and this raised concerns that a future presidential administration could simply reverse course on the Biden administration's 2021 actions that finally allowed for open transgender service. Executive agency rulemaking was further complicated by the Supreme Court's opinion in *Loper Bright Enterprises v. Raimondo* in 2024, which overturned the forty-year-old Chevron doctrine, established in *Chevron USA, Inc. v. Natural Resources Defense Council, Inc.* in 1984.[47] By fundamentally reimagining administrative law, this opinion could reemphasize the importance of congressional action in deciding the future of open transgender service for the armed forces.

To complicate matters more, advocates also expressed concern about the end of the Biden administration, following the annual reauthorization of the National Defense Authorization Act (NDAA) at the end of the 118th Congress in winter 2024. An anti-trans "rider," or amendment, was attached to the bill; this rider disallowed transgender, non-binary, and gender expansive youth from accessing gender affirming care under their military-sponsored TRICARE plan.[48] Following calls to veto the NDAA because of this provision, Biden ultimately signed it into law, and his administration ended by implementing the first anti-LGBTQ+ federal law since the mid-1990s.[49] With the start of the second Trump administration in early 2025, open transgender service remained on tentative ground at best. Within the first hundred days of the second Trump administration, a flurry of executive orders were aimed at excluding transgender people from public life and rolling back Biden-era policies.[50]

And as expected, Trump took actions, once again, to restrict open transgender service in the American military.[51] Given the complexities of this meandering path toward inclusion, the coming decades—regardless of the actions taken throughout the entirety of the second Trump administration—will likely continue to see renewed and competing actions from future presidential administrations, DoD officials, and iterations of Congress.

CONCLUSION

To write a "conclusion" to this book in the current moment feels counterintuitive in many ways, especially with the issue of open transgender service again at the center of public debate. But, publication—with its academic peer review, final revisions, editing, and production-related needs—requires me to stop writing. While I know that this topic will continue to evolve in the coming years, I hope this book helps to shape public debate, academic scholarship, and federal policymaking around the topic of LGBTQ+ inclusion in the American military and intelligence community. Although it feels as though so many contemporary policy questions are still unanswered, I have tried to produce a final chapter that is sufficient and useful, not perfunctory or redundant. First, I revisit the book's research questions, framework, and key findings. Following this, I reexamine the significance of this project both within and beyond the discipline of political science and then highlight some areas of potential future scholarship related to this and adjacent topics related to LGBTQ+ service in the armed forces. Lastly, I offer some parting words for the reader, before transitioning into a more personal narrative about this project's significance in the afterword. I realize that this conclusion may feel unfinished. In many ways, this is a symptom of the current political reality, since the question of open transgender service continues to be debated across presidential administrations and the Department of Defense (DoD). In that respect, this history is very much still yet "to be determined."

THE RESEARCH QUESTION, FRAMEWORK, AND KEY FINDINGS REVISITED

In this book, I have categorized the major policy changes—dubbed the "lavender bans"—that the American military and intelligence community implemented in pursuit of LGBTQ+ exclusion during six periods: World War I, World War II, the early Cold War, the late Cold War, the "Don't Ask, Don't Tell" or DADT period (the early 1990s to 2011), and the present period (2011 to the second Trump administration). I have examined not only the policies but also the corresponding rationales that supported their implementation across each of these distinct periods. Several auxiliary questions have also been directly and indirectly addressed during this analysis of more than a century of American history. What did anti-LGBTQ+ discrimination in the military and intelligence community look like over time? What were the major shifts in these policies over time? How did the rationale for these policies develop? Questions like these and many more helped to influence the intellectual trajectory of this book. Though the book did not address all of these questions directly, they helped to inform how I interacted with the source material and the information and analysis I presented. This book directly answered two specific research questions: (1) What was the rationale for banning LGBTQ+ people from the military and intelligence community in each of these periods? (2) What were the specific policies that emerged in each period?

To answer these questions, this book used a research framework informed by three interdisciplinary bodies of scholarship: feminist scholarship, security studies scholarship, and LGBTQ+ historical scholarship. Both primary and secondary source material proved necessary, particularly since LGBTQ+ history is so often erased, "misremembered," destroyed, or simply not recorded.[1] By using these three areas of scholarship to inform the research framework for this book, I was able to provide clearer answers to the previously mentioned research questions about the rationales for banning LGBTQ+ people from the military and intelligence community and the specific policies that emerged in each period. The answers to both questions, as discussed throughout, varied considerably at different points in American history. For instance, I remain astounded that twenty-four different revisions related to anti-"homosexual" regulations occurred during a four-year period during World War II.[2] Similarly, I am still amazed that the military previously tried to screen for physical traits in order to identify LGBTQ+ people; once more, it bears repeating that such policies almost certainly had a negative impact on intersex people and non-LGBTQ+ people who were presumed to be "queer."

These research frameworks were quite helpful in answering these questions, while also addressing the distinct changes that occurred in the six periods analyzed in this book; I am hopeful that the reader also appreciated how they were integrated and infused throughout each chapter. There are too many unique policy revisions to succinctly summarize each of them here, but for each of these six periods, I can, at least, reiterate the rationales that guided anti-LGBTQ+ policies in the American military and intelligence community. During the World War I period, the primary rationale for banning queer people from the military was that sexual immorality undermined the military's ability to win the war; there was also some evidence of examining for potential physical traits that government officials believed could denote queerness in some way. The notion of a physical manifestation of queerness became more prevalent in the World War II period. During this time, anti-LGBTQ+ policies relied on a rationale built upon a presumption of psychological illness and a physical inability to serve, though there were clear exceptions due to the nature of this war. Shifting once again in the early Cold War period, the rationale from 1947 to the 1970s largely relied upon the idea that LGBTQ+ people were inherently susceptible to Soviet blackmail, which linked the idea of queerness to communism. By the late Cold War period, this rationale shifted once again. During the 1980s, the primary rationale focused on a presumed inability to handle secure information, though a secondary rationale related to the fear of HIV/AIDS emerged by the end of that period. In the DADT period of the early 1990s to 2011, the rationale focused primarily on a concern with "unit cohesion," though earlier concerns about antigay violence and the spread of HIV were originally floated as potential rationales. A secondary but related rationale of privacy, in the context of unit cohesion, was also sometimes cited during this period. The present period, from 2011 onward has been marked by a series of shifting policies that disallowed open transgender service, then allowed, disallowed, and allowed it once more. During this period, the first Trump administration briefly resurrected the "unit cohesion" rationale from the DADT period, supplementing it with a claim that the cost of health care for transgender service members was the real rationale for banning them from open service. Other dramatic shifts then occurred, with further attempts to ban open transgender service in the first Trump administration to a repeal of that policy during the Biden administration. The state of open transgender service remains on tentative ground, given the challenges facing transgender people during the second Trump administration, and this ebb and flow of transgender rights is likely to continue into future presidential administrations.

SIGNIFICANCE WITHIN AND BEYOND THE DISCIPLINE

WITHIN POLITICAL SCIENCE

Given its situation within the discipline of political science, this book is topically significant, as explained in the introduction. LGBTQ+ politics remains an understudied and undervalued area of the broader discipline; this is especially true of American politics scholarship, as discussed in chapter 1.[3] Noted in Julie Novkov and Scott Barclay's "Lesbians, Gays, Bisexuals, and the Transgendered [sic] in Political Science: Report on a Discipline-Wide Survey," numerous problems exist within both the political science classroom and literature.[4] Since I have already discussed their key findings, I will not recount them here, but compared to their early 2010s research, things—at least anecdotally—do not seem considerably better for the discipline. While there has been growth of LGBTQ+ focused political science scholarship since the early 2000s, that growth seems less prolific now, and there is still room for continued improvements across all subfields of the discipline.⁵ With increased identification in the LGBTQ+ community, leaders in the discipline would be wise to prioritize scholars who are working to fill topical knowledge gaps, such as the ones addressed in this book.⁶

While I certainly appreciate that the discipline's professional associations have expanded resources to LGBTQ+ scholars in recent years, the discipline can do more to encourage LGBTQ+ focused teaching, and in the past decade, other scholars have also critiqued the discipline for "losing its edge" in relation to LGBTQ+ politics.⁷ In recent years, there have been improvements in celebrating LGBTQ+ scholarship within the American Political Science Association (APSA), which is a positive development.⁸ I am equally pleased that leaders across the discipline are more actively considering how they can support LGBTQ+ graduate students, since this may help to further cultivate new research across subfields and advancement across the profession.⁹ Despite my critique of the discipline, I care deeply for political science and my colleagues across the APSA, and I firmly believe that the discipline can grow in more academically stimulating ways by more actively engaging LGBTQ+ topics and scholarship. I certainly hope that a book like mine will one day be more normalized within the discipline, and I am encouraged that some such research is continuing to emerge at the time of this writing. More recent examples of such emerging scholarship in political science include Phillip Ayoub and Kristina Stoeckl's "The Global Resistance to LGBTIQ Rights" from 2024, which examines the globalized weaponization of LGBTQ+ issues in political discourse; Zein Murib's "Anti-Trans Attacks: Interrogating 'Gender' in Politics and Gender Scholarship" also from 2024, which focuses on the methodological importance of advancing a more nuanced operationalization of "gender" as an analytical category; and Patrick Egan's "Centering LGBTQ+ Political Behavior in Political Science" from 2025, which argues for the importance of filling research gaps on LGBTQ+ political behavior.¹⁰

Within the broader discipline, this book is also methodologically significant, given the research method that it employs. Richard Valelly, as discussed in the introduction, argues that American political development (APD), a methodological framework and research agenda within political science, has failed to recognize LGBTQ+ politics.¹¹ This research method—which analyzes the durability of certain periods and the shifts between them—is actively employed in this book, which categorizes and analyzes anti-LGBTQ+ policies in the American military and intelligence community in six distinct periods. In response to Valelly's article, this book employs an APD methodological framework in pursuit of its research questions. My hope is that this will actively encourage more LGBTQ+ focused scholarship that utilizes APD, particularly since Valelly's original call to action was well over a decade ago.[12] This specific research method has proved extremely useful for this book, and I, along with Valelly, truly believe that American politics could greatly benefit by engaging the APD methodological framework and research agenda with more LGBTQ+ research questions, especially given the growing importance of LGBTQ+ people in the American electorate.[13] This methodological significance helps to set this book apart from other works by scholars of LGBTQ+ exclusion from the military and intelligence community. As the first academic text (barring some recent journal articles) to examine transgender exclusion in the military within this broader context, this book is also the first to analyze the specific shifting rationales and related policies within the American military and intelligence community from World War I to the second Trump administration. This major component of significance is due, in large part, to the APD methodological framework.

BEYOND POLITICAL SCIENCE

This book is also significant in terms of its timeliness, because of the current events occurring at the time of its production. I would like to draw special attention to that reality here, though it was implied in the introduction. In the earliest iterations of this project from 2015, I intended to end with a discussion of transgender inclusion under the Obama administration, while briefly discussing the potential for a policy shift as a nod to future research and presidential administrations. But midway through my initial research, in summer 2017, the question of a transgender ban quickly arose, seemingly out of nowhere. For an academic, such timeliness of research is almost unheard of, but this project has very much been viewed as a timely, relevant, and important project, given the ongoing public debate about open transgender service. As I mention in chapter 5, my research—via a related project with the Modern Military Association of America during the COVID-19 pandemic—was later employed by the Biden presidential transition team, further underscoring the significance of this research and its apt timing.[14] Given the actions throughout the first hundred days of the second Trump administration, there is a strong likelihood that this book will retain its topical significance well after publication and into forthcoming presidential administrations.[15]

INFORMING FUTURE SCHOLARSHIP

This book examines more than a century of anti-LGBTQ+ policies and associated rationales in the American military and intelligence community. Given this historical scope, there are numerous areas for future scholarship related to this topic. While I certainly cannot provide an exhaustive list of areas for potential scholarly exploration, I note some of the most pressing and (personally) interesting areas under three general subheadings.

PUBLIC OPINION, THE MILITARY, AND PINKWASHING

Certain subfields and areas within the broader discipline of political science offer particularly fertile soil for bearing academic fruit. American politics, international relations, and public law and policy remain the three most obvious areas for such research, though my intellectual interests likely bias me to think of these areas first. Related to this project, a number of interesting questions crisscross through these different subfields. Opinions about LGBTQ+ rights—especially related to marriage but certainly beyond that one topic—have dramatically shifted over the past decade, and scholars of American politics should pay closer attention to this unique political and social moment.[16] Regarding American politics scholarship, two types of questions come to mind. First, how have the American public's opinions about LGBTQ+ inclusion in the military shifted, how do these shifts manifest across discrete identities in the broader LGBTQ+ community, and why? Second, how does the prospect of a transgender ban affect voters' perceptions of a political figure, administration, the military, and other institutions? Regarding international relations, the most immediate question that comes to mind relates to the concept of pinkwashing—appearing to promote LGBTQ+ rights while actually perpetuating harmful practices. Specifically, how does pinkwashing influence American foreign policy, if at all, and what is the impact of this practice, considering the legacy of anti-LGBTQ+ policies in the American military?

IMPACTS ON THE ALL-VOLUNTEER FORCE AND NATIONAL SECURITY FROM BUSH TO TRUMP

Security studies, as an interdisciplinary area of focus, offers multiple potential avenues for emerging LGBTQ+ research in the coming years. Here, I highlight some questions of particular interest, as they relate to the all-volunteer force and national security from the early 2000s to the present. The recommendations here are not an exhaustive list; rather, they are the areas I think would be most valuable to understanding the intersection of security, foreign affairs, and LGBTQ+ rights in the context of America's all-volunteer force and national security. Ranging from the Bush administration to the second Trump administration, I list these questions in chronological order. First, how did DADT undermine national security during the Bush administration and the early days of America's "War on Terror," and what tangible impacts did this policy have on national security beyond what we already know? Second, what effect has service under DADT had on the mental health of LGBTQ+ veterans, and how might the Department of Veterans Affairs (VA) use this knowledge to better serve veterans who experienced trauma related to this policy? Third, what else can be learned from the military's implementation of DADT, and how might these lessons be applied to future debates about open transgender service and future needs at the VA? Fourth, how have shifting policies for open transgender service, from 2016 to the present, affected the Pentagon's resources and national security more broadly? Fifth, what impact have these anti-LGBTQ+ policies had on recruitment efforts to the military's all-volunteer force?

HIV STIGMA, ONGOING LITIGATION, AND SERVICE FOR PEOPLE LIVING WITH HIV

Earlier in the book, I discussed the impact of HIV/AIDS activism on anti-LGBTQ+ policies during the 1992 presidential campaign. Numerous research questions, related to contemporary policies and military service for people living with HIV, come to mind. Originally dubbed Gay-Related Immune Deficiency Syndrome (GRIDS), the virus was presumed to affect only gay men.[17] Clearly, this is not the case. HIV does not exclusively affect LGBTQ+ people, though it does have a disparate impact on the broader LGBTQ+ community. HIV stigmatization and discrimination, which have a well-documented history, regrettably still persist today, and this continues to manifest in outdated policies across the armed forces.[18] The adjacent topic of policies affecting military service for people living with HIV merits more research, particularly given recent progress and continued litigation in federal courts.[19] While I do not have a specific research question in mind, I would be particularly interested in reading an interdisciplinary work that examines this topic—with similar depth to this book's analysis of anti-LGBTQ+ policies—from the intersection of public policy, legal studies, public health, military history, and antiretroviral science.

PARTING WORDS

Regarding LGBTQ+ rights in both the military and civilian society, challenges will certainly continue. Given our current sociopolitical landscape and this detailed history of anti-LGBTQ+ policies, many readers will likely agree. But at the end of my writing, I still feel a certain optimism for the future—in regard to both open transgender service and LGBTQ+ rights more broadly. Considering the realities that faced LGBTQ+ people in the early twentieth century, things are undoubtedly better now; many readers will likely agree with that too. While the LGBTQ+ community will face continued challenges across presidential administrations, I remain hopeful, and I hope the same is true for readers of this book. By remembering our history—including the lavender bans discussed in this book—we can build upon such progress both in and beyond our communities.

AFTERWORD

WASHINGTON, DC, 2025

In the introduction, I opened with an anecdote from summer 2017, when this research was taking shape as a doctoral dissertation. Nearly a decade later, this project has grown into a much larger (and, candidly, better written) book. Beginning as doctoral work from 2015 to 2018 and later evolving into a book manuscript from the early days of the COVID-19 pandemic to 2025, this research has moved far beyond its initial scope. For nearly a decade, it has grown with my career, and—considering my previous discussions of feminist praxis—offering a personal anecdote here seems sensible. While I realize that not every reader will enjoy such a discussion, the beauty of an afterword is that many readers, unless they are uniquely interested in the book or the author, simply skip over it. I, myself, am often guilty of this. So, please consider this afterword as something for the specific reader who is in that "uniquely interested" category.

As an academic who transitioned into public policy and legislative affairs work, I spend a fair amount of time in Washington, DC. During one such trip, I visited the Vietnam Veterans Memorial for a moment of reflection. My doctoral adviser, Christine Sylvester of the University of Connecticut, focuses on this memorial in her latest book, *Curating and Re-Curating the American Wars in Vietnam and Iraq*, which explores the concept of war as experience, the impact of failed national security policies, and how individual people curate their experiences with the tragedies of war. While at the memorial, I reflected upon Christine's work and some kinds words she had shared about my project in relation to her own.[1] While on the National Mall, I also thought about the countless service members, veterans, and civil servants who were negatively affected by a century of anti-LGBTQ+ policies in the American military and intelligence communities. On the long and rainy walk back from the memorial, I felt a deep appreciation for Christine for helping to make this project a reality; without her support and guidance, this book would not exist.

To be frank, this research has had a much wider impact than I could ever have imagined, and I credit the support of so many mentors—including Christine and others named in the acknowledgments—for that. This research, as noted in chapter 5, led to my writing *Freedom to Serve* for the Modern Military Association of America, and subsequently, that work helped create a road map to dismantle the Trump administration's "Trans Ban 2.0" policies in early 2021.[2] Most academics do not have the opportunity to point to tangible impacts from their research, and I have been lucky enough to experience that with my work. While I certainly hope that this book will shift academic conversations about LGBTQ+ issues in security studies and political science more broadly, this experience alone has far exceeded my wildest expectations for this project. For that, I am deeply grateful.

NOTES

INTRODUCTION

1. Donald Trump, "Transgender Tweets," Twitter, July 26, 2017.
2. The modern-day intelligence community is composed of eighteen organizations across the federal government. My discussion of the intelligence community largely focuses on the (1) the nine Department of Defense (DoD) elements, including the National Security Agency (NSA) and intelligence elements for the five service branches of the military (the Air Force, Army, Navy, Marine Corps, and Space Force); (2) one independent agency (the Central Intelligence Agency [CIA]); and (3) three other elements of different federal bodies (the Department of State [DoS], the Department of Justice's [DoJ's] Federal Bureau of Investigation [FBI], and the Department of Homeland Security's [DHS's] intelligence element for the Coast Guard. I do not explore the histories of more recent additions to the intelligence community apparatus (such as the DHS's Office of Intelligence and Analysis, formed in 2007, and the Department of the Treasury's Office of Intelligence and Analysis, formed in 2004), because the question of anti-LGBTQ+ civilian-focused policies was already moot by their creation. For a complete list of organizations in the intelligence community apparatus, see https://www.dni.gov/index.php/what-we-do/members-of-the-ic.
3. Through the remainder of this text, the reader should presume that LGBTQ+ exclusion from the military in each of these periods was inherently discriminatory. While at times I may directly mention specific instances of discrimination against individual members or classes of people in the broader LGBTQ+ community, the blanket exclusion of LGBTQ+ people from the military and intelligence community has historically been a form of categorical discrimination against this community.
4. Mary Hawkesworth, *Feminist Inquiry: From Political Conviction to Methodological Innovation* (New Brunswick, NJ: Rutgers University Press, 2006).

5. Brooke Ackerly and Jacqui True, *Doing Feminist Research in Political and Social Science* (New York: Palgrave Macmillan, 2010). Ackerly and True refer to a feminist praxis as "the practice of feminist scholarship that is informed by critical feminist ... perspectives" that include a feminist research ethic that may or may not be explicitly stated (7).
6. Aaron Belkin, "The Pentagon's Gay Ban Is Not Based on Military Necessity," *Journal of Homosexuality* 41, no. 1 (2001): 103–119.
7. Aaron Belkin and Melissa Sheridan Embser-Herbert, "A Modest Proposal: Privacy as a Flawed Rationale for the Exclusion of Gays and Lesbians from the U.S. Military," *International Security* 27, no. 2 (2002): 178–197.
8. Aaron Belkin and Melissa Levitt, "Homosexuality and the Israeli Defense Forces: Did the Gay Ban Undermine Military Performance?," *Armed Forces & Society* 27, no. 4 (2001): 541–565.
9. Aaron Belkin, "'Don't Ask, Don't Tell': Is the Gay Ban Based on Military Necessity?," *Parameters: U.S. Army War College Quarterly*, Summer 2003, 108–119.
10. Aaron Belkin, "'Don't Ask, Don't Tell': Does the Gay Ban Undermine the Military's Reputation?," *Armed Forces & Society* 34, no. 2 (2007): 276–291.
11. As noted throughout this work, a great deal of the scholarship relating to the American military's treatment of members of the broader LGBTQ+ community centers upon the narratives and experiences of gay men and lesbian women. Given the limitations of primary and secondary source material, my project at times focuses explicitly on this aspect of the community. Other identity categories—including bisexual, transgender, intersex, and more—will certainly be discussed, when historical accuracy can be maintained, but it should be understood that this is one challenge in conducting LGBTQ+ historical scholarship.
12. George Chauncey, Martin B. Duberman, and Martha Vicinus, "Introduction," in *Hidden from History: Reclaiming the Gay & Lesbian Past*, ed. George Chauncey, Martin B. Duberman, and Martha Vicinus (New York: New American Library, 1989), 1–16; Neil Miller, *Out of the Past: Gay and Lesbian History from 1869 to the Present* (New York: Vintage, [1995] 2006).
13. See Allan Berube, "Marching to a Different Drummer: Lesbian and Gay GIs in World War II," in Chauncey, Duberman, and Vicinus, *Hidden from History*, 383–394; Allan Berube, *Coming Out Under Fire: The History of Gay Men and Women in World War II* (Chapel Hill: University of North Carolina Press, [1990] 2010); Margot Canaday, *The Straight State: Sexuality and Citizenship in Twentieth-Century America* (Princeton, NJ: Princeton University Press, 2006); George Chauncey, *Gay New York: Gender, Urban Culture, and the Making of the Gay Male World, 1890–1940* (New York: Basic Books, 1994); David Johnson, *The Lavender Scare: The Cold War Persecution of Gays and Lesbians in the Federal Government* (Chicago: University of Chicago Press, 2004); Sherry Zane, "'I Did It for the Uplift of Humanity and the Navy': Same-Sex Acts and the Origins of the National Security State, 1919–1923," *New England Quarterly* 91, no. 2 (2018): 279–306.
14. Chauncey, *Gay New York*.

15. Canaday, *The Straight State*; Zane, "'I Did It for the Uplift of Humanity and the Navy.'"
16. George Chauncey, "Christian Brotherhood or Sexual Perversion? Homosexual Identities and the Construction of Sexual Boundaries in the World War One Era," *Journal of Social History* 19, no. 2 (1985): 189–211; Zane, "'I Did It for the Uplift of Humanity and the Navy.'"
17. See "Alleged Immoral Conditions at Newport (RI) Naval Training Station," in *Government Versus Homosexuals*, ed. Leslie Parr (North Stratford, NH: Ayer, [1921] 1975); Albert Love and Charles Davenport, *Defects Found in Drafted Men* (Washington, DC: U.S. Government Printing Office, 1920).
18. Bernard Rostker and Scott Harris, *Sexual Orientation and U.S. Military Personnel Policy: Options and Assessment*, National Defense Research Institute (Santa Monica, CA: RAND, 1993).
19. Berube, *Coming Out Under Fire*; Canaday, *The Straight State*.
20. See Berube, "Marching to a Different Drummer;" Berube, *Coming Out Under Fire*; Michael Bronski, *A Queer History of the United States* (Boston: Beacon, 2011); Lillian Faderman, *Odd Girls and Twilight Lovers: A History of Lesbian Life in Twentieth-Century America* (New York: Columbia University Press, [1991] 2012); Gary Lehring, *Officially Gay: The Political Construction of Sexuality by the U.S. Military* (Philadelphia: Temple University Press, 2003); Miller, *Out of the Past*.
21. Johnson, *The Lavender Scare*.
22. Douglas Charles, *Hoover's War on Gays: Exposing the FBI's "Sex Deviates" Program* (Lawrence: University Press of Kansas, 2015); Walter Frank, *Law and the Gay Rights Story: The Long Search for Equal Justice in a Divided Democracy* (New Brunswick, NJ: Rutgers University Press, 2014); Robert Corber, *In the Name of National Security: Hitchcock, Homophobia, and the Political Construction of Gender in Postwar America* (Durham, NC: Duke University Press, 1993); Robert Corber, *Homosexuality in Cold War America* (Durham, NC: Duke University Press, 1997); Michael Kimmel, *Manhood in America: A Cultural History*, 3rd ed. (Oxford: Oxford University Press, 2011). See also S. H. Crittenden, "Report of the Board Appointed to Prepare and Submit Recommendations to the Secretary of the Navy for the Revision of Policies, Procedures, and Directives Dealing with Homosexuals," U.S. Navy Board of Inquiry, March 15, 1957; "Department of Defense Memorandum—1949," in Rostker and Harris, *Sexual Orientation and U.S. Military Personnel Policy*; "Hoey Committee Report," in SY-General 1952 folder, box 1, entry 1508, Office of Security and Consular Affairs, lot file 53-D-233, subject files of the Security Division, 1946–1953, RG 59 (Washington, DC: National Archives and Records Administration, February 1952); Craig Loftin, *Masked Voices: Gay Men and Lesbians in Cold War America* (Albany: State University of New York Press, 2012); Miller, *Out of the Past*.
23. Kate Dyer, "Forward," in *Gays in Uniform: The Pentagon's Secret Reports*, ed. Kate Dyer (Boston: Alyson, 1990): xii–xviii.
24. See also *Dubbs v. Central Intelligence Agency*, 866 F.2d 1114 (1989); Lillian Faderman, *The Gay Revolution: The Story of Struggle* (New York: Simon & Schuster, 2015);

Gregory Herek, "Gay People and Government Security Clearances: A Social Science Perspective," *American Psychologist* 45, no. 9 (1950): 1035–1042; Michael McDaniel, "Preservice Adjustment of Homosexual and Heterosexual Military Accessions: Implications for Security Clearance Suitability," in Dyer, *Gays in Uniform*; Rostker and Harris, *Sexual Orientation and U.S. Military Personnel Policy*; Theodore Sarbin and Kenneth Karols, "Nonconforming Sexual Orientations and Military Suitability," in Dyer, *Gays in Uniform*, 3–97.

25. Faderman, *The Gay Revolution*.
26. See Aaron Belkin, *How We Won: Progressive Lessons from the Repeal of "Don't Ask, Don't Tell"* (Los Angeles: HuffPost Media Group, 2011); Frank, *Law and the Gay Rights Story*; Alexander Nicholson, *Fighting to Serve: Behind the Scenes in the War to Repeal "Don't Ask, Don't Tell"* (Chicago: Chicago Review Press, 2012).
27. Michelle Dietert and Dianne Dentice, "Transgender Military Experience," *SAGE Open* 5, no. 2 (2015); James Parco, David Levy, and Sarah Spears, "Transgender Military Personnel in the Post-DADT Repeal Era," *Armed Forces & Society* 41, no. 2 (2015): 221–242; James Parco, David Levy, and Sarah Spears, "Beyond DADT Repeal: Transgender Evolution Within the U.S. Military," *International Journal of Transgenderism* 17, no. 1 (2016): 4–13; Kayla Quam, "Unfinished Business of Repealing 'Don't Ask, Don't Tell': The Military's Unconstitutional Ban on Transgender Individuals," *Utah Law Review* 3 (2015): 721–741; Adam Yerke and Valory Mitchell, "Transgender People in the Military: Don't Ask? Don't Tell? Don't Enlist!," *Journal of Homosexuality* 60, no. 2 (2013): 436–457.
28. Agnes Schaefer, Radha Iyengar, Srikanth Kadiyala, Jennifer Kavanagh, Charles Engel, Kayla Williams, and Amil Kress, *Assessing the Implications of Allowing Transgender Personnel to Serve Openly*, National Defense Research Institute (Santa Monica, CA: RAND, 2016).
29. U.S. Department of Defense, *Transgender Service in the U.S. Military: An Implementation Handbook* (Washington, DC: Author, September 30, 2016).
30. Timothy Cook, "The Empirical Study of Lesbian, Gay, and Bisexual Politics: Assessing the First Wave of Research," *American Political Science Review* 93, no. 3 (September 1999): 679–692; Paisely Currah, "The State of LGBT/Sexuality Studies in Political Science," *PS: Political Science and Politics* 44 (2011): 13–16; Gary Mucciaroni, "The Study of LGBT Politics and Its Contributions to Political Science," *PS: Political Science and Politics* 44 (2011): 17–21; Julie Novkov and Scott Barclay, "Lesbians, Gays, Bisexuals, and the Transgendered in Political Science: Report on a Discipline-Wide Survey," *PS: Political Science and Politics* 43 (2010): 95–106; Joe Rollins, "Political Science, Political Sex," *PS: Political Science and Politics* 44 (2011): 27–30; Richard Valelly, "LGBT Politics and American Political Development," *Annual Review of Political Science* 15 (2012): 313–332.
31. Valelly, "LGBT Politics and American Political Development."
32. In referring to Novkov and Barclay's "Lesbians, Gays, Bisexuals, and the Transgendered in Political Science: Report on a Discipline-Wide Survey" from 2010, I specifically mention the LGBT rather than the LGBTQ+ community, as their research did

not seek to address the concerns of political scientists who specifically identify as queer. However, when discussing the broader implications of their work and the exclusion of people of diverse genders and sexualities from the discipline of political science, I use the acronym LGBTQ+ to better capture the broader diversity of the community.

33. Novkov and Barclay, "Lesbians, Gays, Bisexuals, and the Transgendered in Political Science."
34. Novkov and Barclay, "Lesbians, Gays, Bisexuals, and the Transgendered in Political Science," 96.
35. Novkov and Barclay, "Lesbians, Gays, Bisexuals, and the Transgendered in Political Science," 100. Regarding this portion of their findings, it is quite likely that at least some of the respondents in the "not familiar" category were affected by social desirability bias. That is, they may have believed that a more "neutral" rather than "negative" response was more socially desirable to report, which could skew those statistics. In sum, a total of 23 percent, or nearly a fourth of the respondents, reported that (1) they believed research on LGBT topics was "not appropriate" or (2) they were "not familiar" enough to make that decision.
36. Novkov and Barclay, "Lesbians, Gays, Bisexuals, and the Transgendered in Political Science," 100–101. Relating this statistic to my discussion in the next chapter of Mary Hawkesworth's 2006 book on feminist inquiry, some might argue that there is nothing inherently wrong with such a low number. However, the critique against my concern may be a manifestation of evidence blindness, discussed in the next chapter. While I agree that a relatively lower number is not altogether surprising, it may be that the lack of discipline-wide support for LGBT scholars, research, and teaching could have drastically affected the number of respondents who might be, or might have been, potentially interested in such topics.
37. Novkov and Barclay, "Lesbians, Gays, Bisexuals, and the Transgendered in Political Science," 101.
38. Cook, "The Empirical Study of Lesbian, Gay, and Bisexual Politics."
39. Cook, "The Empirical Study of Lesbian, Gay, and Bisexual Politics," 680.
40. For instance, many social science researchers analyze "sex" in bimodal terms ("male" or "female"), ignoring intersex identities as a category. Additionally, many of these same researchers fail to draw distinctions between sex assigned at birth and gender identity; oftentimes, these terms are problematically conflated, leading to a variety of errors in data collection.
41. Currah, "The State of LGBT/Sexuality Studies in Political Science," 14.
42. Rollins, "Political Science, Political Sex."
43. Charles Smith, "Gay, Straight, or Questioning? Sexuality and Political Science," *PS: Political Science and Politics* 44 (2011): 35.
44. Smith, "Gay, Straight, or Questioning? Sexuality and Political Science," 35–38.
45. See Manuela Picq and Markus Thiel, eds., *Sexualities in World Politics: How LGBTQ+ Claims Shape International Relations* (New York: Routledge, 2015); Laura Sjoberg, "Towards Trans-Gendering IR?," *International Political Sociology* 6, no. 4 (2012):

337–354; Markus Thiel, "LGBTQ+ Politics and International Relations: Here? Queer? Used to It?," *International Politics Review* 2, no. 2 (2014): 51–60; Cynthia Weber, "Why Is There No Queer International Theory?," *European Journal of International Relations* 21, no. 1 (2014): 27–51; Cynthia Weber, "Queer Intellectual Curiosity as International Relations Method: Developing Queer International Relations Theoretical and Methodological Frameworks," *International Studies Quarterly* 60, no. 1 (2016): 11–23.

46. American Political Science Association, "APSA Kenneth Sherrill Fund: Help Broaden Recognition of LGBT Work in Political Science," *Political Science Now*, December 15, 2015.
47. See Berube, "Marching to a Different Drummer"; Berube, *Coming Out Under Fire*; Canaday, *The Straight State*; Charles, *Hoover's War on Gays*; Chauncey, "Christian Brotherhood or Sexual Perversion?"; Chauncey, *Gay New York*; Johnson, *The Lavender Scare*; Zane, "'I Did It for the Uplift of Humanity and the Navy.'"
48. See Valelly, "LGBT Politics and American Political Development."
49. Valelly, "LGBT Politics and American Political Development."
50. It should be noted that there is no clear definition of American political development (APD) that is generally agreed upon within the subfield of American politics.
51. Some scholars emphasize the necessity of thinking of APD as a subfield of American politics for a number of reasons. As a whole, the subfield of American politics is largely viewed as a quantitatively heavy field of study, and some scholars suggest that conceptualizing APD as a subfield of American politics actually does more to foster intellectual space for qualitative scholars of American politics. While I do not necessarily agree with this distinction of APD as a whole subfield, I do generally agree that the subfield of American politics is stereotypically quantitatively focused, which can very much exclude scholars working on projects such as this one. In short, the APD methodological framework and research agenda ensure that historical work in the subfield of American politics retains space for disciplinary recognition and scholarly debate.
52. See Adam Sheingate, "Institutional Dynamics and American Political Development," *Annual Review of Political Science* 17 (2014): 461–477; Valelly, "LGBT Politics and American Political Development."
53. Sheingate, "Institutional Dynamics and American Political Development," 462.
54. See Karen Orren and Stephen Skowronek, *The Search for American Political Development* (Cambridge: Cambridge University Press, 2004); Sheingate, "Institutional Dynamics and American Political Development"; Sven Steinmo and Kathleen Thelen, "Historical Institutionalism in Comparative Politics," in *Structuring Politics: Historical Institutionalism in Comparative Analysis*, ed. Sven Steinmo, Kathleeen Thelen, and Frank Longstreth (Cambridge: Cambridge University Press, 1992): 1–32.
55. David Mayhew, "Events as Causes: The Case of American Politics," in *Parties & Policies: How the American Government Works*, ed. David Mayhew (New Haven, CT: Yale University Press, 2008): 328–357; Richard Valelly, *Two Reconstructions: The Struggle for Black Enfranchisement* (Chicago: Chicago University Press, 2004): 316.

1. RESEARCHING WITH INTERDISCIPLINARY FRAMEWORKS   139

56. Rogers Smith, *Civic Ideals: Conflicting Visions of Citizenship in U.S. History* (New Haven, CT: Yale University Press, 1997); James Morone, *The Democratic Wish: Popular Participation and the Limits of American Government* (New York: Basic Books, 1990); James Morone, *Hellfire Nation: The Politics of Sin in American History* (New Haven, CT: Yale University Press, 2004).
57. Sheingate, "Institutional Dynamics and American Political Development," 462; see also Orren and Skowronek, *The Search for American Political Development*.
58. The APD methodological framework may be applied to a number of historical topics that may be classified by some type of periodization segmented by change. In other words, this framework can be used to analyze institutions, policies, social change/activism, etc. This flexibility in the APD methodological framework also contributes to some of the confusion around the APD research agenda, since it can be applied so broadly across historical topics of interest.
59. See Phil Everson, Rick Valelly, Arjun Vishwanath, and Jim Wiseman, "NOMINATE and American Political Development: A Primer," *Studies in American Political Development* 30 (2016): 97–115. Note that Rick Valelly, who coauthored this piece, is the same person as Richard Valelly.
60. Valelly, "LGBT Politics and American Political Development."
61. Valelly, "LGBT Politics and American Political Development," 316–318.
62. Valelly, "LGBT Politics and American Political Development," 323–327.
63. Morone, *The Democratic Wish*; Morone, *Hellfire Nation*.
64. Smith, *Civic Ideals*.
65. Valelly, *Two Reconstructions*.
66. As mentioned earlier, more contemporary works that utilize an APD framework are moving toward a mixed methods approach. More specifically, Everson et al.'s "NOMINATE and American Political Development: A Primer" uses the qualitative APD framework in conjunction with NOMINATE, the quantitative scaling application that has a multiplicity of experimental applications. I do not mean to suggest that their work is somehow "less" in line with APD scholarship; rather, it showcases the ways in which APD has been able to develop its research agenda. In my own work, I hope to make a similar contribution, since the APD framework has not, to the best of my knowledge, been used in pursuit of a LGBTQ+ research topic.
67. See Valelly, "LGBT Politics and American Political Development."
68. See Ackerly and True, *Doing Feminist Research in Political and Social Science*.
69. Chauncey, *Gay New York*; see also Berube, "Marching to a Different Drummer;" Berube, *Coming Out Under Fire*; Canaday, *The Straight State*; Johnson, *The Lavender Scare*.

1. RESEARCHING WITH INTERDISCIPLINARY FRAMEWORKS

1. Mary Hawkesworth, *Feminist Inquiry: From Political Conviction to Methodological Innovation* (New Brunswick, NJ: Rutgers University Press, 2006).

2. Some people refuse to accept or acknowledge the actuality of LGBTQ+ history. This societal failure to acknowledge or realize the impact of queer and transgender history may then be augmented by the historical erasure that negatively affects the broader LGBTQ+ community. Later in this chapter, I say more about the difficulties of working with LGBTQ+ history, particularly given issues involving queer and transgender erasure.
3. Hawkesworth, *Feminist Inquiry*, 10.
4. Hawkesworth, *Feminist Inquiry*.
5. For more on the topic of anti-LGBTQ+ censorship today, see New York Public Library, "LGBTQ+ Titles Targeted for Censorship: Stand Against Book Banning," June 23, 2023, https://www.nypl.org/blog/2023/06/23/lgbtq-titles-targeted-censorship-stand-against-book-banning. See also John Ismay, "Who's In and Who's Out at the Naval Academy's Library?," *New York Times*, April 11, 2025, https://www.nytimes.com/2025/04/11/us/politics/naval-academy-banned-books.html.
6. Hawkesworth, *Feminist Inquiry*, 128, 135.
7. Hawkesworth, *Feminist Inquiry*, 129, 136. Hawkesworth further defines social amnesia as "forms of unknowing actively produced and legitimated by dominant discourses" (136).
8. Hawkesworth, *Feminist Inquiry*, 128, 135.
9. As a rather unsurprising "spoiler" for most readers of this book, queer and transgender people have always existed; however, the labels that have been used to describe people of diverse sexualities and genders have varied over time.
10. Justin McCarthy, "Americans' Views on Origins of Homosexuality Remain Split," Gallup, May 28, 2014, https://news.gallup.com/poll/170753/americans-views-origins-homosexuality-remain-split.aspx.
11. LGBTQ+ people have always existed, of course, but language to label and express one's sexuality and/or gender has become more accessible, as previously mentioned.
12. George Chauncey, Martin B. Duberman, and Martha Vicinus, "Introduction," in *Hidden from History: Reclaiming the Gay & Lesbian Past*, ed. George Chauncey, Martin B. Duberman, and Martha Vicinus (New York: New American Library, 1989), 1–16; Neil Miller, *Out of the Past: Gay and Lesbian History from 1869 to Present* (New York: Vintage, [1995] 2006).
13. Joy Resmovits, "California's Students Will Soon Learn More LGBT History in Schools," *Los Angeles Times*, August 23, 2016, https://www.latimes.com/local/education/la-me-2016-california-act-scores-20160823-snap-story.html; see Hawkesworth, *Feminist Inquiry*.
14. Liz Stanly and Sue Wise, *Breaking Out Again: Feminist Ontology and Epistemology*, 2nd ed. (New York: Routledge, [1983] 1993), 120.
15. Stanley and Wise, *Breaking Out Again*, 120–124.
16. Sharlene Hesse-Biber, "A Re-Invitation to Feminist Research," in *Feminist Research Practice: A Primer*, ed. Sharlene Hesse-Biber (Los Angeles: Sage, 2014).
17. Christine Sylvester, *War as Experience: Contributions from International Relations and Feminist Analysis* (London: Routledge, 2012); see also Cynthia Enloe, *Nimo's War*,

1. RESEARCHING WITH INTERDISCIPLINARY FRAMEWORKS

Emma's War: Making Feminist Sense of the Iraq War (Berkeley: University of California Press, 2010); Christine Sylvester, *Curating and Re-Curating the American Wars in Vietnam and Iraq* (Oxford: Oxford University Press, 2019).

18. Brooke Ackerly and Jacqui True, *Doing Feminist Research in Political and Social Science* (New York: Palgrave Macmillan, 2010), 22.
19. Ackerly and True, *Doing Feminist Research in Political and Social Science*, 22–23.
20. For those who are interested, I did identify as a member of the LGBTQ+ community, but as a queer, cisgender man. My transition slightly predated the proposal for this book, and my research and writing have evolved over time.
21. Helene Silverberg, "Gender Studies and Political Science: The History of the 'Behavioralist Compromise,'" in *Discipline and History: Political Science in the United States*, ed. James Farr and Raymon Seidelman (Ann Arbor: University of Michigan Press, 1993).
22. Timothy Cook, "The Empirical Study of Lesbian, Gay, and Bisexual Politics: Assessing the First Wave of Research," *American Political Science Review* 93, no. 3 (September 1999): 679–692; Paisely Currah, "The State of LGBT/Sexuality Studies in Political Science," *PS: Political Science and Politics* 44 (2011): 13–16; Gary Mucciaroni, "The Study of LGBT Politics and Its Contributions to Political Science," *PS: Political Science and Politics* 44 (2011): 17–21; Julie Novkov and Scott Barclay, "Lesbians, Gays, Bisexuals, and the Transgendered in Political Science: Report on a Discipline-Wide Survey," *PS: Political Science and Politics* 43 (2010): 95–106; Joe Rollins, "Political Science, Political Sex," *PS: Political Science and Politics* 44 (2011): 27–30; Richard Valelly, "LGBT Politics and American Political Development," *Annual Review of Political Science* 15 (2012): 313–332.
23. Much of the security studies scholarship used in this project deals exclusively with "Don't Ask, Don't Tell" (DADT) period (the early 1990s to 2011) and the present period (2011 to the second Trump administration). Primary source documents also inform the chapter on these periods; however, much of the security studies scholarship stems from only two periods of analysis. It is my hope that, following the publication of this book, greater developments will occur within the area of security studies, helping to foster more research on this and related topics.
24. Title 10, U.S. Code 654, Public Law 103–160, 107 Statute 1671 (November 30, 1993).
25. Aaron Belkin, "The Pentagon's Gay Ban Is Not Based on Military Necessity," *Journal of Homosexuality* 41, no. 1 (2001): 103–119; see also Janet Halley, *Don't: A Readers Guide to the Military's Anti-Gay Policy* (Durham, NC: Duke University Press, 1999).
26. Aaron Belkin and Melissa Levitt, "Homosexuality and the Israeli Defense Forces: Did the Gay Ban Undermine Military Performance?," *Armed Forces & Society* 27, no. 4 (2001): 541–565.
27. Belkin and Levitt, "Homosexuality and the Israeli Defense Forces," 542.
28. Belkin and Levitt, "Homosexuality and the Israeli Defense Forces," 544.
29. Belkin and Levitt, "Homosexuality and the Israeli Defense Forces," 547.
30. Aaron Belkin and Melissa Sheridan Embser-Herbert, "A Modest Proposal: Privacy as a Flawed Rationale for the Exclusion of Gays and Lesbians from the U.S. Military," *International Security* 27, no. 2 (2002): 178–197.

31. Belkin and Embser-Herbert, "A Modest Proposal," 181.
32. Belkin and Embser-Herbert, "A Modest Proposal," 183, 187–193.
33. Aaron Belkin, "'Don't Ask, Don't Tell': Is the Gay Ban Based on Military Necessity?," *Parameters: U.S. Army War College Quarterly*, Summer 2003, 108–119.
34. Belkin, "'Don't Ask, Don't Tell,'" 109.
35. Belkin and Levitt, "Homosexuality and the Israeli Defense Forces"; Belkin, "'Don't Ask, Don't Tell,'" 110.
36. Belkin, "'Don't Ask, Don't Tell': Is the Gay Ban Based on Military Necessity?, 111. As a reminder, Belkin's work largely focuses on queer inclusion in the military and does not often address the needs of transgender, nonbinary, and/or intersex people.
37. Aaron Belkin, "'Don't Ask, Don't Tell': Does the Gay Ban Undermine the Military's Reputation?," *Armed Forces & Society* 34, no. 2 (2007): 276–291.
38. Aaron Belkin, *How We Won: Progressive Lessons from the Repeal of "Don't Ask, Don't Tell"* (Los Angeles: HuffPost Media Group, 2011).
39. Title 10, U.S. Code 654, Public Law 111–321, 124 Statute 3515, 2516, and 3517 (September 20, 2011).
40. As a reminder, transgender inclusion in the military was a topic of ongoing discussion within the Obama administration and the Pentagon; however, the advent of the Trump administration altered this. Specifically, Trump stated his belief that transgender inclusion in the military was simply the product of "political correctness," so it was relatively unsurprising that his administration did not support the measure. See Yezmin Villarreal, "Donald Trump: Allowing Trans People in the Military Is Due to 'Political Correctness,'" Advocate, October 4, 2016, https://www.advocate.com/election/2016/10/04/donald-trump-allowing-trans-people-military-due-political-correctness.
41. William Walker, *National Security and Core Values in American History* (Cambridge: Cambridge University Press, 2009), 42.
42. Walker, *National Security and Core Values in American* History, 52. As indicated by the quotation marks, these "civilization" projects were focused not on civilization but, rather, on white settler colonialism.
43. Walker, *National Security and Core Values in American History*, 47–63.
44. Walker, *National Security and Core Values in American History*.
45. Title 50, U.S. Code 37, 40 Statute 217 (June 15, 1917); Walker, *National Security and Core Values in American History*, 67.
46. Walker, *National Security and Core Values in American History*, 65–70. As a reminder, the Bolshevik or Russian Revolution began in 1917, with the initial February Revolution followed by the more significant October Revolution. The broader Bolshevik Revolution concluded at the end of the Russian Civil War in 1923.
47. Walker, *National Security and Core Values in American History*, 82; see also Alan Dawley, *Changing the World: American Progressives in War and Revolution* (Princeton, NJ: Princeton University Press, 2005).
48. Title 50, U.S. Code 401, Public Law 80–253 (July 26, 1947).

49. Alan Brinkley, "World War I and the Crisis of Democracy," in *Security v. Liberty: Conflicts Between National Security and Civil Liberties in American History*, ed. Daniel Farber (New York: Russell Sage Foundation, 2008), 27–41.
50. Daniel Farber, "Introduction," in Farber, *Security v. Liberty*, 1–26; Title 50, U.S. Code 37, 40 Statute 553 (May 16, 1918).
51. Farber, "Introduction," 10.
52. Jan Lewis, "Defining the Nation: 1790 to 1898," in Farber, *Security v. Liberty*, 117–164.
53. George Chauncey, "Christian Brotherhood or Sexual Perversion? Homosexual Identities and the Construction of Sexual Boundaries in the World War One Era," *Journal of Social History* 19, no. 2 (1985): 189–211.
54. Chauncey, "Christian Brotherhood or Sexual Perversion?," 190.
55. This is clearly a very outdated notion of sexuality, for a number of reasons. Most obviously, it presumes that "tops" must be dominant, heteronormative, and cisnormative, while presuming the opposite of "bottoms." Interestingly, such an outdated understanding of sexuality also completely fails to conceptualize a wider variety of sexual behaviors and roles that both "tops" and "bottoms" may take in a sexual scene (i.e., power bottoms, among other examples), regardless of historical context. See Janet Hardy and Dossie Easton, *The Ethical Slut: A Practical Guide to Polyamory, Open Relationships, and Other Freedoms in Sex and Love*, 3rd ed. (Berkeley, CA: Ten Speed, 2017); Janet Hardy and Dossie Easton, *The New Bottoming Book* (Emeryville, CA: Greenery, 2001).
56. Chauncey, "Christian Brotherhood or Sexual Perversion?," 193.
57. Margot Canaday, *The Straight State: Sexuality and Citizenship in Twentieth-Century America* (Princeton, NJ: Princeton University Press, 2006), 79. Chauncey's 1985 article is also the basis for placing Canaday's 2006 book and Sherry Zane's 2013 and 2018 research (discussed later) into perspective with one another and with the framework for this book's discussion of the World War I period.
58. Canaday, *The Straight State*, 57.
59. Canaday, *The Straight State*, 62.
60. Canaday, *The Straight State*, 62.
61. Such policies largely targeted queer men; however, these policies and the corresponding search for certain phenotypes also affected intersex people, among others.
62. Sherry Zane, "'I Did It for the Uplift of Humanity and the Navy': Same-Sex Acts and the Origins of the National Security State, 1919–1923," *New England Quarterly* 91, no. 2 (2018): 279–306.
63. Zane, "'I Did It for the Uplift of Humanity and the Navy,'" 5.
64. Zane, "'I Did It for the Uplift of Humanity and the Navy,'" 5, 16.
65. George Chauncey, *Gay New York: Gender, Urban Culture, and the Making of the Gay Male World, 1890–1940* (New York: Basic Books, 1994).
66. Chauncey, *Gay New York*, 2.
67. Chauncey, *Gay New York*, 5.
68. Chauncey, *Gay New York*, 9.

69. Canaday, *The Straight State*; Zane, "'I Did It for the Uplift of Humanity and the Navy.'"
70. Chauncey, "Christian Brotherhood or Sexual Perversion?"; Chauncey, *Gay New York*.
71. *Homosexual* and *transsexual* are dated terms that have largely fallen out of use in modern society. However, these were the labels that people used during this time period, and I have used them here and elsewhere in the book. Although they now have more modern equivalents, such as *queer* and *transgender*, I have avoided applying modern labels to historical discussions, particularly when discussing the advent of historical terms.
72. Robert Beachy, *Gay Berlin: Birthplace of a Modern Identity* (New York: Knopf, 2014).
73. Allan Berube, *Coming Out Under Fire: The History of Gay Men and Women in World War II* (Chapel Hill: University of North Carolina Press, [1990] 2010).
74. Berube, *Coming Out Under Fire*, 149–174.
75. Arthur Dong, *Coming Out Under Fire* (Deep Focus Productions, 1994).
76. Berube, *Coming Out Under Fire*; Canaday, *The Straight State*; Dong, *Coming Out Under Fire*. See also Albert Love and Charles Davenport, *Defects Found in Drafted Men* (Washington, DC: U.S. Government Printing Office, 1920).
77. Lillian Faderman, *Odd Girls and Twilight Lovers: A History of Lesbian Life in Twentieth-Century America* (New York: Columbia University Press, [1991] 2012).
78. Faderman, *Odd Girls and Twilight Lovers*; see also Chauncey, *Gay New York*.
79. Faderman, *Odd Girls and Twilight Lovers*, 118–125.
80. Faderman, *Odd Girls and Twilight Lovers*, 125. Some prominent scholars—most notably, Jack Halberstam and Martha Vicinus—have critiqued Faderman's understanding of lesbianism as too reliant upon sanitized notions of "female friendship." For more on this, see Jack Halberstam, *Female Masculinity* (Durham, NC: Duke University Press, 1998), 5–74; and Martha Vicinus, "'They Wonder to Which Sex I Belong': The Historical Roots of the Modern Lesbian Identity," *Feminist Studies* 18, no. 3 (1992): 467–498.
81. Executive Order 10450, 18 FR 2489, 3 CFR, 1949–1953 Comp: 936 (April 27, 1953).
82. Miller, *Out of the Past*, 235.
83. David Johnson, *The Lavender Scare: The Cold War Persecution of Gays and Lesbians in the Federal Government* (Chicago: University of Chicago Press, 2004).
84. Robert Corber, *In the Name of National Security: Hitchcock, Homophobia, and the Political Construction of Gender in Postwar America* (Durham, NC: Duke University Press, 1993); Robert Corber, *Homosexuality in Cold War America* (Durham, NC: Duke University Press, 1997); K. A. Courdileone, *Manhood and American Political Culture in the Cold War* (New York: Routledge, 2005); Michael Kimmel, *Manhood in America: A Cultural History*, 3rd ed. (Oxford: Oxford University Press, 2011).
85. Johnson, *The Lavender Scare*, 5.
86. Johnson, *The Lavender Scare*.
87. Johnson, *The Lavender Scare*, 21. These were people who were presumed to be "homosexual," but that does not mean they actually were. Throughout all of these periods, anti-LGBTQ+ policies have had unintended consequences affecting straight, cisgender, non-intersex people who were presumed to be queer, transgender, and/or intersex.

1. RESEARCHING WITH INTERDISCIPLINARY FRAMEWORKS   145

88. Johnson, *The Lavender Scare*, 117.
89. Some of the concerns and historical moments that led to a new rationale for excluding LGBTQ+ people from the military and intelligence community are seeing a resurgence today. More specifically, some members of the Trump administration's first-term transition team had previously called for a modern-day version of the House Un-American Activities Committee, which was a vehicle for the Red Scare (and a partial impetus for the Lavender Scare as well) in the 1950s; see Gregory Krieg, "Newt Gingrich Wants New House Un-American Activities Committee," CNN, June 14, 2016, https://www.cnn.com/2016/06/14/politics/newt-gingrich-house-un-american-activities-committee/index.html. Concerns about a link between queer identities and communist ideology also briefly reentered the popular discourse by way of some conservative activists in 2016; see Dawn Ennis, "Antigay Texas Activist: Soviets Created Gays to Destroy U.S., Like 'Termites,'" LGBTQ Nation, 2016, https://www.lgbtqnation.com/2016/11/antigay-texas-activist-soviets-created-gays-destroy-u-s-like-termites/.
90. Douglas Charles, *Hoover's War on Gays: Exposing the FBI's "Sex Deviates" Program* (Lawrence: University Press of Kansas, 2015).
91. Charles, *Hoover's War on Gays*; see also Johnson, *The Lavender Scare*.
92. Walter Frank, *Law and the Gay Rights Story: The Long Search for Equal Justice in a Divided Democracy* (New Brunswick, NJ: Rutgers University Press, 2014).
93. Randy Shilts, *Conduct Unbecoming: Gays & Lesbians in the U.S. Military* (New York: Ballantine, 1994).
94. "Alleged Immoral Conditions at Newport (RI) Naval Training Station," in *Government Versus Homosexuals*, ed. Leslie Parr (North Stratford, NH: Ayer, [1921] 1975); Love and Davenport, *Defects Found in Drafted Men*; see also Canaday, *The Straight State*; Chauncey, "Christian Brotherhood or Sexual Perversion?"; Zane, "'I Did It for the Uplift of Humanity and the Navy.'"
95. Title 10, U.S. Code Chapter 47 (1950).
96. Dong, *Coming Out Under Fire*.
97. Craig Loftin, *Letters to ONE: Gay and Lesbian Voices from the 1950s and 1960s* (Albany: State University of New York Press, 2012).
98. "Hoey Committee Report" in SY-General 1952 folder, Box 1, Entry 1508, Office of Security and Consular Affairs, Lot File 53-D-233, Subject Files of the Security Division, 1946–1953, RG 59 (Washington, DC: National Archives and Records Administration, February 1952).
99. S. H. Crittenden, "Report of the Board Appointed to Prepare and Submit Recommendations to the Secretary of the Navy for the Revision of Policies, Procedures, and Directives Dealing with Homosexuals," United States Navy Board of Inquiry, March 15, 1957.
100. Kate Dyer, ed., *Gays in Uniform: The Pentagon's Secret Reports* (Boston: Alyson, 1990).
101. Director of Central Intelligence Directive Number 1/14 (Washington, DC: Central Intelligence Agency, 1987); *Dubbs v. Central Intelligence Agency*, 866 F.2d 1114 (1989).
102. Bernard Rostker and Scott Harris, *Sexual Orientation and U.S. Military Personnel Policy: Options and Assessment*, National Defense Research Institute (Santa Monica, CA: RAND, 1993).

103. Bernard Rostker and Scott Harris, *Sexual Orientation and U.S. Military Personnel Policy: An Update of RAND's 1993 Study*, National Defense Research Institute (Santa Monica, CA: RAND, 2010); Agnes Schaefer, Radha Iyengar, Srikanth Kadiyala, Jennifer Kavanagh, Charles Engel, Kayla Williams, and Amil Kress, *Assessing the Implications of Allowing Transgender Personnel to Serve Openly*, National Defense Research Institute (Santa Monica, CA: RAND, 2016); U.S. Department of Defense, *Transgender Service in the U.S. Military: An Implementation Handbook* (Washington, DC: Author, September 30, 2016).

2. THE EARLY YEARS OF ANTI-LGBTQ+ MILITARY POLICY

1. This folk-speech phrase likely refers to "Dorothy" from L. Frank Baum's Oz series of books from 1900 to 1920 and later the protagonist, played by Judy Garland, in the 1939 film *The Wonderful Wizard of Oz*. The belief is that queer-coded references from the books and film gained popularity in queer, particularly male, subcultures. The question "Are you a friend of Dorothy?" could be used in casual conversation to safely determine if someone was queer; its use was most widespread in the mid-twentieth century among people presumed to be, though not exclusively identifying as, queer men. While this is the most commonly accepted origin story, others suggest it might be a reference to the gay-friendly soirées hosted by Dorothy Parker, literary critic and founding member of the Algonquin Round Table, in the New York social scene of the Roaring Twenties. See James Deutsch, "Are You a Friend of Dorothy? Folk Speech of the LGBT Community," *Folklife*, October 25, 2016, https://folklife.si.edu/talkstory/2016/are-you-a-friend-of-dorothy-folk-speech-of-the-lgbt-community.
2. While I realize that some elders within the broader LGBTQ+ community may—because of their lived experience—view this word as derogatory, I use it in this book for two principal reasons. First, it is an historical term that was utilized throughout portions of the early twentieth century, and it is both linguistically and historically accurate when used in relation to discussions of this time period. Second, the word has been reclaimed by members of the broader LGBTQ+ community in an effort to defuse its negative connotations in American history and culture.
3. David Shneer and Caryn Aviv, "Bulldykes, Faggots, and Faires, Oh My!: Calling and Being Called Queer in America Now and Then," in *American Queer: Now and Then*, ed. David Shneer and Caryn Aviv (Boulder, CO: Paradigm, 2006), 2.
4. David Shneer and Caryn Aviv, "The Birds and the . . . Birds: Queer Love, Sex, and Romance in America, Now and Then," in Schneer and Aviv, *American Queer*, 91–94.
5. Shneer and Aviv, "The Birds and the . . . Birds," 92; see also George Chauncey, *Gay New York: Gender, Urban Culture, and the Making of the Gay Male World, 1890–1940* (New York: Basic Books, 1994); Lillian Faderman, *Odd Girls and Twilight Lovers: A History of Lesbian Life in Twentieth-Century America* (New York: Columbia University Press, [1991] 2012); Shneer and Aviv, "Bulldykes, Faggots, and Faires, Oh My!"

6. Chauncey, *Gay New York*, 15–16; Shneer and Aviv, "The Birds and the . . . Birds"; Siobhan Somerville, *Queering the Color Line: Race and the Invention of Homosexuality in American Culture* (Durham, NC: Duke University Press, 2000), 142–143.
7. Shneer and Aviv, "Bulldykes, Faggots, and Faires, Oh My!," 3.
8. Shneer and Aviv, "Bulldykes, Faggots, and Faires, Oh My!," 4.
9. George Chauncey, "Christian Brotherhood or Sexual Perversion? Homosexual Identities and the Construction of Sexual Boundaries in the World War One Era," *Journal of Social History* 19, no. 2 (1985): 189. See also Vicki Eaklor, *Queer America: A People's GLBT History of the United States* (New York: New Press, 2008), 53. For more information about early queer American history and the use of language, see John D'Emilio and Estelle Freedman, *Intimate Matters: A History of Sexuality in America*, 3rd ed. (Chicago: University of Chicago Press, [1988] 2012); Jonathan Katz, *Gay American History: Lesbians and Gay Men in the U.S.A.* (New York: Meridan, [1976] 1992); Neil Miller, *Out of the Past: Gay and Lesbian History from 1869 to the Present* (New York: Vintage, [1995] 2006); Susan Stryker, *Transgender History* (Berkeley, CA: Seal, 2008).
10. Shneer and Aviv, "Bulldykes, Faggots, and Faires, Oh My!," 3. See also Chauncey, "Christian Brotherhood or Sexual Perversion?"; Chauncey, *Gay New York*.
11. Shneer and Aviv, "Bulldykes, Faggots, and Faires, Oh My!," 3. See also Chauncey, "Christian Brotherhood or Sexual Perversion?"
12. Chauncey, "Christian Brotherhood or Sexual Perversion?"; Chauncey, *Gay New York*.
13. Chauncey, *Gay New York*, 50–63.
14. Robert Beachy, *Gay Berlin: Birthplace of a Modern Identity* (New York: Knopf, 2014), xiv–xvi.
15. Beachy, *Gay Berlin*, 160–219.
16. Beachy, *Gay Berlin*; see also Benjamin Cantu, *Eldorado: Everything the Nazis Hate* (Film Base Berlin and Netflix Studios, 2023).
17. For anecdotal information describing the culture of Berlin under the Weimar Republic and its influence in the cultural memory of the everyday queer experience, see Christopher Isherwood, *Goodbye to Berlin* (New York: New Directions, [1939] 2012). This book is based on Isherwood's interactions with the Berlin queer community over several years. In the past decade or so, this progressivism in relation to LGBTQ+ communities in pre-Nazi Berlin has been depicted in a variety of television shows and films; for more on this, see Tom Hooper, *The Danish Girl* (Focus Features and Universal Pictures, 2015); Geoffrey Sax, *Christopher and His Kind* (BBC Two, 2011).
18. Beachy, *Gay Berlin*, ix–xvi.
19. Jack Halberstam, *Female Masculinity* (Durham, NC: Duke University Press, 1998), 82.
20. Beachy, *Gay Berlin*; see also Cantu, *Eldorado*; Chauncey, *Gay New York*.
21. Magnus Hirschfeld, "Die Intersexuelle Konstitution," *Jahrbuch fur Sexuelle Zwischenstufen Unterbesonderer Berucksichtigung der Homosexualit* 23 (1923): 3–27; see also Beachy, *Gay Berlin*; Cantu, *Eldorado*.
22. Hirschfeld, "Die Intersexuelle Konstitution"; see also Magnus Hirschfeld, *Die Transvestiten—Eine Untersuchung uber den Erotischen Verkleidungstrieb: Mit Umfangreichem Casuistischen und Historischen Material* (Berlin: Alfred Pulvermacher, 1910).

23. David Cauldwell, "Psychopathia Transexualis," *Sexology* 16 (1949): 274–280: Stryker, *Transgender History*.
24. Beachy, *Gay Berlin*; Cantu, *Eldorado*; Stryker, *Transgender History*.
25. Halberstam, *Female Masculinity*, 85.
26. Beachy, *Gay Berlin*.
27. Chauncey, *Gay New York*; Faderman, *Odd Girls and Twilight Lovers*.
28. Shneer and Aviv, "Bulldykes, Faggots, and Faires, Oh My!," 3.
29. Chauncey, *Gay New York*, 16.
30. Chauncey, *Gay New York*, 16; see also Shneer and Aviv, "Bulldykes, Faggots, and Faires, Oh My!."
31. Beachy, *Gay Berlin*; Chauncey, *Gay New York*, 16; see also Shneer and Aviv, "Bulldykes, Faggots, and Faires, Oh My!"
32. Chauncey, *Gay New York*, 15–16; Eaklor, *Queer America*, 53; Somerville, *Queering the Color Line*, 142–143.
33. Beachy, *Gay Berlin*; Chauncey, *Gay New York*; Shneer and Aviv, "Bulldykes, Faggots, and Faires, Oh My!"
34. Faderman, *Odd Girls and Twilight Lovers*.
35. "Case of Stephen Brug, Chief Boatswain's Mate, USN," Record of Proceedings of a General Court-Martial Convened at U.S. Naval Training State, Newport, R.I, By Order of Secretary of the Navy (Washington, DC: National Archives and Records Administration, November 18–21, 1919), 48.
36. Margot Canaday, *The Straight State: Sexuality and Citizenship in Twentieth-Century America* (Princeton, NJ: Princeton University Press, 2006), 79; see also Chauncey, *Gay New York*, 99–130; Shneer and Aviv, "Bulldykes, Faggots, and Faires, Oh My!," 3.
37. Chauncey, *Gay New York*, 189; see also Eaklor, *Queer America*, 53.
38. Chauncey, *Gay New York*, 190; see also Canaday, *The Straight State*, 79.
39. Canaday, *The Straight State*, 62; Sherry Zane, "'I Did It for the Uplift of Humanity and the Navy,'" MIT Press Podcast, September 18, 2018.
40. James Morone, *Hellfire Nation: The Politics of Sin in American History* (New Haven, CT: Yale University Press, 2004), 222–349.
41. Canaday, *The Straight State*; Chauncey, *Gay New York*; Sherry Zane, "'I Did It for the Uplift of Humanity and the Navy': Same-Sex Acts and the Origins of the National Security State, 1919–1923," *New England Quarterly* 91, no. 2 (2018): 279–306; Zane, MIT Press Podcast.
42. Canaday, *The Straight State*, 62.
43. With regard to female impersonation or "drag," other scholars, examining the role of drag queens in the Canadian military in World War II, have demonstrated how drag shows and female impersonation shows were expressly used to raise morale and to provide the enlisted service members with a sense of lightheartedness. See Laurel Halladay, "A Lovely War: Male to Female Cross-Dressing and Canadian Military Entertainment in World War II," in *The Drag Queen Anthology: The Absolutely Fabulous but Flawlessly Customary World of Female Impersonators*, ed. Steven Schacht and Lisa Underwood (Binghamton, NY: Haworth, 2004), 19–34; Paul Jackson, *One of the Boys:*

2. THE EARLY YEARS OF ANTI-LGBTQ+ MILITARY POLICY 149

Homosexuality in the Military During World War II, 2nd ed. (Montreal: Mc-Gill Queen's University Press, [2004] 2010). For general discussions of drag prior to World War II and the drag balls of the 1920s and 1930s, see Chauncey, *Gay New York*. Chauncey describes drag as an imitation and appropriation of the more dominant cisnormative and heteronormative culture of balls with a distinctly dynamic queer and gender-variant tinge; for this specific reference, see Chauncey, *Gay New York*, 25. Over the decades following this critique, drag shows would find their own place in both American and, likely to the surprise of the World War I–era vice squads, military culture.

44. Canaday, *The Straight State*, 62; see also Albert Love and Charles Davenport, *Defects Found in Drafted Men* (Washington, DC: U.S. Government Printing Office, 1920).
45. Canaday, *The Straight State*; Zane, "'I Did It for the Uplift of Humanity and the Navy.'"
46. Canaday, *The Straight State*.
47. Love and Davenport, *Defects Found in Drafted Men*, 59.
48. Canaday, *The Straight State*; Love and Davenport, *Defects Found in Drafted* Men; Zane, "'I Did It for the Uplift of Humanity and the Navy.'"
49. Morone, *Hellfire Nation*, 222–349.
50. Allan Berube, *Coming Out Under Fire: The History of Gay Men and Women in World War II* (Chapel Hill: University of North Carolina Press, [1990] 2010).
51. Canaday, *The Straight State*, 64; Berube, *Coming Out Under Fire*, 13–14. For more information about the experiences of these people, see Canaday, *The Straight State*, 62–64. While certainty about these people's sexed identities is lost to history, it may be the case that some draft and medical advisory boards were encountering intersex people, who may not fit neatly into the biological categories assumed to characterize the sex "male."
52. According to interAct Advocates for Intersex Youth, "intersex is an umbrella term for differences in sex traits or reproductive anatomy," and "there are many possible differences in genitalia, hormones, internal anatomy, or chromosomes, compared to the usual two ways that human bodies develop." The term *intersex* describes people who have natural variations in their external genitalia (phallus, clitoris, etc.), internal reproductive system, hormones (and resulting secondary sex characteristics), and/or chromosomes. See interAct Advocates for Intersex Youth, "What Is Intersex?," https://interactadvocates.org/faq/.
53. Canaday, *The Straight State*; see also National Parks Service, "Women in World War I," https://www.nps.gov/articles/women-in-world-war-i.htm.
54. Canaday, *The Straight State*, 64.
55. Bernard Rostker and Scott Harris, *Sexual Orientation and U.S. Military Personnel Policy: Options and Assessment*, National Defense Research Institute (Santa Monica, CA: RAND, 1993), 3–4.
56. Rhonda Evans, "U.S. Military Policies Concerning Homosexuals: Development, Implementation and Outcomes," Report for the Center for the Study of Sexual Minorities in the Military (Santa Barbara: University of California at Santa Barbara, 2002),

117; see also David Burrelli, "An Overview of the Debate on Homosexuals in the U.S. Military," in *Gays and Lesbians in the Military: Issues, Concerns, and Contrasts*, ed. Wilbur Scott and Sandra Stanley (Hawthorne, NY: Aldine de Gruyter, 1994), 17–31; Rostker and Harris, *Sexual Orientation and U.S. Military Personnel Policy*, 3–4.

57. Chauncey, "Christian Brotherhood or Sexual Perversion?"; Zane, "'I Did It for the Uplift of Humanity and the Navy,' "; Zane, MIT Press Podcast.
58. Chauncey, "Christian Brotherhood or Sexual Perversion?"; Zane, "'I Did It for the Uplift of Humanity and the Navy'"; Zane, MIT Press Podcast.
59. "Case of Harold J. Trubshaw, Hospital Apprentice 2nd class, USNRF," Record of Proceedings of a General Court-Martial Convened at U.S. Naval Training State, Newport, R.I., By Order of Secretary of the Navy (Washington, DC: National Archives and Records Administration, October 28–30, 1919), C(a).
60. Chauncey, "Christian Brotherhood or Sexual Perversion?"; Zane, "'I Did It for the Uplift of Humanity and the Navy'"; Zane, MIT Press Podcast.
61. Chauncey, "Christian Brotherhood or Sexual Perversion?"; Zane, "'I Did It for the Uplift of Humanity and the Navy' "; Zane, MIT Press Podcast.
62. Zane, "'I Did It for the Uplift of Humanity and the Navy'"; see also Zane, MIT Press Podcast.
63. Zane, "'I Did It for the Uplift of Humanity and the Navy'"; see also Letter to President Woodrow Wilson, January 11, 1920, Bishop Perry Papers, Subject Series 29, Series No. VIII, Box 9, Folder 331 at the University of Rhode Island Library Special Collections; Zane, MIT Press Podcast.
64. "Alleged Immoral Conditions at Newport (R.I.) Naval Training Station," Report of the Committee on Naval Affairs of the United States Senate, 67th Congress, reprinted in *Government Versus Homosexuals*, ed. Leslie Parr (North Stratford, NH: Ayer, [1921] 1975), 5; see also Zane, "'I Did It for the Uplift of Humanity and the Navy'"; Zane, MIT Press Podcast.
65. Title 50, U.S. Code 37, 40 Statute 217 (June 15, 1917); Title 50, U.S. Code 37, 40 Statute 553 (May 16, 1918); "Alleged Immoral Conditions at Newport (R.I.) Naval Training Station"; Daniel Farber, "Introduction," in *Security v. Liberty: Conflicts Between National Security and Civil Liberties in American History*, ed. Daniel Farber (New York: Russell Sage Foundation, 2008), 1–26; Zane, "'I Did It for the Uplift of Humanity and the Navy.'"
66. Zane, "'I Did It for the Uplift of Humanity and the Navy'"; Zane, MIT Press Podcast.
67. Zane, "'I Did It for the Uplift of Humanity and the Navy,' "; Zane, MIT Press Podcast.
68. Chauncey, "Christian Brotherhood or Sexual Perversion?,"193.
69. Shneer and Aviv, "Bulldykes, Faggots, and Faires, Oh My!," 3; *see also* Chauncey, "Christian Brotherhood or Sexual Perversion?."
70. "Case of Harold J. Trubshaw," C-C(a).
71. "Case of Harold J. Trubshaw."
72. Chauncey, "Christian Brotherhood or Sexual Perversion?"; Chauncey, *Gay New York*; see also Zane, "'I Did It for the Uplift of Humanity and the Navy.'"

73. "Alleged Immoral Conditions at Newport (R.I.) Naval Training Station"; see also Zane, "'I Did It for the Uplift of Humanity and the Navy.'"
74. Zane, "'I Did It for the Uplift of Humanity and the Navy.'"
75. Chauncey, *Gay New York*; see also "Alleged Immoral Conditions at Newport (R.I.) Naval Training Station"; Chauncey, "Christian Brotherhood or Sexual Perversion?"; Zane, "'I Did It for the Uplift of Humanity and the Navy'"; Shneer and Aviv, "Bulldykes, Faggots, and Faires, Oh My!"; Zane, MIT Press Podcast.
76. Chauncey, *Gay New York*; Eaklor, *Queer America*; Shneer and Aviv, "Bulldykes, Faggots, and Faires, Oh My!;" Shneer and Aviv, "The Birds and the . . . Birds."
77. Zane, "'I Did It for the Uplift of Humanity and the Navy'"; see also Canaday, *The Straight State*; Zane, MIT Press Podcast.
78. Rostker and Harris, *Sexual Orientation and U.S. Military Personnel Policy*, 4; Canaday, *The Straight State*; Chauncey, "Christian Brotherhood or Sexual Perversion?"; Zane, "'I Did It for the Uplift of Humanity and the Navy,"; Zane, MIT Press Podcast.
79. Canaday, *The Straight State*; Love and Davenport, *Defects Found in Drafted Men*, 59; Morone, *Hellfire Nation*, 222–349; Zane, "'I Did It for the Uplift of Humanity and the Navy.'"
80. Canaday, *The Straight State*, 89.
81. Canaday, *The Straight State*, 87.
82. Arthur Dong, *Coming Out Under Fire* (Deep Focus Productions, 1994).
83. Beachy, *Gay Berlin*; Chauncey, *Gay New York*; Faderman, *Odd Girls and Twilight Lovers*.
84. Originally developed in World War I, blue discharges—sometimes called "blue tickets"—were neither honorable nor dishonorable discharges; their name derives from the fact that they were printed on blue paper. See National Park Service, "Blue and 'Other Than Honorable' Discharges," https://www.nps.gov/articles/000/blue-and-other-than-honorable-discharges.htm.
85. Canaday, *The Straight State*, 58; see also Rostker and Harris, *Sexual Orientation and U.S. Military Personnel Policy*, 4–5.
86. "Alleged Immoral Conditions at Newport (R.I.) Naval Training Station."
87. Rostker and Harris, *Sexual Orientation and U.S. Military Personnel Policy*, 5. Following the conclusion of World War II, the Department of War (DoW) became the Department of Defense (DoD), and the Army Air Corps became the Air Force, a separate unit within the DoD. See U.S. Department of Defense, "The History of the Department of Defense," 2021, https://www.defense.gov/Multimedia/Experience/The-History-of-the-Department-of-Defense/.
88. For more on the growth of the military during this period, see Barry M. Stentiford, "Selective Service: Before the All-Volunteer Force," *Military Review*, November–December 2023, https://www.armyupress.army.mil/portals/7/military-review/Archives/English/Nov-Dec-23/Selective-Service/Selective-Service-UA1.pdf.
89. Berube, *Coming Out Under Fire*. See also Rostker and Harris, *Sexual Orientation and U.S. Military Personnel Policy*, 5; Gary Lehring, *Officially Gay: The Political Construction of Sexuality by the U.S. Military* (Philadelphia: Temple University Press, 2003), 75; Miller, *Out of the Past*, 215.

90. Canaday, *The Straight State*.
91. Lehring, *Officially Gay*, 44; see also Carolyn Herbst Lewis, *Prescription for Heterosexuality: Sexual Citizenship in the Cold War Era* (Chapel Hill: University of North Carolina Press, 2010). The medical model of "diagnosing" someone as homosexual would continue to spur research and medical practice outside the context of the American military as well; for more information about this in post–World War II America, see Lewis, *Prescription for Heterosexuality*.
92. Canaday, *The Straight State*, 88.
93. In late antiquity, the presence of an enlarged clitoris resulted in the word *tribade*. As a practice, *tribadism*—the rubbing of external genitalia for sexual pleasure—became associated with sexual activities between queer women and sapphics. However, this was not inherently equivalent to contemporary notions of lesbianism. For more on this topic, see Halberstam, *Female Masculinity*, 59–65.
94. For firsthand information about the intrusiveness of this process, see Dong, *Coming Out Under* Fire. This film allowed affected service members from World War II to speak about this process and their experiences in the military.
95. Berube, *Coming Out Under Fire*, 387.
96. Douglas Stuart, *Creating the National Security State: A History of the Law That Transformed America* (Princeton, NJ: Princeton University Press, 2012), 40.
97. Stuart, *Creating the National Security State*, 31.
98. Stuart, *Creating the National Security State*, 37.
99. Stuart, *Creating the National Security State*, 40.
100. Allan Berube, "Marching to a Different Drummer: Lesbian and Gay GIs in World War II," in *Hidden from History: Reclaiming the Gay & Lesbian Past*, ed. George Chauncey, Martin B. Duberman, and Martha Vicinus (New York: New American Library, 1989), 383–394.
101. Faderman, *Odd Girls and Twilight Lovers*, 120–125; see also Gabrielle Camp, "Women on the Home Front: The Women's Army Corps and Lesbian Community During and After World War II," April 27, 2023, Florida State University Libraries; Women's Army Corps, "Sex Hygiene Course," Pamphlet 35-1 (Washington, DC: Department of War, 1945), 24–27.
102. Faderman, *Odd Girls and Twilight Lovers*, 123.
103. Berube, "Marching to a Different Drummer," 388.
104. Berube, "Marching to a Different Drummer," 388; see also Berube, *Coming Out Under Fire*; Miller, *Out of the Past*, 210–217.
105. Berube, "Marching to a Different Drummer," 389; Faderman, *Odd Girls and Twilight Lovers*, 123. See also Berube, *Coming Out Under Fire*; Dong, *Coming Out Under Fire*; Women's Army Corps, "Sex Hygiene Course."
106. Faderman, *Odd Girls and Twilight Lovers*, 119–125.
107. Faderman, *Odd Girls and Twilight Lovers*, 123; Miller, *Out of the Past*, 210. See also Camp, "Women on the Home Front"; Dong, *Coming Out Under Fire*.
108. There were almost certainly service members who were discharged under other premises, policies, and administrative mechanisms. During World War II, some

discharges given for a variety of reasons, including homosexuality, were so-called blue discharges, which were neither honorable nor dishonorable. Yet the presence of this discharge potentially raised questions and excluded former service members from receiving certain veteran's benefits. See Berube, *Coming Out Under Fire*, 230.
109. Berube, "Marching to a Different Drummer," 391.
110. Miller, *Out of the Past*, 211. See also Canaday, *The Straight State*; Faderman, *Odd Girls and Twilight Lovers*. For more on the screening process and expectations of WAAC/WAC, see Beth Bailey, "'A Higher Moral Character': Respectability and the Women's Army Corps," *Managing Sex in the U.S. Military*, ed. Beth Bailey, Alesha Doan, Shannon Portillo, and Kara Dixon Vuic (Lincoln: University of Nebraska Press, 2022), 71–94.
111. Berube, "Marching to a Different Drummer," 389. See also Douglas Charles, *Hoover's War on Gays: Exposing the FBI's "Sex Deviates" Program* (Lawrence: University Press of Kansas, 2015).
112. Berube, "Marching to a Different Drummer," 393; see also Charles, *Hoover's War on Gays*.
113. Charles, *Hoover's War on Gays*; see also Walter Frank, *Law and the Gay Rights Story: The Long Search for Equal Justice in a Divided Democracy* (New Brunswick, NJ: Rutgers University Press, 2014).
114. Berube, *Coming Out Under Fire*, 112–113; see also Dong, *Coming Out Under Fire*.
115. Halladay, "A Lovely War," 19–34; Jackson, *One of the Boys*, 211–220.
116. Jackson, *One of the Boys*, 211.
117. Julie Satow, *When Women Ran Fifth Avenue: Glamour and Power at the Dawn of American Fashion* (New York: Doubleday, 2024), 111–112; see also Joe David Rice, "Good Lord and Taylor!," *About You*, June 30, 2020, https://aymag.com/good-lord-and-taylor/.
118. Berube, *Coming Out Under Fire*; see also Dong, *Coming Out Under Fire*.
119. Faderman, *Odd Girls and Twilight Lovers*, 125–130.
120. Faderman, *Odd Girls and Twilight Lovers*, 125.
121. Faderman, *Odd Girls and Twilight Lovers*, 125–126.
122. Faderman, *Odd Girls and Twilight Lovers*, 126.
123. Faderman, *Odd Girls and Twilight Lovers*, 126.
124. Chauncey, *Gay New York*.
125. Chauncey, *Gay New York*; Dong, *Coming Out Under Fire*; Faderman, *Odd Girls and Twilight Lovers*; see also Berube, *Coming Out Under Fire*.
126. Faderman, *Odd Girls and Twilight Lovers*; Miller, *Out of the Past*, 211; Rostker and Harris, *Sexual Orientation and U.S. Military Personnel Policy*, 5.
127. Stuart, *Creating the National Security State*, 7.
128. Stuart, *Creating the National Security State*, 172–230.

3. THE COLD WAR, COMMUNISTS, AND QUEER BOOGEYMEN

1. Title 50, U.S. Code 401, Public Law 80-253 (July 26, 1947).
2. *Congressional Record* 96, pt. 4, 81st Congress, 2nd session (March 29 to April 24, 1950), 4527–4528.

3. Gregory Herek, "Gay People and Government Security Clearances: A Social Science Perspective," *American Psychologist* 45, no. 9 (1950): 1035–1042; see also David Johnson, *The Lavender Scare: The Cold War Persecution of Gays and Lesbians in the Federal Government* (Chicago: University of Chicago Press, 2004).
4. Kate Dyer, "Forward," in *Gays in Uniform: The Pentagon's Secret Reports*, ed. Kate Dyer (Boston: Alyson, 1990): xii–xviii; Bernard Rostker and Scott Harris, *Sexual Orientation and U.S. Military Personnel Policy: Options and Assessment*, National Defense Research Institute (Santa Monica, CA: RAND, 1993), 6; Johnson, *Lavender Scare*.
5. Dyer, "Forward," xv.
6. Dyer, "Forward"; Johnson, *The Lavender Scare*; Rostker and Harris, *Sexual Orientation and U.S. Military Personnel Policy*.
7. Judith Adkins, "Congressional Investigations and the Lavender Scare," in *Prologue* 48, no. 2 (Washington, DC: National Archives and Records Administration, 2016); Johnson, *The Lavender Scare*; Neil Miller, *Out of the Past: Gay and Lesbian History from 1869 to Present* (New York: Vintage, [1995] 2006), 238–239.
8. Miller, *Out of the Past*, 91–93; see also Rob Epstein and Jeffrey Friedman, *Paragraph 175* (Telling Pictures, 2000); Richard Plant, *The Pink Triangle: The Nazi War Against Homosexuals* (New York: Holt, 1986).
9. Adkins, "Congressional Investigations and the Lavender Scare"; Johnson, *The Lavender Scare*.
10. Adkins, "Congressional Investigations and the Lavender Scare," 2.
11. Alfred Kinsey, *Sexual Behavior in the Human Male* (Indianapolis: Indiana University Press, [1948] 1998).
12. Adkins, "Congressional Investigations and the Lavender Scare"; Johnson, *The Lavender Scare*.
13. "Department of Defense Memorandum," October 11, 1949, reprinted in Rostker and Harris, *Sexual Orientation and U.S. Military Personnel Policy*.
14. Adkins, "Congressional Investigations and the Lavender Scare"; see also K. A. Courdileone, *Manhood and American Political Culture in the Cold War* (New York: Routledge, 2005), 67–87.
15. See Adkins, "Congressional Investigations and the Lavender Scare"; Courdileone, *Manhood and American Political Culture in the Cold War*, 67–87; Johnson, *The Lavender Scare*; Miller, *Out of the Past*, 234–239.
16. Johnson, *The Lavender Scare*, 1; see also Adkins, "Congressional Investigations and the Lavender Scare."
17. Johnson, *The Lavender Scare*, 18; see also Adkins, "Congressional Investigations and the Lavender Scare."
18. Adkins, "Congressional Investigations and the Lavender Scare"; see also Courdileone, *Manhood and American Political Culture in the Cold War*, 67–87; Johnson, *The Lavender Scare*.
19. Adkins, "Congressional Investigations and the Lavender Scare"; see also Johnson, *The Lavender Scare*; Miller, *Out of the Past*.

20. While the Lavender Scare describes the fear of LGBTQ+ people in intelligence roles in the federal government, the early Cold War saw the spread of this presumed connection between homosexual identity and communist ideology in other ways too. For instance, the state of Florida led an investigation of people believed to be communist sympathizers, "homosexual," and/or generally un-American during the early years of the Cold War; see Stacy Braukman, *Communists and Perverts Under the Palms: The Johns Committee in Florida, 1956–1965* (Gainesville: University Press of Florida, 2013). During the Cold War and in the same state, anticommunist sentiments led to the mass dismissal of queer educators; see Karen Graves, *And They Were Wonderful Teachers: Florida's Purge of Gay and Lesbian Teachers* (Champaign: University of Illinois Press, 2009). In short, this fear of LGBTQ+ people in the so-called Lavender Scare existed in the cultural consciousness well beyond Washington, DC; along with the Red Scare, it served as a definitive moment that had consequences well beyond the federal government.
21. Johnson, *The Lavender Scare*, 21.
22. *Congressional Record*, 4527.
23. *Congressional Record*, 4527.
24. The political rhetoric, along with the contributions of World War II military psychiatrists and psychologists, later contributed to the classification of homosexuality as a mental health disorder in the psychiatric community's first publication of the *Diagnostic and Statistical Manual of Mental Disorders (DSM)*.
25. *Congressional Record*, 4527.
26. *Congressional Record*, 4528.
27. *Congressional Record*, 4528.
28. Executive Order 9835, 12 FR 1935 (March 25, 1947).
29. Alan Harper, *The Politics of Loyalty: The White House and the Communist Issue, 1946–1952* (Santa Barbara, CA: Praeger, 1970); Michael Hogan, *A Cross of Iron: Harry S. Truman and the Origins of the National Security State, 1945–1954* (Cambridge: Cambridge University Press, 2000).
30. Adkins, "Congressional Investigations and the Lavender Scare"; see also Johnson, *The Lavender Scare*.
31. Lillian Faderman, *Odd Girls and Twilight Lovers: A History of Lesbian Life in Twentieth-Century America* (New York: Columbia University Press, [1991] 2012), 141.
32. Adkins, "Congressional Investigations and the Lavender Scare," 5.
33. Adkins, "Congressional Investigations and the Lavender Scare"; see also Johnson, *The Lavender Scare*.
34. Adkins, "Congressional Investigations and the Lavender Scare," 6; see also Johnson, *The Lavender Scare*.
35. Adkins, "Congressional Investigations and the Lavender Scare," 3; see also Johnson, *The Lavender Scare*; Miller, *Out of the Past*, 234–239.
36. Adkins, "Congressional Investigations and the Lavender Scare"; Johnson, *The Lavender Scare*.

37. Adkins, "Congressional Investigations and the Lavender Scare," 8. The psychiatric community released the first *Diagnostic and Statistical Manual of Mental Disorders*, or *DSM*, in 1952, the year this committee began its inquiry. This handbook for diagnosing mental health issues and related conditions officially classified non-straight behavior and/or identity as a sociopathic personality disturbance; for more information, see. American Psychiatric Association, *Diagnostic and Statistical Manual of Mental Disorders* (Washington, DC: Author, 1952). For more information on the role of sexuality and medicine throughout the early Cold War period, see Carolyn Herbst Lewis, *Prescription for Heterosexuality: Sexual Citizenship in the Cold War Era* (Chapel Hill: University of North Carolina Press, 2010). For more on the impact of the *DSM*'s first publication in relation to the Hoey Committee's goals, see Adkins, "Congressional Investigations and the Lavender Scare"; Johnson, *The Lavender Scare*.
38. Adkins, "Congressional Investigations and the Lavender Scare"; Johnson, *The Lavender Scare*.
39. Douglas Charles, *Hoover's War on Gays: Exposing the FBI's "Sex Deviates" Program* (Lawrence: University Press of Kansas, 2015); see also Courdileone, *Manhood and American Political Culture in the Cold War*, 72–73; Walter Frank, *Law and the Gay Rights Story: The Long Search for Equal Justice in a Divided Democracy* (New Brunswick, NJ: Rutgers University Press, 2014). Charles's *Hoover's War on Gays* is the definitive text on the subject, detailing the origins, purpose, and impact of this program. While not all of the information falls within the scope of my project, it confirms that this FBI program was actively framing queer people, in the context of service to the federal government, as security risks to the nation.
40. Subcommittee on Investigations to the Committee on Expenditures in the Executive Departments, 81st Congress, *Employment of Homosexuals and Other Sex Perverts in Government* (Washington, DC: U.S. Government Printing Office, 1950).
41. Adkins, "Congressional Investigations and the Lavender Scare"; Johnson, *The Lavender Scare*. See also "Draft of Proposed Manual for Special Agents," SY-General 1954 Folder, Box 1, Entry 1508, Office of Security and Consular Affairs, Lot File 53-D-233, Subject Files of the Security Division, 1946–1953, RG 59 (Washington, DC: National Archives and Records Administration, February 1952).
42. *Employment of Homosexuals and Other Sex Perverts in Government*, 3.
43. *Employment of Homosexuals and Other Sex Perverts in Government*.
44. *Employment of Homosexuals and Other Sex Perverts in Government*, 4; see also *Congressional Record*, 4527–4528.
45. George Chauncey, *Gay New York: Gender, Urban Culture, and the Making of the Gay Male World, 1890–1940* (New York: Basic Books, 1994); Faderman, *Odd Girls and Twilight Lovers*, 125–130. See also Fenton Bailey and Randy Barbato, *The Strange History of Don't Ask, Don't Tell* (HBO Documentary Films, 2012).
46. *Employment of Homosexuals and Other Sex Perverts in Government*, 6–8; see also Adkins, "Congressional Investigations and the Lavender Scare"; Johnson, *The Lavender Scare*.
47. *Employment of Homosexuals and Other Sex Perverts in Government*, 3.

48. *Employment of Homosexuals and Other Sex Perverts in Government*, 7; see also Johnson, *The Lavender Scare*; Miller, *Out of the Past*, 238–239. Estimates suggest that the military saw the dismissal of roughly two thousand queer service members per year in the early 1950s (Miller, *Out of the Past*, 238–239). The actual number of people purged from the military and from the federal government has been lost to history, but this number is a verifiable conservative estimate based on data available at the time of Miller's writing. I am unaware of any estimates that differ drastically from this number in one direction or the other. For information on the impact and importance of "blue discharges" issued to gay men and lesbian women throughout the 1950s and 1960s, see Craig Loftin, *Masked Voices: Gay Men and Lesbians in Cold War America* (Albany: State University of New York Press, 2012).
49. Adkins, "Congressional Investigations and the Lavender Scare"; Johnson, *The Lavender Scare*.
50. Adkins, "Congressional Investigations and the Lavender Scare," 13.
51. S. H. Crittenden, "Report of the Board Appointed to Prepare and Submit Recommendations to the Secretary of the Navy for the Revision of Policies, Procedures, and Directives Dealing with Homosexuals," U.S. Navy Board of Inquiry, March 15, 1957; Dyer, "Forward"; Johnson, *The Lavender Scare*.
52. Adkins, "Congressional Investigations and the Lavender Scare"; Johnson, *The Lavender Scare*.
53. Executive Order 10450, 18 FR 2489, 3 CFR, 1949–1953 Comp: 936 (April 27, 1953); Adkins, "Congressional Investigations and the Lavender Scare"; Johnson, *The Lavender Scare*.
54. For simplicity, I refer to this as a Navy Board of Inquiry. Its official name was the Board Appointed to Prepare and Submit Recommendations to the Secretary of the Navy for the Revision of Policies, Procedures, and Directives Dealing with Homosexuals.
55. Crittenden, "Report of the Board Appointed to Prepare and Submit Recommendations"; see also Johnson, *The Lavender Scare*.
56. Johnson, *The Lavender Scare*; see also Dyer, "Forward," xv–xvi; Rostker and Harris, *Sexual Orientation and U.S. Military Personnel Policy*, 6.
57. Johnson, *The Lavender Scare*, 115; see also Crittenden, "Report of the Board Appointed to Prepare and Submit Recommendations."
58. Crittenden, "Report of the Board Appointed to Prepare and Submit Recommendations"; see also Johnson, *The Lavender Scare*; Miller, *Out of the Past*, 238–239.
59. Lawrence Gibson, *Get Off My Ship: Ensign Verg vs. the U.S. Navy* (New York: Avon, 1978).
60. Dyer, "Forward."
61. Dyer, "Forward."
62. Department of Defense, DoD Directive 1332.14, reprinted in *Code of Federal Regulations*, Title 31, parts 40–399 (Washington, DC: U.S. Government Printing Office, 1959).
63. Jeffrey Davis, "Military Policy Towards Homosexuals: Scientific, Historical, and Legal Perspectives," *Military Law Review* 131 (1991); Rhonda Evans, "U.S. Military

Policies Concerning Homosexuals: Development, Implementation and Outcomes," Report for the Center for the Study of Sexual Minorities in the Military (Santa Barbara: University of California at Santa Barbara, 2002), 117.

64. Rostker and Harris, *Sexual Orientation and U.S. Military Personnel Policy*, 6–7.
65. Adkins, "Congressional Investigations and the Lavender Scare"; Johnson, *The Lavender Scare*.
66. See Alex Dixon, "July Marks the 40th Anniversary of All-Volunteer Military," U.S. Army (2013), https://www.army.mil/article/106813/july_marks_40th_anniversary_of_all_volunteer_army. In 1975, Leonard Matlovich became the first gay service member to out himself in protest to the military's exclusionary stance against gay men and lesbian women; see Miller, *Out of the Past*, 411–415; Randy Shilts, *Conduct Unbecoming: Gays & Lesbians in the U.S. Military* (New York: Ballantine, 1994).
67. Rostker and Harris, *Sexual Orientation and U.S. Military Personnel Policy*, 7; see also C. J. Williams and M. S. Weinberg, *Homosexuals and the Military: A Study of Less Than Honorable Discharge* (New York: Harper & Row, 1971).
68. For more detailed information on the ways queer histories and visibility intersected with popular culture during the first portion of the Cold War period, see Robert Corber, *In the Name of National Security: Hitchcock, Homophobia, and the Political Construction of Gender in Postwar America* (Durham, NC: Duke University Press, 1993); Robert Corber, *Homosexuality in Cold War America* (Durham, NC: Duke University Press, 1997). Corber in particular discusses how gay male subculture produced cultural products for the broader American culture despite ongoing efforts to render members of the queer community invisible.
69. *One, Inc. v. Olesen*, 355 U.S. 371 (1958); *Manual Enterprises, Inc. v. Day*, 370 U.S. 478 (1962). For more information on the impact of *ONE* magazine on people's ability to communicate about a variety of issues, including military service, love, etc., see Craig Loftin, *Letters to ONE: Gay and Lesbian Voices from the 1950s and 1960s* (Albany: State University of New York Press, 2012).
70. *Stoumen v. Reilly*, 37 Cal. 2d 713 (1951); *Vallegra v. Dept. of Alcoholic Beverage* Control, 53 Cal. 2d 313 (1959); see also Frank, *Law and the Gay Rights Story*. While the right to congregate in a gay bar was affirmed by the court by way of the First Amendment, the *Vallegra* ruling held that public displays of queer sexual desires could be grounds to arrest someone in a queer bar, even though it allowed the bar to exist. The rulings in these cases are of direct importance to visibility, activism, and resistance in relation to the broader LGBTQ+ community, as some of the earliest forms of resistance from this community in the 1960s revolved around queer bars (the Stonewall Inn, for instance).
71. David Carter, *Stonewall: The Riots That Shaped the Gay Revolution* (New York: St. Martin's, 2004); Lillian Faderman, *The Gay Revolution: The Story of Struggle* (New York: Simon & Schuster, 2015); Frank, *Law and the Gay Rights Story*; Victor Silverman and Susan Stryker, *Screaming Queens: The Riot at Compton's Cafeteria* (San Francisco: Frameline, 2005). See also Susan Stryker, *Transgender History* (Berkeley, CA: Seal, 2008). For primary source information and footage of the first queer action directed at the White House, see Kirsten Appleton, "What It Was Like at the First Gay Rights

3. THE COLD WAR, COMMUNISTS, AND QUEER BOOGEYMEN   159

Demonstration Outside the White House 50 Years Ago," ABC News, April 17, 2015, https://abcnews.go.com/Politics/gay-rights-demonstration-white-house-50-years-ago/story?id=30379792. This protest centered on the rights of queer employees of the federal workforce, which is clearly of importance to this project.

72. Bernard Rostker, "50 Years Without the Draft: Behind the Bold Move That Ended Conscription, and What's Next for the All-Volunteer Force," Association of the United States Army, June 21, 2023, https://www.ausa.org/articles/50-years-without-draft-behind-bold-move-ended-conscription-and-whats-next-all-volunteer.
73. Rory Dicker, *A History of U.S. Feminisms* (Berkeley, CA: Seal, 2016); Frank, *Law and the Gay Rights Story*.
74. Judy Carter, *The Homo Handbook: Getting in Touch with Your Inner Homo—A Survival Guide for Lesbians and Gay Men* (New York: Fireside, 2006), 184; see also Shilts, *Conduct Unbecoming*.
75. Shilts, *Conduct Unbecoming*, 214.
76. Rostker and Harris, *Sexual Orientation and U.S. Military Personnel Policy*, 6–7.
77. Roger Anders, "The Federal Energy Administration," U.S. Department of Energy, November 1980, https://www.energy.gov/management/articles/federal-energy-administration.
78. Rostker and Harris, *Sexual Orientation and U.S. Military Personnel Policy*, 6–7; Shilts, *Conduct Unbecoming*, 375–392.
79. Director of Security, Central Intelligence Agency, "Letter to Julie Dubbs," 1981. See also https://law.justia.com/cases/federal/appellate-courts/F2/866/1114/205315/.
80. Central Intelligence Agency, Director of Central Intelligence Directive (DCID) Number 1/14 (Washington, DC: Central Intelligence Agency, 1984, 1987, 1994); *Dubbs v. Central Intelligence Agency*, 866 F.2d 1114 (1989); Michael McDaniel, *Preservice Adjustment of Homosexual and Heterosexual Military Accessions: Implications for Security Clearance Suitability* (Monterey, CA: PERSEREC, 1989); Theodore Sarbin and Kenneth Karols, *Nonconforming Sexual Orientation and Military Suitability* (Monterey, CA: PERSEREC, 1988).
81. A year before the founding of PERSEREC, Reagan's secretary of defense, Caspar Weinberger, ordered what was then the largest screening program for HIV/AIDS in the world. As a result, virtually the entire military was tested for HIV/AIDS. While this was not the primary rationale for banning queer people from the military and active duty positions in the intelligence community, it became a secondary rationale and an emerging concern by the height of the HIV/AIDS crisis. This further influenced the discussions about the policy that eventually came to be known as "Don't Ask, Don't Tell" in the early 1990s. See Shilts, *Conduct Unbecoming*, 504.
82. Dyer, "Forward," xvi.
83. Herek, "Gay People and Government Security Clearances," 1035.
84. Crittenden, "Report of the Board Appointed to Prepare and Submit Recommendations."
85. McDaniel, *Preservice Adjustment of Homosexual and Heterosexual Military Accessions*; Sarbin and Karols, *Nonconforming Sexual Orientation and Military Suitability*.
86. Herek, "Gay People and Government Security Clearances," 1038. The concern about service members' nondisclosure of their sexuality is important because this would

have an impact on later iterations of the military's ban against LGBTQ+ people. These reports would influence later studies and the implementation of the military's "Don't Ask, Don't Tell" policy, which set supposed boundaries that encouraged service members not to disclose or "tell" their anything about their sexuality.

87. Dyer, "Forward," xvi; see also Sarbin and Karols, *Nonconforming Sexual Orientation and Military Suitability*. The report by Sarbin and Karols effectively affirmed the findings of the Crittenden Report thirty years earlier. Thus, while the Department of Defense imposed an exclusionary ban against gay men and lesbian women under an outdated rationale, the department funded a study that confirmed a report that had disproved that rationale decades before.

88. Dyer, "Forward," xvi; see also McDaniel, *Preservice Adjustment of Homosexual and Heterosexual Military Accessions*. McDaniel's reasoning was that queer people might actually be more careful and discreet with sensitive information because of the need to exercise caution in their day-to-day lives regarding disclosure of their own identity. As noted by OutServe—Servicemembers Legal Defense Network, "Fact Sheet About Department of Defense-Commissioned Reports," 2012, the first report was received so badly by Pentagon officials that this second report was never submitted for review.

89. Dyer, "Forward," xvii.

90. Dyer, "Forward," xvii; see also Stephen LeSueur, "But No Immediate Change Expected: DoD Ban Against Gays Weakened by Cheney's Lackluster Defense of Policy," *Inside the Pentagon* 7, no. 33 (1991): 3–5.

91. Central Intelligence Agency, DCID Number 1/14, 1984, 1987.

92. Herek, "Gay People and Government Security Clearances," 1036; see also *Dubbs v. Central Intelligence Agency*.

93. For more on the political views and influence of the Moral Majority, see Matthew Avery Sutton, *Jerry Falwell and the Rise of the Religious Right: A Brief History with Documents* (New York: Macmillan, 2013); Andrew Francis Bell, "Radical Religious Beliefs: The Rise and Fall of Jerry Falwell and the Moral Majority" (master's thesis, Eastern Tennessee State University, 2008). See also "The 1980 Republican Platform: Implications for the Civil Rights of Gay Americans—Gay Vote 1980: The National Convention Project" in Douglas Bandow Files, 1981–1982, box 3, folder title: homosexuals/gay rights, Ronald Reagan Presidential Library, Simi Valley, CA.

94. William Turner, "'Adolph Reagan?' Ronald Reagan, AIDS, and Lesbian/Gay Civil Rights," SSRN, July 13, 2009, https://papers.ssrn.com/sol3/papers.cfm?abstract_id=1433567, 8–9.

95. *Dubbs v. Central Intelligence Agency*.

96. Central Intelligence Agency, DCID Number 1/14, 1994. This directive was superseded by DCID 6/4 in 1998.

97. Scott Calonico, *When AIDS Was Funny* (documentary, 2015). Speakes's jokes in response to Kinsolving's questions about the Reagan administration's lack of concern for the HIV/AIDS epidemic, often insinuating that simply being gay and/or HIV-positive was downright comical, have been widely circulated. Decades later, the refusal of some to accurately remember the legacy of the Reagan administration's failure to

respond to the HIV/AIDS epidemic has remained a topic of critique in the broader LGBTQ+ community. In fact, former secretary of state and then presidential candidate Hillary Clinton, when attending First Lady Nancy Reagan's funeral, was actively criticized for failing to publicly acknowledge this. See Jessica Taylor and Danielle Kurtzleben, "Clinton's Comments on Nancy Reagan and HIV/AIDS Cause an Uproar," NPR, March 11, 2016, https://www.npr.org/2016/03/11/470141514/clintons-comments-on-nancy-reagan-and-hiv-aids-cause-an-uproar.

98. David France, *How to Survive a Plague: The Inside Story of How Citizens and Science Tamed AIDS* (New York: Knopf, 2016); David France, *How to Survive a Plague* (documentary, 2012); Deborah Gould, *Moving Politics: Emotion and ACT UP's Fight Against AIDS* (Chicago: University of Chicago Press, 2009); see also Frank, *Law and the Gay Rights Story*. For more on the role of the Moral Majority during the AIDS crisis, see Turner, "'Adolph Reagan?'"

99. Shilts, *Conduct Unbecoming*, 504.

100. France, *How to Survive a Plague* (2016); France, *How to Survive a Plague* (2012); Gould, *Moving Politics*; see also "HIV and AIDS—United States, 1981–2000," *Mortality and Morbidity Weekly Report* 50, no. 1 (2001): 430–434.

101. France, *How to Survive a Plague* (2012); see also France, *How to Survive a Plague* (2016).

102. Bailey and Barbato, *The Strange History of Don't Ask, Don't Tell*.

103. Rostker and Harris, *Sexual Orientation and U.S. Military Personnel Policy*.

104. Bailey and Barbato, *The Strange History of Don't Ask, Don't Tell*; France, *How to Survive a Plague* (2012).

4. IT'S MILITARY READINESS AND UNIT COHESION, *NOT* DISCRIMINATION

1. Bernard Rostker and Scott Harris, *Sexual Orientation and U.S. Military Personnel Policy: Options and Assessment*, National Defense Research Institute (Santa Monica, CA: RAND, 1993).

2. Title 10, U.S. Code 654, Public Law 103–160, 107 Statute 1671 (November 30, 1993).

3. Dan Choi, "Injustice Anywhere Is a Threat to Justice Everywhere," *HuffPost*, March 18, 2010, http://www.huffingtonpost.com/lt-dan-choi/injustice-anywhere-is-a-t_b_425424.html. For additional narratives concerning queer exclusion from the military under "Don't Ask, Don't Tell," see Steve Estes, *Ask & Tell: Gay and Lesbian Veterans Speak Out* (Chapel Hill: University of North Carolina Press, 2009). This oral history project uses the narratives of queer veterans to highlight the discriminatory treatment they faced while serving in the military. While my project explores the policies and related rationales that banned LGBTQ+ people from the military and intelligence community, this particular text engages the resulting lived experience of these service members and veterans.

4. Aaron Belkin, "The Pentagon's Gay Ban Is Not Based on Military Necessity," *Journal of Homosexuality* 41, no. 1 (2001): 104; see also *Dignity & Respect: A Training Guide on*

Homosexual Conduct Policy, prepared for the Assistant Secretary of the Army, Manpower and Reserve Affairs (Washington, DC: Department of the Army, 2001).

5. *Dignity & Respect*; see also Title 10, U.S. Code 654 (1993). During portions of this discussion, I use the term *soldier* rather than *service member* because the Army was specifically referring to the policy as applied to its service members, who are soldiers. When discussing DADT and its application across all or multiple service branches (i.e., the Air Force, Army, Coast Guard, Marine Corps, Navy, and eventually Space Force), I use the more general term *service member*.

6. Aaron Belkin, " 'Don't Ask, Don't Tell': Is the Gay Ban Based on Military Necessity?," *Parameters: U.S. Army War College Quarterly*, Summer 2003, 108–119; see also Belkin, "The Pentagon's Gay Ban Is Not Based on Military Necessity." As reiterated in interview testimony, the initial implementation of "Don't Ask, Don't Tell" was intended to render sexuality a nonissue by ensuring that (1) the military did not ask about sexuality and (2) service members did not say anything about their sexuality; for more on this firsthand account, see Fenton Bailey and Randy Barbato, *The Strange History of Don't Ask, Don't Tell* (HBO Documentary Films, 2012).ß

7. Human Rights Watch, "Uniform Discrimination: The 'Don't Ask, Don't Tell' Policy of the U.S. Military," January 5, 2003, https://www.hrw.org/report/2003/01/06/uniform-discrimination/dont-ask-dont-tell-policy-us-military.

8. Belkin, "The Pentagon's Gay Ban Is Not Based on Military Necessity"; Aaron Belkin and Melissa Sheridan Embser-Herbert, "A Modest Proposal: Privacy as a Flawed Rationale for the Exclusion of Gays and Lesbians from the U.S. Military," *International Security* 27, no. 2 (2002): 178–197.

9. Rostker and Harris, *Sexual Orientation and U.S. Military Personnel Policy*.

10. Rostker and Harris, *Sexual Orientation and U.S. Military Personnel Policy*. Regarding the use of limited data from the civilian population, the researchers at the RAND Corporation note that there is "a high rate of failure to report anti-homosexual violence" (27). Rostker and Harris point out that there are broad, systemic reasons that might influence someone's decision not to report an act of violence as a specifically homophobic act. Similarly, the Southern Poverty Law Center has previously noted that the number of hate crimes that are reported pales in comparison to the actual number; see Southern Poverty Law Center, "Report: FBI Hate Crime Statistics Vastly Understate Problem," January 31, 2006, https://www.splcenter.org/resources/reports/report-fbi-hate-crime-statistics-vastly-understate-problem/. More recent analyses of FBI hate crime data indicate that LGBT people are the most likely people to be targeted with hate crimes in America today; see Haeyoun Park and Iaryna Mykhyalyshyn, "L.G.B.T. People Are More Likely to Be Targets of Hate Crimes Than Any Other Group," *New York Times*, June 16, 2016, https://www.nytimes.com/interactive/2016/06/16/us/hate-crimes-against-lgbt.html. The concern with anti-LGBTQ violence addressed in the RAND Corporation report of 1993 is still a pervasive issue in both civilian and military life.

11. Rostker and Harris, *Sexual Orientation and U.S. Military Personnel Policy*, 280–281.

12. Rostker and Harris, *Sexual Orientation and U.S. Military Personnel Policy*, 272–282.

13. The concern over an increase in the prevalence of HIV within the military generally involved the preconceived notion that queer men in particular are inherently at risk for HIV. While the HIV/AIDS epidemic did drastically affect men in the queer community during the 1980s, the reasons for this impact included the community's lower condom usage prior to the advent of the virus and the failure of the federal government to directly address the issue as a public health crisis. The idea that the inclusion of queer people more generally might lead to a widespread impact of HIV/AIDS on the armed forces was also premised on the idea that queer men might engage in unprotected sexual intercourse with their straight counterparts, which reiterates the stereotype of the hypersexualized queer male.
14. Rostker and Harris, *Sexual Orientation and U.S. Military Personnel Policy*, 28.
15. While all civilian applicants were tested for HIV upon accession into the military, the researchers at RAND noted that the number of applicants who tested positive had declined since the inception of this policy, citing data from the Walter Reed Army Institute of Research. At the start of the policy in 1985, 1.58 out of 1,000 applicants tested HIV-positive; by the end of 1992, that number had decreased to 0.44 out of 1,000 applicants. They suggest that people living with HIV may have self-selected not to apply for accession into the military, given the blanket policy regarding HIV status and enlistment requirements. See Rostker and Harris, *Sexual Orientation and U.S. Military Personnel Policy*, 248–249.
16. Bailey and Barbato, *The Strange History of Don't Ask, Don't Tell*.
17. Ramon Hinojosa, "Doing Hegemony: Military, Men, and Constructing a Hegemonic Masculinity," *Journal of Men's Studies* 18, no. 2 (2010): 179–194; Brandon Locke, "The Military-Masculinity Complex: Hegemonic Masculinity and the United States Armed Forces, 1940–1963" (PhD diss., University of Nebraska at Lincoln, 2013).
18. Aaron Belkin, "'Don't Ask, Don't Tell': Does the Gay Ban Undermine the Military's Reputation?," *Armed Forces & Society* 34, no. 2 (2007): 278.
19. Aaron Belkin and Melissa Levitt, "Homosexuality and the Israeli Defense Forces: Did the Gay Ban Undermine Military Performance?," *Armed Forces & Society* 27, no. 4 (2001): 544.
20. Another concern that emerged within the debates concerning DADT was the question of whether queer service members might be given some type of relaxed treatment on the basis of their sexuality and/or gender expression. Advocates of queer inclusion in the military were quick to note that these service members would be held to the same tactical standards and training metrics; see Belkin, "'Don't Ask, Don't Tell:' Is the Gay Ban Based on Military Necessity?," 111. This was not a prevalent concern during the debates around DADT, but it was an issue that was sometimes brought up in a more roundabout manner.
21. Belkin, "The Pentagon's Gay Ban Is Not Based on Military Necessity"; Elizabeth Kier, "Homosexuals in the U.S. Military: Open Integration and Combat Effectiveness," *International Security* 23, no. 2 (1998): 5–39.
22. Belkin and Embser-Herbert, "A Modest Proposal," 183. Given the history and conceptualization of queer identities as a security threat during World War I, this concern is

also quite ironic, especially considering that the American military instructed the straight sailors of Section A "to allow immoral acts to be performed upon them" to identify and then court-martial queer sailors; see "Alleged Immoral Conditions at Newport (R.I.) Naval Training Station," in *Government Versus Homosexuals*, ed. Leslie Parr (North Stratford, NH: Ayer, [1921] 1975), 5.

23. Belkin and Embser-Herbert, "A Modest Proposal," 187–194.
24. The myth of the gay male predator relies upon the idea that queer men are sexually deviant, perverted, etc. Encompassed within this myth is the falsehood that queer men might also engage in pedophilia, a pervasive falsehood that has deep roots in American cultural history. Even though these falsehoods have been disproven, the myth of the gay male predator still arises. See Olga Khazan, "Milo Yiannopoulos and the Myth of the Gay Pedophile," *Atlantic*, February 21, 2017, https://www.theatlantic.com/health/archive/2017/02/milo-yiannopoulos-and-the-myth-of-the-gay-pedophile/517332/.
25. Bailey and Barbato, *The Strange History of Don't Ask, Don't Tell*; Johnny Symons, *Ask Not* (Persistent Visions, 2008).
26. Belkin and Embser-Herbert, "A Modest Proposal," 187–194; see also Khazan, "Milo Yionnopoulos and the Myth of the Gay Pedophile."
27. Frank T. Pimentel, "Constitution as Chaperone: President Clinton's Flirtation with Gays in the Military," *Notre Dame Law School Journal of Legislation* 20, no. 1 (1994).
28. A dramatized version of Winchell's relationship with Calpernia Adams and the subsequent murder was portrayed in the made-for-TV film, *Soldier's Girl*; see Frank Pierson, *Soldier's Girl* (Bachrach and Gottlieb Productions, 2003).
29. Robert Pear, "President Admits 'Don't Ask, Don't Tell' Policy Has Been Failure," *New York Times*, December 12, 1999, http://www.nytimes.com/1999/12/12/us/president-admits-don-t-ask-policy-has-been-failure.html.
30. Chris Black, "Pentagon to Review 'Don't Ask, Don't Tell' Policy," CNN, December 13, 1999, http://archives.cnn.com/1999/US/12/13/pentagon.gays/index.html.
31. Black, "Pentagon to Review 'Don't Ask, Don't Tell' Policy"; see also Elizabeth Becker, "Pentagon Orders Training to Prevent Harassment of Gays," *New York Times*, February 2, 2000, http://www.nytimes.com/2000/02/02/us/pentagon-orders-training-to-prevent-harassment-of-gays.html.
32. Bailey and Barbato, *The Strange History of Don't Ask, Don't Tell*; Symons, *Ask Not*.
33. Becker, "Pentagon Orders Training to Prevent Harassment of Gays."
34. For those unfamiliar with the reference to "hanging chads," the 2000 presidential election ended with a contested vote count in the state of Florida. At the time, Florida used a so-called butterfly ballot that involved pushing a utensil through the paper. A recount involved concerns over hanging chads, or small bits of paper that remained attached to the paper ballots. The election was ultimately decided by the Supreme Court of the United States, which declared that Bush had won Florida.
35. James Dao and Eric Schmitt, "The 43rd President: The Defense Department; Bush Says He Is Taking Time on Defense Pick to 'Get it Right,'" *New York Times*,

December 23, 2000, http://www.nytimes.com/2000/12/23/us/43rd-president-defense-department-bush-says-he-taking-time-defense-pick-get-it.html.
36. The Log Cabin Republicans are a group of LGBTQ+ Republicans.
37. Dao and Schmitt, "The 43rd President"; Craig Rimmerman, *From Identity to Politics: Lesbian & Gay Movements in the U.S.* (Philadelphia: Temple University Press, 2002).
38. While Rumsfeld was nominated and confirmed as secretary of defense relatively quickly, other key posts in the Bush administration's DoD would not be filled until late spring and early summer; see Alex Tippet, "What the 9/11 Commission Found: Slow Confirmations Imperil U.S. National Security," Center for Presidential Transition, December 16, 2020, https://presidentialtransition.org/blog/what-the-9-11-commission-found-slow-confirmations-imperil-u-s-national-security/.
39. To my knowledge, the Army did not specifically state that the comic book was a direct response to the murder of Winchell; however, the 2001 publication followed shortly after the year of anti-harassment trainings throughout the Pentagon, which had been spurred by his death. Consequently, this brutal murder had at least an indirect impact on the eventual publication of the training manual nearly two years later.
40. Department of Defense, *Dignity & Respect*, 3.
41. Department of Defense, *Dignity & Respect*, 13.
42. Bailey and Barbato, *The Strange History of Don't Ask, Don't Tell*.
43. As noted in the comic book, the unit's commanding officer had the sole authority to determine whether the person filing the accusation was a credible source. This created a number of issues for queer service members who served without discussing or disclosing their sexuality. If someone filed an accusation that was deemed credible by the commanding officer, the officer would then examine sufficient evidence to determine if the soldier's actions were in accordance with the policy—even if the soldier disclosed their diverse sexuality—"to determine the sincerity" of the claim; see *Dignity & Respect*, 24.
44. National Commission on Terrorist Attacks Upon the United States, *The 9/11 Commission Report* (Washington, DC: U.S. Government Printing Office, 2004).
45. Nathaniel Frank, *Unfriendly Fire: How the Gay Ban Undermines the Military and Weakens America* (New York: Thomas Dunne, 2009), 215.
46. *The 9/11 Commission Report*, 77; see also Frank, *Unfriendly Fire*.
47. Bailey and Barbato, *The Strange History of Don't Ask, Don't Tell*; Frank, *Unfriendly Fire*, 215–236; Associated Press, "Report: More Gay Linguists Discharged Than First Thought," NBC News, January 13, 2005, http://www.nbcnews.com/id/6824206/ns/us_news-security/t/report-more-gay-linguistsdischarged-first-thought/.
48. Frank, *Unfriendly Fire*, 220. To the chagrin of queer activists and service members alike, the percentage of new enlistees receiving moral waivers also rose throughout the Bush administration, while queer service members were continuing to be discharged under DADT. See Bailey and Barbato, *The Strange History of Don't Ask, Don't Tell*; see also Bryan Bender, "Almost 12% of U.S. Army Recruits Required Waivers for Criminal Records," *New York Times*, July 13, 2007, http://www.nytimes.com/2007/07

/13/world/americas/13iht-13recruits.6652316.html. Following the transition to an all-volunteer force, the American military retained the use of so-called moral waivers to assist with recruiting during times of need. As explained by Lieutenant Colonel John Haefner, a moral waiver is an "exception to regulations that otherwise excluded from enlistment those not meeting legal standards and moral societal norms" expected of recruits; see John Haefner, "Moral Waivers in Army Recruiting: It Is About Family," Strategy Research Project, U.S. Army War College, 2013, 8. In 2007, nearly 12 percent of new enlistees in the Army were given moral waivers for criminal records. This number had risen from 7.9 percent in the year before and roughly 4.6 percent in 2003. At the same time, the military was continuing to discharge qualified service members under DADT. See Bailey and Barbato, *The Strange History of Don't Ask, Don't Tell*.

49. Frank, *Unfriendly Fire*, 220; see also Bailey and Barbato, *The Strange History of Don't Ask, Don't Tell*.
50. Sheryl Stolberg, "Obama Pledges Again to End 'Don't Ask, Don't Tell,'" *New York Times*, October 11, 2010, http://www.nytimes.com/2009/10/11/us/politics/11speech.html.
51. Aaron Belkin, *How We Won: Progressive Lessons from the Repeal of "Don't Ask, Don't Tell"* (Los Angeles: HuffPost Media Group, 2011). In 2009, the Commission on Military Justice, also known as the Cox Commission, recommended once again that the military remove the punitive measures for consensual sodomy, as listed under Article 125 of the Uniform Code of Military Justice; see Lisa Novak, "Panel Urges Ending UCMJ's Sodomy Ban," *Stars and Stripes*, October 27, 2009. Although the Supreme Court had already invalidated laws penalizing consensual sodomy in 2003 by way of *Lawrence v. Texas*, the military still retained its statutes. The criminalization of consensual sodomy was later removed from the UCMJ via the National Defense Authorization Act (NDAA) for 2014. See *Lawrence v. Texas*, 539 U.S. 558 (2003); David Vergun, "Legislation Changing UCMJ, Especially for Sex Crimes," U.S. Army, January 8, 2014, https://www.army.mil/article/117919/legislation_changing_ucmj_especially_for_sex_crimes.
52. Bailey and Barbato, *The Strange History of Don't Ask, Don't Tell*; Belkin, *How We Won*.
53. Roxana Tiron and Russell Berman, "House Votes to Repeal 'Don't Ask, Don't Tell' Policy on Gay Service Members," *The Hill*, May 28, 2010, http://thehill.com/homenews/house/100397-house-votes-to-repeal-dont-ask-dont-tell; see also Belkin, *How We Won*.
54. Belkin, *How We Won*.
55. Senator John McCain of Arizona, then a ranking member of this committee, also requested that RAND review its 1993 report. Given that he later led a filibuster against queer inclusion in the armed forces, it seems likely that McCain had hoped RAND would reiterate the unit cohesion rationale that had led to the creation of DADT, which was simply a distorted version of a compromise allowing closeted queer people to serve. It is somewhat ironic that McCain had a hand in approaching the office of the secretary of defense to commission this updated study, since the findings in RAND's 2010 report ultimately aided in the repeal of DADT. See Bailey and Barbato, *The Strange History of Don't Ask, Don't Tell*; see also Bernard Rostker, *Sexual Orientation*

4. IT'S MILITARY READINESS AND UNIT COHESION   167

and U.S. Military Personnel Policy: An Update of RAND's 1993 Study, National Defense Research Institute (Santa Monica, CA: RAND, 2010), xix.

56. Rostker, *Sexual Orientation and U.S. Military Personnel Policy*.
57. In surveying LGBT service members for the updated 2010 report, RAND researchers discussed the difficulties of working with this population—i.e., the need to retain confidentiality of respondents and the sampling issues that arose; see Rostker, *Sexual Orientation and U.S. Military Personnel Policy*, 255–256. Despite these difficulties, the survey results provide useful insights relating to the opinions of closeted LGBTQ+ people serving in the military prior to the repeal of DADT; however, there are practical sampling issues that should be acknowledged in considering this portion of RAND's updated report.
58. Rostker, *Sexual Orientation and U.S. Military Personnel Policy*, 264.
59. Rostker, *Sexual Orientation and U.S. Military Personnel Policy*, 16.
60. Nicole Allen, "Senate Republicans Block 'Don't Ask, Don't Tell' Repeal," *Atlantic*, September 21, 2010, https://www.theatlantic.com/politics/archive/2010/09/senate-republicans-block-dont-ask-dont-tell-repeal/63342/.
61. Daneil Kreps, "Lady Gaga Rallies Against 'Don't Ask, Don't Tell,'" *Rolling Stone*, September 20, 2010, http://www.rollingstone.com/music/news/lady-gaga-rallies-against-dont-ask-dont-tell-20100920.
62. "A Message from Lady Gaga to the Senate," YouTube, September 16, 2010, https://www.youtube.com/watch?v=GG5VK2lquEc.
63. Belkin, *How We Won*; for more on the stories of LGBTQ+ service members during this period, see Josh Seefried, *Our Time: Breaking the Silence of "Don't Ask, Don't Tell"* (New York: Penguin, 2011) and Vincent Cianni, *Gays in the Military: Photographs and Interviews* (New York: Daylight, 2014).
64. Belkin, *How We Won*; Lisa Daniel, "Repeal of 'Don't Ask, Don't Tell' Offers Few Risks, Report Finds," American Forces Press Service, November 29, 2010, https://www.dvidshub.net/news/514457/repeal-dont-ask-dont-tell-offers-few-risks-report-finds; Ed O'Keefe and Greg Jaffe, "Sources: Pentagon Group Finds There Is Minimal Risk to Lifting Gay Ban During War," *Washington Post*, November 11, 2010, http://www.washingtonpost.com/wp-dyn/content/article/2010/11/10/AR2010111007381.html.
65. Given the timing of this remark concerning the federal courts, it is highly likely that the secretary of defense was tacitly referring to *Collins v. United States*, a case filed by the American Civil Liberties Union (ACLU) in early November 2010 and eventually settled out of court in 2013. In this case, the ACLU asserted that a gay Air Force staff sergeant, who was honorably discharged under DADT, had received lower separation pay than his peers. The government eventually settled the case as a class action lawsuit in 2013. See ACLU, "Collins v. United States—Class Action for Military Separation Pay," November 8, 2010, https://www.aclu.org/cases/collins-v-united-states-class-action-military-separation-pay; Carlo Muñoz, "'Don't Ask, Don't Tell' Discharges to Receive Full Back Pay from DoD," *The Hill*, January 7, 2013, http://thehill.com/policy/defense/275971-service-members-discharged-under-dont-ask-dont-tell-to-receive-full-back-pay.

66. Liz Halloran, "Gates to Senate: End 'Don't Ask, Don't Tell' Before Courts Do," NPR, November 30, 2010, https://www.npr.org/2010/11/30/131697322/pentagon-study-dismisses-risk-of-openly-gay-troops; see also Belkin, *How We Won*.
67. Ed O'Keefe and Paul Kane, "Senate Delivers Potentially Fatal Blow to 'Don't Ask, Don't Tell' Repeal Efforts," *Washington Post*, December 10, 2010, http://www.washingtonpost.com/wp-dyn/content/article/2010/12/09/AR2010120906555.html; see also Belkin, *How We Won*; C-SPAN, "Senate Session," December 9, 2010, https://www.c-span.org/video/?296995-1/senate-session.
68. Michael O'Brien, "Lieberman Plans Standalone Repeal of 'Don't Ask, Don't Tell,'" *The Hill*, December 9, 2010, http://thehill.com/blogs/blog-briefing-room/news/133001-lieberman-plans-standalone-repeal-of-dont-ask-dont-tell; Ed O'Keefe and Craig Whitlock, "New Bill Introduced to End 'Don't Ask, Don't Tell,'" *Washington Post*, December 11, 2010, http://www.washingtonpost.com/wp-dyn/content/article/2010/12/10/AR2010121007163.html. See also Belkin, *How We Won*.
69. Title 10, U.S. Code 654, Public Law 111–321, 124 Statute 3515, 3516, and 3517 (September 20, 2011); CNN, "House Democrats Push 'Don't Ask, Don't Tell' Repeal," December 14, 2010; Jennifer Steinhauer, "House Votes to Repeal 'Don't Ask, Don't Tell,'" *New York Times*, December 15, 2010, http://www.nytimes.com/2010/12/16/us/politics/16military.html. See also Belkin, *How We Won*.
70. Ed O'Keefe, "'Don't Ask, Don't Tell' Is Repealed by Senate; Bill Awaits Obama's Signing," *Washington Post*, December 19, 2010, http://www.washingtonpost.com/wp-dyn/content/article/2010/12/18/AR2010121801729.html. See also Bailey and Barbato, *The Strange History of Don't Ask, Don't Tell*; Belkin, *How We Won*.
71. William Branigin, Debbi Wilgoren, and Perry Bacon, "Obama Signs DADT Repeal Before Big, Emotional Crowd," *Washington Post*, December 22, 2010, http://www.washingtonpost.com/wp-dyn/content/article/2010/12/22/AR2010122201888.html.
72. U.S. Department of Defense, "Statement by Secretary Robert Gates on Senate Vote to Repeal 'Don't Ask, Don't Tell,'" December 24, 2010, https://web.archive.org/web/20101224204231/http://www.defense.gov/releases/release.aspx?releaseid=14154.

5. A MEANDERING PATH TOWARD TRANS INCLUSION

1. Secretary of Defense Ash Carter, "Remarks on Ending the Ban on Transgender Service in the Military," U.S. Department of Defense, June 30, 2016, https://www.defense.gov/News/Speeches/Speech/Article/821833/remarks-on-ending-the-ban-on-transgender-service-in-the-us-military/.
2. Bernard Rostker, "A Year After the Repeal of 'Don't Ask, Don't Tell,'" RAND, September 20, 2012, https://www.rand.org/blog/2012/09/a-year-after-repeal-of-dont-ask-dont-tell.html.
3. Michael Schmidt and Charlie Savage, "Eric Fanning Confirmed as Secretary of the Army," *New York Times*, May 17, 2016, https://www.nytimes.com/2016/05/18/us/eric-fanning-army-secretary.html; Laura Wagner, "Senate Confirms Eric Fanning, First

Openly Gay Leader of Military Service," NPR, May 17, 2016, https://www.npr.org/sections/thetwo-way/2016/05/17/478456199/senate-confirms-eric-fanning-first-openly-gay-leader-of-military-service.
4. Kristina Wong, "Confirmation Hearing for Army Secretary Pick Eric Fanning Next Week," *The Hill*, January 17, 2016, http://thehill.com/business-a-lobbying/266200-confirmation-hearing-for-army-secretary-pick-eric-fanning-next-week.
5. Secretary of Defense Ash Carter, "Statement by Secretary of Defense Ash Carter on DOD Transgender Policy," U.S. Department of Defense, July 13, 2015, https://www.defense.gov/News/News-Releases/News-Release-View/Article/612778/.
6. Secretary of Defense Ash Carter, "Statement on DOD Transgender Policy."
7. U.S. Department of Defense, Memorandum: "Transgender Service Members," July 28, 2015, https://web.archive.org/web/20171105172248/https://www.defense.gov/Portals/1/features/2016/0616_policy/memo-transgender-service-directive-28-July-2015.pdf. The same year, Carter also announced a number of modernizations in combat regulations for women in the military; see Christopher Hamner, "Brothers in Arms? Combat, Masculinity, and Change in the Twenty-First-Century American Military," *Managing Sex in the U.S. Military*, ed. Beth Bailey, Alesha Doan, Shannon Portillo, and Kara Dixon Vuic (Lincoln: University of Nebraska Press, 2022): 275–306.
8. Agnes Schaefer, Radha Iyengar, Srikanth Kadiyala, Jennifer Kavanagh, Charles Engel, Kayla Williams, and Amil Kress, *Assessing the Implications of Allowing Transgender Personnel to Serve Openly*, National Defense Research Institute (Santa Monica, CA: RAND, 2016).
9. Schaefer et al., *Assessing the Implications of Allowing Transgender Personnel to Serve Openly*, 69–70.
10. Jennifer Rizzo and Zachery Cohen, "Pentagon Ends Transgender Ban," CNN, June 30, 2016, https://www.cnn.com/2016/06/30/politics/transgender-ban-lifted-us-military/index.html; see also Assistant Secretary of Defense, Memorandum: "Guidance for Treatment of Gender Dysphoria for Active and Reserve Competent Service Members," July 29, 2016, https://web.archive.org/web/20170112211346/https://www.defense.gov/Portals/1/features/2016/0616_policy/Guidance_for_Treatment_of_Gender_Dysphoria_Memo_FINAL_SIGNED.pdf.
11. Secretary of Defense, Memorandum: "Directive-Type Memorandum (DTM) 16-005 Military Service of Transgender Service Members," 2016, https://web.archive.org/web/20181021195834/https://dod.defense.gov/portals/1/features/2016/0616_policy/dtm-16-005.pdf.
12. Memorandum: "Military Service of Transgender Service Members"; see also Memorandum: "Guidance for Treatment of Gender Dysphoria".
13. Office of the Under Secretary of Defense for Personnel and Readiness, "DoD Instruction 1300.28: In-Service Transition for Transgender Service Members," October 1, 2016, https://www.esd.whs.mil/Portals/54/Documents/FOID/Reading%20Room/Personnel_Related/15-F-1724_DoD_Instruction_1300.25.pdf.
14. "DoD Instruction 1300.28: In-Service Transition for Transgender Service Members," 2016.

15. Memorandum: "Guidance for Treatment of Gender Dysphoria"; see also "DoD Instruction 1300.28: In-Service Transition for Transgender Service Members," 2016.
16. U.S. Department of Defense, *Transgender Service in the U.S. Military: An Implementation Handbook* (Washington, DC: Author, September 30, 2016).
17. Yezmin Villarreal, "Donald Trump: Allowing Trans People in the Military Is Due to 'Political Correctness,'" Advocate, October 4, 2016, https://www.advocate.com/election/2016/10/04/donald-trump-allowing-trans-people-military-due-political-correctness. When asked about Trump's commentary, Secretary of the Army Fanning, in November 2016, remained skeptical that Trump would reverse Secretary of Defense Carter's work regarding transgender inclusion in the military. See Chris Johnson, "Fanning Skeptical Trump Will Undo LGBT Inclusion in Military," *Washington Blade*, November 17, 2016, http://www.washingtonblade.com/2016/11/17/fanning-skeptical-trump-will-undo-lgbt-inclusion-in-military/. Even so, members of the broader LGBTQ+ community feared this would occur, as other harbingers began to appear. The nomination of former general James Mattis in December 2016 was cause for alarm, given his historical opposition to women and queer people serving in the armed forces; see Nico Lang, "Trump's Secretary of Defense Pick Opposes LGBT People, Women Serving in the Military," Advocate, December 2, 2016, https://www.advocate.com/politics/2016/12/02/trumps-secretary-defense-pick-opposes-lgbt-people-women-serving-military.
18. Administration of Barack Obama, 2017, "Executive Order 13764—Amending the Civil Service Rules, Executive Order 13488, and Executive Order 13467 To Modernize the Executive Branch-Wide Governance Structure and Processes for Security Clearances, Suitability and Fitness for Employment, and Credentialing, and Related Matters," January 17, 2017, https://www.govinfo.gov/content/pkg/DCPD-201700051/pdf/DCPD-201700051.pdf.
19. Sandhya Somashekhar, Emma Brown, and Moriah Balingit, "Trump Administration Rolls Back Protections for Transgender Students," *Washington Post*, February 22, 2017, https://www.washingtonpost.com/local/education/trump-administration-rolls-back-protections-for-transgender-students/2017/02/22/550a83b4-f913-11e6-bf01-d47f8cf9b643_story.html.
20. Andrew de Grandpre and Karen Jowers, "Trump's Transgender Directive and What's at Stake Within the U.S. Military," *Military Times*, February 23, 2017, https://www.militarytimes.com/news/your-military/2017/02/23/trump-s-transgender-directive-and-what-s-at-stake-within-the-u-s-military/.
21. Andrew de Grandpre and Karen Jowers, "At Military Schools, Transgender Bathroom Decisions Will Be Made Case by Case Basis," *Military Times*, February 25, 2017, https://web.archive.org/web/20170809042734/https://www.militarytimes.com/news/your-military/2017/02/25/at-military-schools-transgender-bathroom-decisions-will-be-made-case-by-case/.
22. Travis Tritten, "Trump Army Nominee Under Fire for Newly Uncovered Transgender Comments," *Washington Examiner*, April 20, 2017, https://www

.washingtonexaminer.com/news/792140/trump-army-nominee-under-fire-for-newly-uncovered-transgender-comments/; see also Sheri Swokowski, "Trump's Anti-LGBT Army Secretary Nominee Thinks Veterans Like Me Have 'a Disease,'" *Washington Post*, April 21, 2017, https://www.washingtonpost.com/posteverything/wp/2017/04/21/trumps-anti-lgbt-army-secretary-nominee-thinks-veterans-like-me-have-a-disease/.

23. John Paul Brammer and Brooke Sopelsa, "Trump's Army Secretary Pick, Mark Green, Withdraws Name from Consideration," NBC News, May 5, 2017, https://www.nbcnews.com/feature/nbc-out/trump-s-army-secretary-pick-slammed-anti-transgender-islamophobic-n754806. Similar to the Clinton, Bush, and Obama administrations from the early 1990s to the mid-2010s, Trump had multiple nominees and eventual appointees for secretary of the army. Trump's first nominee for the post was Vincent Viola, who withdrew his name from consideration in February 2017; see Ryan Browne and Eli Watkins, "Vincent Viola Withdraws from Secretary of Army Nomination," CNN, February 4, 2017, https://www.cnn.com/2017/02/03/politics/vincent-viola-withdraws-from-secretary-of-army-nomination/index.html.

24. Brian McBride, "17 Times the Trump-Pence Administration Attacked the LGBTQ Community in 2017," Human Rights Campaign, December 22, 2017, https://www.hrc.org/blog/17-times-the-trump-pence-administration-attacked-the-lgbtq-community-in-201.

25. Dan Lamothe, "On Eve of Deadline, Pentagon Delays Plan to Allow Transgender Recruits by 6 Months," *Washington Post*, June 30, 2017, https://www.washingtonpost.com/news/checkpoint/wp/2017/06/30/mattis-delays-pentagons-decision-to-allow-transgender-recruits-six-more-months/?utm_term=.39154266031b.

26. Donald Trump, "Transgender Tweets," Twitter, July 26, 2017.

27. de Grandpre and Jowers, "Trump's Transgender Directive."

28. Jeremy Diamond, "Trump to Reinstate US Military Ban on Transgender People," CNN, July 26, 2017, https://www.cnn.com/2017/07/26/politics/trump-military-transgender/index.html.

29. Jeff Schogol, "The Military Spends More on Giving Retirees Erections Than on Transgender Troops," *Military Times*, July 26, 2017, https://www.militarytimes.com/news/2017/07/26/the-military-spends-more-on-giving-retirees-erections-than-on-transgender-troops/; Aaron Belkin, Frank Barrett, Mark Eitelberg, and Marc Ventresca, "Discharging Transgender Troops Would Cost $960 Million," Palm Center, August 2017, http://www.palmcenter.org/wp-content/uploads/2017/08/cost-of-firing-trans-troops-3.pdf.

30. ACLU, "Federal Court Blocks All Aspects of Trump's Transgender Military Ban," November 21, 2017, https://www.aclu.org/news/federal-court-blocks-all-aspects-trumps-transgender-military-ban.

31. David Savage, "Military Poised to Accept Transgender Troops, Despite Trump Tweets, as Courts Block Ban," *Los Angeles Times*, December 26, 2017, http://www.latimes.com/politics/la-na-pol-transgender-military-20171226-story.html.

32. Chris Kenning, "Transgender U.S. Military Recruits Enlist Amid Uncertainty," *Reuters*, January 14, 2018, https://www.reuters.com/article/us-usa-military-transgender/transgender-u-s-military-recruits-enlist-amid-uncertainty-idUSKBN1F30I0.
33. Quoted in A4TE, "Trump Administration to Defend 'Trans Ban 2.0' Later This Month," February 8, 2018, https://transequality.org/news/trump-administration-to-defend-trans-ban-20-later-this-month.
34. Office of the Deputy Secretary of Defense, Memorandum: "Directive-Type Memorandum (DTM) 19–004—Military Service by Transgender Persons and Persons with Gender Dysphoria," March 12, 2019, https://drive.google.com/file/d/1tQugAtmmg-cDrhwQVRPtCGNBA6c7b3x2/view.
35. Palm Center, "The Making of a Ban: How DTM-19-004 Works to Push Transgender People Out of Military Service," March 20, 2019, https://www.palmcenter.org/wp-content/uploads/2019/04/The-Making-of-a-Ban.pdf; see also Memorandum: "Directive-Type Memorandum (DTM) 19–004."
36. Palm Center, "The Making of a Ban"; see also Office of the Under Secretary of Defense for Personnel and Readiness "DoD Instruction 1300.28: Military Service by Transgender Persons and Persons with Gender Dysphoria," September 4, 2020, https://www.esd.whs.mil/Portals/54/Documents/FOID/Reading%20Room/Personnel_Related/15-F-1724_DoD_Instruction_1300.25.pdf; Hallie Jackson and Courtney Kube, "Trump's Controversial Transgender Military Policy Goes Into Effect," *NBC News*, April 12, 2019, https://www.nbcnews.com/feature/nbc-out/trump-s-controversial-transgender-military-policy-goes-effect-n993826; Memorandum: "Directive-Type Memorandum (DTM) 19–004."
37. Dorian Rhea Debussy, *Freedom to Serve: The Definitive Guide to LGBTQ+ Military Service*, ed. Jennifer Dane and Emily Starbuck Gerson (Washington, DC: Modern Military Association of America, 2023).
38. Cathy Marcello, "Breaking Barriers: Freedom to Serve Guide 3.0 Unveiled with Vital LGBTQ+ Updates," *Modern Military Magazine*, February 2024, 30–33; see also Queer Forty, "The Definitive Guide to LGBTQ Military Service Has Now Been Updated and Expanded," October 20, 2023, https://queerforty.com/the-definitive-guide-to-lgbtq-military-service-has-now-been-updated-and-expanded; Modern Military Association of America, "MMAA Releases 3rd Edition of *Freedom to Serve: The Definitive Guide to LGBTQ Military Service*," 2023, https://modernmilitary.org/2023/10/mmaa-releases-3rd-edition-of-freedom-to-serve-the-definitive-guide-to-lgbtq-military-service/.
39. David Crary and Elana Schor, "Lifting Near-Total Ban on Transgender People from Military Service Among Biden Plans to Protect LGBTQ Rights," *Military Times*, November 29, 2020, https://www.militarytimes.com/news/pentagon-congress/2020/11/29/lifting-near-total-ban-on-transgender-people-from-military-service-among-biden-plans-to-protect-lgbtq-rights/.
40. Executive Office of the President, White House, "Executive Order on Enabling All Qualified Americans to Serve Their Country in Uniform," January 25, 2021,

https://bidenwhitehouse.archives.gov/briefing-room/presidential-actions/2021/01/25/executive-order-on-enabling-all-qualified-americans-to-serve-their-country-in-uniform/; see also White House, "Fact Sheet: President Biden Signs Executive Order Enabling All Qualified Americans to Serve Their Country in Uniform," January 25, 2021, https://bidenwhitehouse.archives.gov/briefing-room/statements-releases/2021/01/25/fact-sheet-president-biden-signs-executive-order-enabling-all-qualified-americans-to-serve-their-country-in-uniform/.

41. White House, "A Proclamation on Transgender Day of Visibility, 2021," March 31, 2021, https://bidenwhitehouse.archives.gov/briefing-room/presidential-actions/2021/03/31/a-proclamation-on-transgender-day-of-visibility-2021/.

42. Laurel Wamsley, "Pentagon Releases New Policies Enabling Transgender People to Serve in the Military," NPR, March 31, 2021, https://www.npr.org/2021/03/31/983118029/pentagon-releases-new-policies-enabling-transgender-people-to-serve-in-the-milit; see also Office of the Under Secretary of Defense for Personnel and Readiness, "DoD Instruction 1300.28: In-Service Transition for Transgender Service Members," March 31, 2021, https://web.archive.org/web/20210407095728/https://www.esd.whs.mil/Portals/54/Documents/DD/issuances/dodi/130028p.pdf; Secretary of Defense, "DoD Instruction 6130.03: Medical Standards for Military Service: Appointment, Enlistment, or Induction," March 31, 2021, https://web.archive.org/web/20220318183306/https://www.defense.gov/News/Releases/Release/Article/2557220/dod-announces-policy-updates-for-transgender-military-service/.

43. Matt Lavietes, "Dr. Rachel Levine Becomes Nation's First Transgender Four-Star Officer," NBC News, October 19, 2021, https://www.nbcnews.com/nbc-out/out-health-and-wellness/dr-rachel-levine-becomes-nations-first-transgender-four-star-officer-rcna3283.

44. Mael Embser-Herbert and Bree Fram, eds., *With Honor and Integrity: Transgender Troops in Their Own Words* (New York: New York University Press, 2022); see also Bree Fram and Mael Sheridan, eds., *With Valor and Visibility: The Next Chapter of Transgender Military Service* (Alexandria, VA: Forged in Fire, 2025).

45. Minami Funakoshi and Disha Raychaudhuri, "The Rise of Anti-Trans Bills in the U.S.," Reuters, August 19, 2023, https://www.reuters.com/graphics/USA-HEALTHCARE/TRANS-BILLS/zgvorreyapd/; see also Tatyana Tandanpolie, "'Flood' of Anti-LGBTQ+ Bills Shows GOP Wants to 'Eradicate Trans People from Public Life': Advocate," *Salon*, January 6, 2024, https://www.salon.com/2024/01/06/flood-of-anti-lgbtq-bills-shows-wants-to-eradicate-trans-people-from-public-life-advocate/.

46. *Dobbs v. Jackson Women's Health Organization*, 597 U.S. ___ (2022), 142 S. Ct. 2228; Kyleanne Hunter, Sarah Meadows, Rebecca Collins, and Isabelle Gonzalez, "How the *Dobbs* Decision Could Affect U.S. National Security," RAND, September 13, 2022, https://www.rand.org/pubs/perspectives/PEA2227-1.html. For more on reproductive rights and family issues in the military's all-volunteer force, see John Worsencroft, "'We Recruit Individuals But Retain Families': Managing Marriage and Family in the All-Volunteer Force," in *Managing Sex in the U.S. Military*, ed. Beth Bailey, Alesha

Doan, Shannon Portillo, and Kara Dixon Vuic (Lincoln: University of Nebraska Press, 2022), 95–118.

47. *Loper Bright Enterprises v. Raimondo*, 603 U.S. ___ (2024), 144 S. Ct. 2244; *Chevron USA, Inc. v. Natural Resources Defense Council, Inc.*, 467 U.S. 837 (1984).
48. Brooke Migdon, "Military with Transgender Connections See NDAA Provision as 'Slap in the Face,'" *The Hill*, December 11, 2024, https://thehill.com/policy/defense/5035326-transgender-health-care-bill/.
49. Sam Lau, "President Biden Signs Defense Bill Blocking Health Care for Trans Military Children, First Anti-LGBTQ+ Federal Law Enacted Since 'Defense of Marriage Act,'" Human Rights Campaign, December 24, 2024, https://www.hrc.org/press-releases/president-biden-signs-defense-bill-blocking-health-care-for-trans-military-children-first-anti-lgbtq-federal-law-enacted-since-defense-of-marriage-act.
50. Orian Rummler and Kate Sosin, "All the Ways Trump Wants to Exclude Trans People from Public Life," The 19th, March 5, 2025, https://19thnews.org/2025/03/trump-anti-trans-executive-orders/; see also Federal Register, "2025 Donald J. Trump Executive Orders," https://www.federalregister.gov/presidential-documents/executive-orders/donald-trump/2025.
51. Andrew Chung, "Trump Asks US Supreme Court to Enforce Transgender Military Ban," Reuters, April 24, 2025, https://www.reuters.com/world/us/trump-asks-us-supreme-court-allow-enforcement-transgender-military-ban-2025-04-24/.

CONCLUSION

1. George Chauncey, Martin B. Duberman, and Martha Vicinus, "Introduction," in *Hidden from History: Reclaiming the Gay & Lesbian Past*, ed. George Chauncey, Martin B. Duberman, and Martha Vicinus (New York: New American Library, 1989), 1–16.
2. Bernard Rostker and Scott Harris, *Sexual Orientation and U.S. Military Personnel Policy: Options and Assessment*, National Defense Research Institute (Santa Monica, CA: RAND, 1993), 5.
3. Timothy Cook, "The Empirical Study of Lesbian, Gay, and Bisexual Politics: Assessing the First Wave of Research," *American Political Science Review* 93, no. 3 (September 1999): 679–692; Paisely Currah, "The State of LGBT/Sexuality Studies in Political Science," *PS: Political Science and Politics* 44, no. 1 (January 2011): 13–16; Gary Mucciaroni, "The Study of LGBT Politics and Its Contributions to Political Science," *PS: Political Science and Politics* 44, no. 1 (January 2011): 17–21; Julie Novkov and Scott Barclay, "Lesbians, Gays, Bisexuals, and the Transgendered in Political Science: Report on a Discipline-Wide Survey," *PS: Political Science and Politics* 43, no. 1 (January 2010): 95–106; Joe Rollins, "Political Science, Political Sex," *PS: Political Science and Politics* 44, no. 1 (January 2011): 27–30; Richard Valelly, "LGBT Politics and American Political Development," *Annual Review of Political Science* 15, no. 1 (May 2012): 313–332.

4. Novkov and Barclay, "Lesbians, Gays, Bisexuals, and the Transgendered in Political Science."
5. American Political Science Association, "Recent Works Published on LGBT Topics," https://apsanet.org/diversity/apsa-status-committees/status-of-lesbians-gays-bisexuals-and-transgender-individuals-in-the-profession/.
6. Jeffrey Jones, "LGBTQ+ Identification in U.S. Now at 7.6%," Gallup, March 13, 2024, https://news.gallup.com/poll/611864/lgbtq-identification.aspx.
7. Lesbian, Gay, Bisexual, Transgender, and Queer Caucus, "About Us," American Political Science Association, n.d., https://connect.apsanet.org/lgbtq-caucus/about-us/; see also Committee on the Status of Lesbian, Gay, Bisexual, and Transgender Individuals in the Profession, "Statement on Discriminatory Legislation Against the LGBTQ Community and Its Implications for Our Professional Conference Siting Decisions," American Political Science Association, 2021, https://docs.google.com/document/d/1kUcEU8i2MDhcR8bJ-1hcIfe94manTiolprETsqQaLdU/edit?tab=t.0; James McQuiston, "Redesigning the Political Science Curriculum to Incorporate LGBTQ+ Issues," *PS: Political Science and Politics* 58, no. 3 (July 2025): 400–405; Barry Tadlock, Jami Taylor, and Maria Brettschneider, "Where Has the Field Gone? An Investigation of LGBTQ Political Science Research," *LGBTQ Politics*, ed. Maria Brettschneider, Susan Burgess, and Christine Keating (New York: New York University Press, 2017), 212–233.
8. Queer J. Thomas, "Celebrating Fifty Years of LGBTQ+ Scholarship: Kenneth Sherrill, an LGBTQ+ Leader Who Has No Trouble Finding Followers," *Political Science Today* 3, no. 3 (August 2023), 3–4.
9. Monique Newton, Brian Harrison, and Edward Kammerer, "Political Science & LGBTQ+ Identity: Thoughts & Suggestions for LGBTQ+ Graduate Students," *Strategies for Navigating Graduate School and Beyond*, ed. Kevin Lorentz, Daniel Mallinson, Julia Marin Hellwege, Davin Phoenix, and J. Cherie Strachan (Washington, DC: American Political Science Association, 2022), 371–378; Kimberly Creasap and Dorian Rhea Debussy, "LGBTQ+ Advocacy on Campus and Beyond," *Higher Education Careers Beyond the Professoriate*, ed. Karen Cardozo, Katherine Kearns, Shannan Palma (West Lafayette, IN: Purdue University Press, 2024), 293–304.
10. Phillip Ayoub and Kristina Stoeckl, "The Global Resistance to LGBTIQ Rights," *Journal of Democracy* 35, no. 1 (January 2024), 59–73; Zein Murib, "Anti-Trans Attacks: Interrogating 'Gender' in Politics and Gender Scholarship," *Politics & Gender* 20, no. 3 (September 2024), 740–744; Patrick Egan, "Centering LGBTQ+ Political Behavior in Political Science," *PS: Political Science & Politics* 58, no. 3 (July 2025). See also Philip Edward Jones, "Language and LGBTQ Politics: The Effect of Changing Group Labels on Public Attitudes," *American Politics Research* 52, no. 5 (2024), 590–594.
11. Valelly, "LGBT Politics and American Political Development."
12. Valelly, "LGBT Politics and American Political Development."
13. Dorian Rhea Debussy, "LGBTQ+ Voters in These 4 States Could Swing the 2024 Presidential Election," Advocate, November 2, 2024, https://www.advocate.com/election

/lgbtq-voters-in-4-states-swing-election; see also Valelly, "LGBT Politics and American Political Development."

14. Cathy Marcello, "Breaking Barriers: Freedom to Serve Guide 3.0 Unveiled with Vital LGBTQ+ Updates," *Modern Military Magazine*, February 2024, 30–33; Queer Forty, "The Definitive Guide to LGBTQ Military Service Has Now Been Updated and Expanded," October 20, 2023, https://queerforty.com/the-definitive-guide-to-lgbtq-military-service-has-now-been-updated-and-expanded; Modern Military Association of America, "MMAA releases 3rd edition of *Freedom to Serve: The Definitive Guide to LGBTQ Military Service*," 2023, https://modernmilitary.org/2023/10/mmaa-releases-3rd-edition-of-freedom-to-serve-the-definitive-guide-to-lgbtq-military-service/.

15. Orian Rummler and Kate Sosin, "All the Ways Trump Wants to Exclude Trans People from Public Life," The 19th, March 5, 2025, https://19thnews.org/2025/03/trump-anti-trans-executive-orders/; see also "2025 Donald J. Trump Executive Orders," Federal Register, https://www.federalregister.gov/presidential-documents/executive-orders/donald-trump/2025.

16. Gallup, "LGBTQ+ Rights," 2025, https://news.gallup.com/poll/1651/gay-lesbian-rights.aspx.

17. David France, *How to Survive a Plague: The Inside Story of How Citizens and Science Tamed AIDS* (New York: Knopf, 2016); David France, *How to Survive a Plague* (Washington, DC: Independent Lens, 2012); Deborah Gould, *Moving Politics: Emotion and ACT UP's Fight Against AIDS* (Chicago: University of Chicago Press, 2009).

18. Anish Mahajan, Jennifer Sayles, Vishal Patel, Robert Remien, Daniel Ortiz, Greg Szekeres, and Thomas Coates, "Stigma in the HIV/AIDS Epidemic: A Review of the Literature and Recommendations for the Way Forward," *AIDS* 22 (August 2008): S67–S79, https://pmc.ncbi.nlm.nih.gov/articles/PMC2835402/pdf/nihms168647.pdf; Bach Xuan Tran, Hai Thanh Phan, Carl Latkin, Huong Lan Thi Nguyen, Chi Linh Hoang, Cyrus S. H. Ho, and Roger C. M. Ho, "Understanding Global HIV Stigma and Discrimination: Are Contextual Factors Sufficiently Studied?," *International Journal of Environmental Research and Public Health* 16 (2019), https://pmc.ncbi.nlm.nih.gov/articles/PMC6603743/pdf/ijerph-16-01899.pdf; UN AIDS, "HIV and Stigma and Discrimination," Human Rights Fact Sheet Series 2024, https://www.unaids.org/sites/default/files/media_asset/07-hiv-human-rights-factsheet-stigma-discrmination_en.pdf; Nicholas Morjal, "HIV and Converging Policies," *Army Lawyer* 5 (2020); Secretary of Defense, Memorandum: "Policy Regarding Human Immunodeficiency Virus-Positive Personnel Within the Armed Forces," June 6, 2022, https://media.defense.gov/2022/Jun/07/2003013398/-1/-1/1/POLICY-REGARDING-HUMAN-IMMUNODEFICIENCY-VIRUS-POSITIVE-PERSONNEL-WITHIN-THE-ARMED-FORCES.PDF.

19. *Roe and Voe v. Austin*, 947 F.3d 207 (2020); *Harrison v. Austin*, 597 F.3d 884 (2022); see also U.S. Department of Justice, Office of the Solicitor General, Letter to Speaker Nancy Pelosi, June 6, 2022, https://www.justice.gov/oip/page/file/1510856/dl#:~:text=Austin%2C%20No.-,18%2Dcv%2D641%20(E.D.,Va.).

AFTERWORD

1. Christine Sylvester, *Curating and Re-Curating the American Wars in Vietnam and Iraq* (Oxford: Oxford University Press, 2019), viii.
2. Dorian Rhea Debussy, *Freedom to Serve: The Definitive Guide to LGBTQ+ Military Service*, ed. Jennifer Dane and Emily Starbuck Gerson (Washington, DC: Modern Military Association of America, 2023).

BIBLIOGRAPHY

The 1980 Republic Platform: Implications for the Civil Rights of Gay Americans—Gay Vote 1980: The National Convention Project. Douglas Bandow Files, 1981–1982, Box 3, Folder Title: Homosexuals/Gay Rights. Ronald Reagan Presidential Library, Simi Valley, CA.

A4TE, "Trump Administration to Defend 'Trans Ban 2.0' Later This Month." February 8, 2018. https://transequality.org/news/trump-administration-to-defend-trans-ban-20-later-this-month.

Ackerly, Brooke, and Jacqui True. *Doing Feminist Research in Political and Social Science.* New York: Palgrave Macmillan, 2010.

ACLU, "Collins v. United States—Class Action for Military Separation Pay." November 8, 2010. https://www.aclu.org/cases/collins-v-united-states-class-action-military-separation-pay.

———. "Federal Court Blocks All Aspects of Trump's Transgender Military Ban." November 21, 2017. https://www.aclu.org/news/federal-court-blocks-all-aspects-trumps-transgender-military-ban.

Adkins, Judith. "Congressional Investigations and the Lavender Scare." *Prologue* 48, no. 2. Washington, DC: National Archives and Records Administration, 2016.

Administration of Barack Obama, 2017. "Executive Order 13764—Amending the Civil Service Rules, Executive Order 13488, and Executive Order 13467 To Modernize the Executive Branch-Wide Governance Structure and Processes for Security Clearances, Suitability and Fitness for Employment, and Credentialing, and Related Matters." January 17, 2017. https://www.govinfo.gov/content/pkg/DCPD-201700051/pdf/DCPD-201700051.pdf.

"Alleged Immoral Conditions at Newport (RI) Naval Training Station." In *Government Versus Homosexuals*, ed. Leslie Parr. North Stratford, NH: Ayer, [1921] 1975.

Allen, Nicole. "Senate Republicans Block 'Don't Ask, Don't Tell' Repeal." *Atlantic*, September 21, 2010. https://www.theatlantic.com/politics/archive/2010/09/senate-republicans-block-dont-ask-dont-tell-repeal/63342/.

American Political Science Association. "APSA Kenneth Sherrill Fund: Help Broaden Recognition of LGBT Work in Political Science." *Political Science Now*, December 15, 2015.

———. "Recent Works Published on LGBT Politics." https://apsanet.org/diversity/apsa-status-committees/status-of-lesbians-gays-bisexuals-and-transgender-individuals-in-the-profession/.

American Psychiatric Association. *Diagnostic and Statistical Manual of Mental Disorders*. Washington, DC: Author 1952.

Anders, Roger. "The Federal Energy Administration." U.S. Department of Energy, November 1980. https://www.energy.gov/management/articles/federal-energy-administration.

Appleton, Kirsten. "What It Was Like at the First Gay Rights Demonstration Outside the White House 50 Years Ago." ABC News, April 17, 2015. https://abcnews.go.com/Politics/gay-rights-demonstration-white-house-50-years-ago/story?id=30379792.

Assistant Secretary of Defense. Memorandum: "Guidance for Treatment of Gender Dysphoria for Active and Reserve Competent Service Members." July 29, 2016. https://web.archive.org/web/20170112211346/https://www.defense.gov/Portals/1/features/2016/0616_policy/Guidance_for_Treatment_of_Gender_Dysphoria_Memo_FINAL_SIGNED.pdf.

Associated Press. "Report: More Gay Linguists Discharged Than First Thought." NBC News. January 13, 2005. http://www.nbcnews.com/id/6824206/ns/us_news-security/t/report-more-gay-linguistsdischarged-first-thought/.

Ayoub, Phillip, and Kristina Stoeckl. "The Global Resistance to LGBTIQ Rights." *Journal of Democracy* 35, no. 1 (2024): 59–73.

Bailey, Beth. "'A Higher Moral Character': Respectability and the Women's Army Corps." In *Managing Sex in the U.S. Military*, ed. Beth Bailey, Alesha Doan, Shannon Portillo, and Kara Dixon Vuic, 71–94. Lincoln: University of Nebraska Press, 2022.

Bailey, Fenton, and Randy Barbato. *The Strange History of Don't Ask, Don't Tell*. HBO Documentary Films, 2012.

Beachy, Robert. *Gay Berlin: Birthplace of a Modern Identity*. New York: Knopf, 2014.

Becker, Elizabeth. "Pentagon Orders Training to Prevent Harassment of Gays." *New York Times*, February 2, 2000. http://www.nytimes.com/2000/02/02/us/pentagon-orders-training-to-prevent-harassment-of-gays.html.

Belkin, Aaron. "'Don't Ask, Don't Tell': Does the Gay Ban Undermine the Military's Reputation?" *Armed Forces & Society* 34, no. 2 (2007): 276–291.

———. "'Don't Ask, Don't Tell': Is the Gay Ban Based on Military Necessity?" *Parameters: U.S. Army War College Quarterly*, Summer 2003, 108–119.

———. *How We Won: Progressive Lessons from the Repeal of "Don't Ask, Don't Tell."* Los Angeles: HuffPost Media Group, 2011.

———. "The Pentagon's Gay Ban Is Not Based on Military Necessity." *Journal of Homosexuality* 41, no. 1 (2001): 103–119.

Belkin, Aaron, Frank Barrett, Mark Eitelberg, and Marc Ventresca. "Discharging Transgender Troops Would Cost $960 Million." Palm Center. August 2017. http://www.palmcenter.org/wp-content/uploads/2017/08/cost-of-firing-trans-troops-3.pdf.

Belkin, Aaron, and Melissa Sheridan Embser-Herbert. "A Modest Proposal: Privacy as a Flawed Rationale for the Exclusion of Gays and Lesbians from the U.S. Military." *International Security* 27, no. 2 (2002): 178–197.

Belkin, Aaron, and Melissa Levitt. "Homosexuality and the Israeli Defense Forces: Did the Gay Ban Undermine Military Performance?" *Armed Forces & Society* 27, no. 4 (2001): 541–565.

Bell, Andrew Francis. "Radical Religious Rebels: The Rise and Fall of Jerry Falwell and the Moral Majority." Master's thesis, Eastern Tennessee State University, 2008.

Bender, Bryan. "Almost 12% of U.S. Army Recruits Required Waivers for Criminal Records." *New York Times*, July 13, 2007. http://www.nytimes.com/2007/07/13/world/americas/13iht-13recruits.6652316.html.

Berube, Allan. *Coming Out Under Fire: The History of Gay Men and Women in World War II*. Chapel Hill: University of North Carolina Press, [1990] 2010.

———. "Marching to a Different Drummer: Lesbian and Gay GIs in World War II." In *Hidden from History: Reclaiming the Gay & Lesbian Past*, ed. George Chauncey, Martin B. Duberman, and Martha Vicinus, 383–394. New York: New American Library, 1989.

Black, Chris. "Pentagon to Review 'Don't Ask, Don't Tell' Policy." CNN. December 13, 1999. http://archives.cnn.com/1999/US/12/13/pentagon.gays/index.html.

Brammer, John Paul, and Brooke Sopelsa. "Trump's Army Secretary Pick, Mark Green, Withdraws Name from Consideration." NBC News. May 5, 2017. https://www.nbcnews.com/feature/nbc-out/trump-s-army-secretary-pick-slammed-anti-transgender-islamophobic-n754806.

Branigin, William, Debbi Wilgoren, and Perry Bacon. "Obama Signs DADT Repeal Before Big, Emotional Crowd." *Washington Post*, December 22, 2010. http://www.washingtonpost.com/wp-dyn/content/article/2010/12/22/AR2010122201888.html.

Braukman, Stacy. *Communists and Perverts under the Palms: The Johns Committee in Florida, 1956–1965*. Gainesville: University Press of Florida, 2013.

Brinkley, Alan. "World War I and the Crisis of Democracy." In *Security v. Liberty: Conflicts Between National Security and Civil Liberties in American History*, ed. Daniel Farber, 27–41. New York: Russell Sage Foundation, 2008.

Bronski, Michael. *A Queer History of the United States*. Boston: Beacon, 2011.

Browne, Ryan, and Eli Watkins, "Vincent Viola Withdraws from Secretary of Army Nomination," CNN. February 4, 2017, https://www.cnn.com/2017/02/03/politics/vincent-viola-withdraws-from-secretary-of-army-nomination/index.html.

Burrell, David. "An Overview of the Debate on Homosexuals in the U.S. Military." In *Gays and Lesbians in the Military: Issues, Concerns, and Contrasts*, ed. Wilbur Scott and Sandra Stanley, 17–31. Hawthorne: Walter de Gruyter, 1994.

C-SPAN. "Senate Session," December 9, 2010. https://www.c-span.org/video/?296995-1/senate-session.

Calonico, Scott. *When AIDS Was Funny*. 2015.

Camp, Gabrielle. "Women on the Home Front: The Women's Army Corps and Lesbian Community During and After World War II." April 27, 2023. Tallahassee: Florida State University Libraries.

Canaday, Margot. *The Straight State: Sexuality and Citizenship in Twentieth-Century America*. Princeton, NJ: Princeton University Press, 2006.
Cantu, Benjamin. *Eldorado: Everything the Nazis Hate*. Film Base Berlin and Netflix Studios, 2023.
Carter, David. *Stonewall: The Riots That Shaped the Gay Revolution*. New York: St. Martin's, 2004.
Carter, Judy. *The Homo Handbook: Getting in Touch with Your Inner Homo—A Survival Guide for Lesbians and Gay Men*. New York: Fireside, 2006.
"Case of Harold J. Trubshaw, Hospital Apprentice 2nd class, USNRF." Record of Proceedings of a General Court-Martial Convened at U.S. Naval Training State, Newport, R.I.By Order of Secretary of the Navy. Washington, DC: National Archives and Records Administration, October 28–30, 1919.
"Case of Stephen Brug, Chief Boatswain's Mate, USN." Record of Proceedings of a General Court-Martial Convened at U.S. Naval Training State, Newport, R.I. By Order of Secretary of the Navy. Washington, DC: National Archives and Records Administration, November 18–21, 1919.
Cauldwell, David. "Psychopathia Transexualis." *Sexology* 16 (1949): 274–280.
Charles, Douglas. *Hoover's War on Gays: Exposing the FBI's "Sex Deviates" Program*. Lawrence: University Press of Kansas, 2015.
Chauncey, George. "Christian Brotherhood or Sexual Perversion? Homosexual Identities and the Construction of Sexual Boundaries in the World War One Era." *Journal of Social History* 19, no. 2 (1985): 189–211.
———. *Gay New York: Gender, Urban Culture, and the Making of the Gay Male World, 1890–1940*. New York: Basic Books, 1994.
Chauncey, George, Martin B. Duberman, and Martha Vicinus. "Introduction." In *Hidden from History: Reclaiming the Gay & Lesbian Past*, ed. George Chauncey, Martin B. Duberman, and Martha Vicinus, 1–16. New York: New American Library, 1989.
Chevron USA, Inc. v. Natural Resources Defense Council, Inc. 467 U.S. 837 (1984).
Choi, Dan. "Injustice Anywhere Is a Threat to Justice Everywhere." *HuffPost*, March 18, 2011. http://www.huffingtonpost.com/lt-dan-choi/injustice-anywhere-is-a-t_b_425424.html.
Chung, Andrew. "Trump Asks US Supreme Court to Enforce Transgender Military Ban." Reuters. April 24, 2025. https://www.reuters.com/world/us/trump-asks-us-supreme-court-allow-enforcement-transgender-military-ban-2025-04-24/.
Cianni, Vincent. *Gays in the Military: Photographs and Interviews*. New York: Daylight, 2014.
CNN. "House Democrats Push 'Don't Ask, Don't Tell' Repeal." December 14, 2010. http://www.cnn.com/2010/POLITICS/12/14/gays.military/index.html.
Committee on the Status of Lesbian, Gay, Bisexual, and Transgender Individuals in the Profession. "Statement on Discriminatory Legislation Against the LGBTQ Community and Its Implications for Our Professional Conference Siting Decisions." American Political Science Association, 2021. https://docs.google.com/document/d/1kUcEU8i2MDhcR8bJ-1hcIfe94manTiolprETsqQaLdU/edit?tab=t.0.
Congressional Record 96, pt. 4. 81st Congress, 2nd session. March 29 to April 24, 1950.

Cook, Timothy. "The Empirical Study of Lesbian, Gay, and Bisexual Politics: Assessing the First Wave of Research." *American Political Science Review* 93, no. 3 (September 1999): 679–692.

Corber, Robert. *Homosexuality in Cold War America*. Durham, NC: Duke University Press, 1997.

———. *In the Name of National Security: Hitchcock, Homophobia, and the Political Construction of Gender in Postwar America*. Durham, NC: Duke University Press, 1993.

Courdileone, K. A. *Manhood and American Political Culture in the Cold War*. New York: Routledge, 2005.

Crary, David, and Elana Schor. "Lifting Near-Total Ban on Transgender People from Military Service Among Biden Plans to Protect LGBTQ Rights." *Military Times*, November 29, 2020. https://www.militarytimes.com/news/pentagon-congress/2020/11/29/lifting-near-total-ban-on-transgender-people-from-military-service-among-biden-plans-to-protect-lgbtq-rights/.

Creasap, Kimberly, and Dorian Rhea Debussy. "LGBTQ+ Advocacy on Campus and Beyond." In *Higher Education Careers Beyond the Professoriate*, ed. Karen Cardozo, Katherine Kearns, and Shannan Palma, 293–304. West Lafayette, IN: Purdue University Press, 2024.

Crittenden, S. H. "Report of the Board Appointed to Prepare and Submit Recommendations to the Secretary of the Navy for the Revision of Policies, Procedures, and Directives Dealing with Homosexuals." U.S. Navy Board of Inquiry. March 15, 1957.

Currah, Paisely. "The State of LGBT/Sexuality Studies in Political Science." *PS: Political Science and Politics* 44 (2011): 13–16.

Daniel, Lisa. "Repeal of 'Don't Ask, Don't Tell' Offers Few Risks, Report Finds." American Forces Press Service, November 29, 2010. http://archive.defense.gov/news/newsarticle.aspx?id=61899.

Dao, James, and Eric Schmitt. "The 43rd President: The Defense Department; Bush Says He Is Taking Time on Defense Pick to 'Get it Right.'" *New York Times*, December 23, 2000. http://www.nytimes.com/2000/12/23/us/43rd-president-defense-department-bush-says-he-taking-time-defense-pick-get-it.html.

Davis, Jeffrey. "Military Policy Towards Homosexuals: Scientific, Historical, and Legal Perspectives." *Military Law Review* 131 (1991).

Dawley, Alan. *Changing the World: American Progressives in War and Revolution*. Princeton, NJ: Princeton University Press, 2005.

de Grandpre, Andrew, and Karen Jowers. "At Military Schools, Transgender Bathroom Decisions Will Be Made Case by Case Basis." *Military Times*, February 25, 2017. https://web.archive.org/web/20170809042734/https://www.militarytimes.com/news/your-military/2017/02/25/at-military-schools-transgender-bathroom-decisions-will-be-made-case-by-case/.

———. "Trump's Transgender Directive and What's at Stake Within the U.S. Military." *Military Times*, February 23, 2017. https://www.militarytimes.com/news/your-military/2017/02/23/trump-s-transgender-directive-and-what-s-at-stake-within-the-u-s-military/.

Debussy, Dorian Rhea. *Freedom to Serve: The Definitive Guide to LGBTQ+ Military Service.* Ed. Jennifer Dane and Emily Starbuck Gerson. Washington, DC: Modern Military Association of America, 2023.

———. "LGBTQ+ Voters in These 4 States Could Swing the 2024 Presidential Election." *Advocate*, 2024. https://www.advocate.com/election/lgbtq-voters-in-4-states-swing-election.

D'Emilio, John, and Estelle Freedman. *Intimate Matters: A History of Sexuality in America.* 3rd ed. Chicago: University of Chicago Press, [1988] 2012.

Department of Defense. DoD Directive 1332.14. Reprinted in *Code of Federal Regulations*, Title 31, Parts 40–399. Washington, DC: U.S. Government Printing Office, 1959.

"Department of Defense Memorandum." October 11, 1949. Reprinted in Bernard Rostker and Scott Harris, *Sexual Orientation and U.S. Military Personnel Policy: Options and Assessment.* National Defense Research Institute. Santa Monica, CA: RAND, 1993.

Deutsch, James. "Are You a Friend of Dorothy? Folk Speech of the LGBT Community." *Folklife*, October 25, 2016. https://folklife.si.edu/talkstory/2016/are-you-a-friend-of-dorothy-folk-speech-of-the-lgbt-community.

Diamond, Jeremy. "Trump to Reinstate US Military Ban on Transgender People." CNN. July 26, 2017. https://www.cnn.com/2017/07/26/politics/trump-military-transgender/index.html.

Dicker, Rory. *A History of U.S. Feminisms.* Berkely, CA: Seal, 2016.

Dietert, Michelle, and Dianne Dentice. "Transgender Military Experience." *SAGE Open* 5, no. 2 (2015).

Dignity & Respect: A Training Guide on Homosexual Conduct Policy. Prepared for the Assistant Secretary of the Army, Manpower and Reserve Affairs. Washington, DC: Department of the Army, 2001.

Director of Central Intelligence Directive (DCID) Number 1/14. Washington, DC: Central Intelligence Agency, 1984.

Director of Central Intelligence Directive (DCID) Number 1/14. Washington, DC: Central Intelligence Agency, 1987. https://www.jagcnet.army.mil/Sites/trialjudiciary.nsf/xsp/.ibmmodres/domino/OpenAttachment/sites/trialjudiciary.nsf/2A901902D7BF56B885257B480066DE3D/Attachments/R%205200.2-R%2019870101.pdf.

Director of Central Intelligence Directive (DCID) Number 1/14. Washington, DC: Central Intelligence Agency, 1994. https://www.cia.gov/library/readingroom/docs/DOC_0000200002.pdf.

Director of Security. Central Intelligence Agency. "Letter to Julie Dubbs." 1981.

Dixon, Alex. "July Marks the 40th Anniversary of All-Volunteer Military." U.S. Army, 2013. https://www.army.mil/article/106813/july_marks_40th_anniversary_of_all_volunteer_army.

Dobbs v. Jackson Women's Health Organization. 597 U.S. ___ (2022), 142 S. Ct. 2228.

Dong, Arthur. *Coming Out Under Fire.* Deep Focus Productions, 1994.

"Draft of Proposed Manual for Special Agents." SY-General 1954 Folder, Box 1, Entry 1508. Office of Security and Consular Affairs, Lot File 53-D-233. Subject Files of the Security Division, 1946–1953, RG 59. Washington, DC: National Archives and Records Administration, February 1952.

Dubbs v. Central Intelligence Agency. 866 F.2d 1114 (1989).
Dyer, Kate. "Forward." In *Gays in Uniform: The Pentagon's Secret Reports*, ed. Kate Dyer, xii–xviii. Boston: Alyson, 1990.
———, ed. *Gays in Uniform: The Pentagon's Secret Reports.* Boston: Alyson, 1990.
Eaklor, Vicki. *Queer America: A People's GLBT History of the United States.* New York: New Press, 2008.
Egan, Patrick. "Centering LGBTQ+ Political Behavior in Political Science." *PS: Political Science & Politics* 58, no. 3 (July 2025).
Embser-Herbert, Mael, and Bree Fram, eds. *With Honor and Integrity: Transgender Troops in Their Own Words.* New York: New York University Press, 2022.
Enloe, Cynthia. *Nimo's War, Emma's War: Making Feminist Sense of the Iraq War.* Berkeley: University of California Press, 2010.
Ennis, Dawn. "Antigay Texas Activist: Soviets Created Gays to Destroy U.S., Like 'Termites.'" LGBTQ Nation, 2016. https://www.LGBTQ+nation.com/2016/11/antigay-texas-activist-soviets-created-gays-destroy-u-s-like-termites/.
Epstein, Rob, and Jeffrey Friedman. *Paragraph 175.* Telling Pictures, 2000.
Estes, Steve. *Ask & Tell: Gay and Lesbian Veterans Speak Out.* Chapel Hill: University of North Carolina Press, 2009.
Evans, Rhonda. "U.S. Military Policies Concerning Homosexuals: Development, Implementation and Outcomes." Report for the Center for the Study of Sexual Minorities in the Military. Santa Barbara: University of California at Santa Barbara, 2002.
Everson, Phil, Rick Valelly, Arjun Vishwanath, and Jim Wiseman. "NOMINATE and American Political Development: A Primer." *Studies in American Political Development* 30 (2016): 97–115.
Executive Office of the President, White House. "Executive Order on Enabling All Qualified Americans to Serve Their Country in Uniform." January 25, 2021. https://www.whitehouse.gov/briefing-room/presidential-actions/2021/01/25/executive-order-on-enabling-all-qualified-americans-to-serve-their-country-in-uniform/.
Executive Order 9835. 12 FR 1935. March 25, 1947.
Executive Order 10450. 18 FR 2489. 3 CFR, 1949–1953. Comp: 936. April 27, 1953.
Faderman, Lillian. *The Gay Revolution: The Story of Struggle.* New York: Simon & Schuster, 2015.
———. *Odd Girls and Twilight Lovers: A History of Lesbian Life in Twentieth-Century America.* New York: Columbia University Press, [1991] 2012.
Farber, Daniel. "Introduction." In *Security v. Liberty: Conflicts Between National Security and Civil Liberties in American History*, ed. Daniel Farber, 1–26. New York: Russell Sage Foundation, 2008.
Federal Register. "2025 Donald J. Trump Executive Orders." https://www.federalregister.gov/presidential-documents/executive-orders/donald-trump/2025.
Forty, Queer. "The Definitive Guide to LGBTQ Military Service Has Now Been Updated and Expanded." October 20, 2023. https://queerforty.com/the-definitive-guide-to-lgbtq-military-service-has-now-been-updated-and-expanded.
Fram, Bree, and Mael Sheridan, eds. *With Valor and Visibility: The Next Chapter of Transgender Military Service.* Alexandria, VA: Forged in Fire, 2025.

France, David. *How to Survive a Plague*. Washington, DC: Independent Lens, 2012.
——. *How to Survive a Plague: The Inside Story of How Citizens and Science Tamed AIDS*. New York: Knopf, 2016.
Frank, Nathaniel. *Unfriendly Fire: How the Gay Ban Undermines the Military and Weakens America*. New York: Thomas Dunne, 2009.
Frank, Walter. *Law and the Gay Rights Story: The Long Search for Equal Justice in a Divided Democracy*. New Brunswick, NJ: Rutgers University Press, 2014.
Funakoshi, Minami, and Disha Raychaudhuri. "The Rise of Anti-Trans Bills in the US." Reuters. August 19, 2023. https://www.reuters.com/graphics/USA-HEALTHCARE/TRANS-BILLS/zgvorreyapd/.
Gallup. "LGBTQ+ Rights." 2025. https://news.gallup.com/poll/1651/gay-lesbian-rights.aspx.
Gays in Uniform: The Pentagon's Secret Reports, ed. Kate Dyer. Boston: Alyson Publication, Inc., 1990.
Gibson, Lawrence. *Get Off My Ship: Ensign Verg vs. the U.S. Navy*. New York: Avon, 1978.
Gould, Deborah. *Moving Politics: Emotion and ACT UP's Fight Against AIDS*. Chicago: University of Chicago Press, 2009.
Graves, Karen. *And They Were Wonderful Teachers: Florida's Purge of Gay and Lesbian Teachers*. Champaign: University of Illinois Press, 2009.
Haefner, John. "Moral Waivers in Army Recruiting: It Is About Family." Strategy Research Project. U.S. Army War College. 2013.
Halberstam, Jack. *Female Masculinity*. Durham, NC: Duke University Press, 1998.
Halladay, Laurel. "A Lovely War: Male to Female Cross-Dressing and Canadian Military Entertainment in World War II." In *The Drag Queen Anthology: The Absolutely Fabulous but Flawlessly Customary World of Female Impersonators*, ed. Steven Schacht and Lisa Underwood, 19–34. Binghamton, NY: Haworth, 2004.
Halley, Janet. *Don't: A Readers Guide to the Military's Anti-Gay Policy*. Durham, NC: Duke University Press, 1999.
Halloran, Liz. "Gates to Senate: End 'Don't Ask, Don't Tell' Before Courts Do." NPR, November 30, 2010. https://www.npr.org/2010/11/30/131697322/pentagon-study-dismisses-risk-of-openly-gay-troops.
Hamner, Christopher. "Brothers in Arms? Combat, Masculinity, and Change in the Twenty-First-Century American Military." In *Managing Sex in the U.S. Military*, ed. Beth Bailey, Alesha Doan, Shannon Portillo, and Kara Dixon Vuic, 275–306. Lincoln: University of Nebraska Press, 2022.
Hardy, Janet, and Dossie Easton. *The Ethical Slut: A Practical Guide to Polyamory, Open Relationships, and Other Freedoms in Sex and Love*. 3rd ed. Berkeley, CA: Ten Speed, 2017.
——. *The New Bottoming Book*. Emeryville, CA: Greenery, 2001.
Harper, Alan. *The Politics of Loyalty: The White House and the Communist Issue, 1946–1952*. Santa Barbara, CA: Praeger, 1970.
Harrison v. Austin. 597 F.3d 884 (2022).
Hawkesworth, Mary. *Feminist Inquiry: From Political Conviction to Methodological Innovation*. New Brunswick, NJ: Rutgers University Press, 2006.

Herek, Gregory. "Gay People and Government Security Clearances: A Social Science Perspective." *American Psychologist* 45, no. 9 (1950): 1035–1042.

Hesse-Biber, Sharlene. "A Re-Invitation to Feminist Research." In *Feminist Research Practice: A Primer*, ed. Sharlene Hesse-Biber. Los Angeles: Sage, 2014.

Hinojosa, Ramon. "Doing Hegemony: Military, Men, and Constructing a Hegemonic Masculinity." *Journal of Men's Studies* 18, no. 2 (2010): 179–194.

Hirschfeld, Magnus. "Die Intersexuelle Konstitution." *Jahrbuch fur Sexuelle Zwischenstufen Unterbesonderer Berucksichtigung der Homosexualit* 23 (1923): 3–27.

———. "Die Transvestiten—Eine Untersuchung uber den Erotischen Verkleidungstrieb: Mit Umfangreichem Casuistischen und Historischen Material." Berlin: Alfred Pulvermacher, 1910.

"HIV and AIDS—United States, 1981–2000." *Mortality and Morbidity Weekly Report* 50, no. 1 (2001): 430–434.

"Hoey Committee Report." SY-General 1952 folder, Box 1, Entry 1508. Office of Security and Consular Affairs, Lot File 53-D-233. Subject Files of the Security Division, 1946–1953, RG 59. Washington, DC: National Archives and Records Administration, February 1952.

Hogan, Michael. *A Cross of Iron: Harry S. Truman and the Origins of the National Security State, 1945–1954*. Cambridge: Cambridge University Press, 2000.

Hooper, Tom. *The Danish Girl*. Focus Features and Universal Pictures, 2015.

Human Rights Watch. "Uniform Discrimination: The 'Don't Ask, Don't Tell' Policy of the U.S. Military." January 5, 2003. https://www.hrw.org/report/2003/01/06/uniform-discrimination/dont-ask-dont-tell-policy-us-military.

Hunter, Kyleanne, Sarah Meadows, Rebecca Collins, and Isabelle Gonzalez. "How the *Dobbs* Decision Could Affect U.S. National Security." RAND. September 13, 2022. https://www.rand.org/pubs/perspectives/PEA2227-1.html.

interAct Advocates for Intersex Youth. "What Is Intersex?" https://interactadvocates.org/faq/.

Isherwood, Christopher. *Goodbye to Berlin*. New York: New Directions, [1939] 2012.

Ismay, John. "Who's In and Who's Out at the Naval Academy's Library?" *New York Times*, April 11, 2025. https://www.nytimes.com/2025/04/11/us/politics/naval-academy-banned-books.html

Jackson, Hallie, and Courtney Kube. "Trump's Controversial Transgender Military Policy Goes Into Effect." NBC News. April 12, 2019. https://www.nbcnews.com/feature/nbc-out/trump-s-controversial-transgender-military-policy-goes-effect-n993826.

Jackson, Paul. *One of the Boys: Homosexuality in the Military during World War II*. 2nd ed. Montreal: Mc-Gill Queen's University Press, [2004] 2010.

Johnson, Chris. "Fanning Skeptical Trump Will Undo LGBT Inclusion in Military." *Washington Blade*, 2016. http://www.washingtonblade.com/2016/11/17/fanning-skeptical-trump-will-undo-lgbt-inclusion-in-military/

Johnson, David. *The Lavender Scare: The Cold War Persecution of Gays and Lesbians in the Federal Government*. Chicago: University of Chicago Press, 2004.

Jones, Jeffrey. "LGBTQ+ Identification in U.S. Now at 7.6%." Gallup, March 13, 2024. https://news.gallup.com/poll/611864/lgbtq-identification.aspx.

Jones, Philip Edward. "Language and LGBTQ Politics: The Effect of Changing Group Labels on Public Attitudes." *American Politics Research* 52, no. 5 (2024): 590–594.

Katz, Jonathan. *Gay American History: Lesbians and Gay Men in the U.S.A.* New York: Meridan, [1976] 1992.

Kenning, Chris. "Transgender U.S. Military Recruits Enlist Amid Uncertainty." Reuters. January 14, 2018. https://www.reuters.com/article/us-usa-military-transgender/transgender-u-s-military-recruits-enlist-amid-uncertainty-idUSKBN1F30Io.

Khazan, Olga. "Milo Yiannopoulos and the Myth of the Gay Pedophile." *Atlantic*, February 21, 2017. https://www.theatlantic.com/health/archive/2017/02/milo-yiannopoulos-and-the-myth-of-the-gay-pedophile/517332/.

Kier, Elizabeth. "Homosexuals in the U.S. Military: Open Integration and Combat Effectiveness." *International Security* 23, no. 2 (1998): 5–39.

Kimmel, Michael. *Manhood in America: A Cultural History*. 3rd ed. Oxford: Oxford University Press, 2011.

Kinsey, Alfred. *Sexual Behavior in the Human Male*. Indianapolis: Indiana University Press, [1948] 1998.

Kreps, Daniel. "Lady Gaga Rallies Against 'Don't Ask, Don't Tell.'" *Rolling Stone*, September 20, 2010. http://www.rollingstone.com/music/news/lady-gaga-rallies-against-dont-ask-dont-tell-20100920.

Krieg, Gregory. "Newt Gingrich Wants New House Un-American Activities Committee." CNN. June 14, 2016. https://www.cnn.com/2016/06/14/politics/newt-gingrich-house-un-american-activities-committee/index.html.

Lamothe, Dan. "On Eve of Deadline, Pentagon Delays Plan to Allow Transgender Recruits by 6 Months." *Washington Post*, June 30, 2017. https://www.washingtonpost.com/news/checkpoint/wp/2017/06/30/mattis-delays-pentagons-decision-to-allow-transgender-recruits-six-more-months/?utm_term=.39154266031b.

Lang, Nico. "Trump's Secretary of Defense Pick Opposes LGBT People, Women Serving in the Military." Advocate. December 2, 2016. https://www.advocate.com/politics/2016/12/02/trumps-secretary-defense-pick-opposes-lgbt-people-women-serving-military.

Lau, Sam. "President Biden Signs Defense Bill Blocking Health Care for Trans Military Children, First Anti-LGBTQ+ Federal Law Enacted Since 'Defense of Marriage Act.'" Human Rights Campaign. December 24, 2024. https://www.hrc.org/press-releases/president-biden-signs-defense-bill-blocking-health-care-for-trans-military-children-first-anti-lgbtq-federal-law-enacted-since-defense-of-marriage-act.

Lavietes, Matt. "Dr. Rachel Levine Becomes Nation's First Transgender Four-Star Officer." NBC News. October 19, 2021. https://www.nbcnews.com/nbc-out/out-health-and-wellness/dr-rachel-levine-becomes-nations-first-transgender-four-star-officer-rcna3283.

Lawrence v. Texas. 539 U.S. 558 (2003).

Lehring, Gary. *Officially Gay: The Political Construction of Sexuality by the U.S. Military*. Philadelphia: Temple University Press, 2003.

Lesbian, Gay, Bisexual, Transgender, and Queer Caucus. "About Us." American Political Science Association. https://connect.apsanet.org/lgbtq-caucus/about-us/.

LeSueur, Stephen. "But No Immediate Change Expected: DoD Ban Against Gays Weakened by Cheney's Lackluster Defense of Policy." *Inside the Pentagon* 7, no. 33 (1991): 3–5.

Letter to President Woodrow Wilson. January 11, 1920. Bishop Perry Papers. Subject Series 29, Series No. VIII. Box 9, Folder 331. University of Rhode Island Library Special Collections.

Lewis, Carolyn Herbst. *Prescription for Heterosexuality: Sexual Citizenship in the Cold War Era.* Chapel Hill: University of North Carolina Press, 2010.

Lewis, Jan. "Defining the Nation: 1790 to 1898." In *Security v. Liberty: Conflicts Between National Security and Civil Liberties in American History,* ed. Daniel Farber, 117–164. New York: Russell Sage Foundation, 2008.

Locke, Brandon. *The Military-Masculinity Complex: Hegemonic Masculinity and the United States Armed Forces, 1940–1963.* PhD diss., University of Nebraska at Lincoln, 2013.

Loftin, Craig. *Letters to ONE: Gay and Lesbian Voices from the 1950s and 1960s.* Albany: State University of New York Press, 2012.

———. *Masked Voices: Gay Men and Lesbians in Cold War America.* Albany: State University of New York Press, 2012.

Loper Bright Enterprises v. Raimondo. 603 U.S. ___ (2024). 144 S. Ct. 2244.

Love, Albert, and Charles Davenport. *Defects Found in Drafted Men.* Washington, DC: U.S. Government Printing Office, 1920.

Mahajan, Anish, Jennifer Sayles, Vishal Patel, Robert Remien, Daniel Ortiz, Greg Szekeres, and Thomas Coates. "Stigma in the HIV/AIDS Epidemic: A Review of the Literature and Recommendations for the Way Forward." *AIDS* 22 (August 2008): S67–S79. https://pmc.ncbi.nlm.nih.gov/articles/PMC2835402/pdf/nihms168647.pdf.

Manual Enterprises, Inc. v. Day. 370 U.S. 478 (1962).

Marcello, Cathy. "Breaking Barriers: Freedom to Serve Guide 3.0 Unveiled with Vital LGBTQ+ Updates." *Modern Military Magazine,* February 2024, 30–33.

Mayhew, David. "Events as Causes: The Case of American Politics." In *Parties & Policies: How the American Government Works,* ed. David Mayhew, 328–357. New Haven, CT: Yale University Press, 2008.

McBride, Brian. "17 Times the Trump-Pence Administration Attacked the LGBTQ Community in 2017." Human Rights Campaign. December 22, 2017. https://www.hrc.org/blog/17-times-the-trump-pence-administration-attacked-the-lgbtq-community-in-201.

McCarthy, Justin. "Americans' Views on Origins of Homosexuality Remain Split." Gallup. May 28, 2014. https://news.gallup.com/poll/170753/americans-views-origins-homosexuality-remain-split.aspx.

McDaniel, Michael. *Preservice Adjustment of Homosexual and Heterosexual Military Accessions: Implications for Security Clearance Suitability.* Defense Personnel Security Research and Education Center. Monterey, CA: PERSEREC, 1989.

———. "Preservice Adjustment of Homosexual and Heterosexual Military Accessions: Implications for Security Clearance Suitability." In *Gays in Uniform: The Pentagon's Secret Reports,* ed. Kate Dyer. Boston: Alyson, 1990.

McQuiston, James. "Redesigning the Political Science Curriculum to Incorporate LGBTQ+ Issues." *PS: Political Science and Politics* 58, no. 3 (July 2025): 400–405.

"A Message from Lady Gaga to the Senate." YouTube. September 16, 2010. https://www.youtube.com/watch?v=GG5VK2lquEc.

Migdon, Brooke. "Military with Transgender Connections See NDAA as 'Slap in the Face.'" *The Hill*, December 11, 2024. https://thehill.com/policy/defense/5035326-transgender-health-care-bill/.

Miller, Neil. *Out of the Past: Gay and Lesbian History from 1869 to Present*. New York: Vintage, [1995] 2006.

Modern Military Association of America. "MMAA Releases 3rd Edition of *Freedom to Serve: The Definitive Guide to LGBTQ Military Service*." 2023. https://modernmilitary.org/2023/10/mmaa-releases-3rd-edition-of-freedom-to-serve-the-definitive-guide-to-lgbtq-military-service/.

Morjal, Nicholas. "HIV and Converging Policies. *Army Lawyer* 5 (2020).

Morone, James. *The Democratic Wish: Popular Participation and the Limits of American Government*. New York: Basic Books, 1990.

———. *Hellfire Nation: The Politics of Sin in American History*. New Haven, CT: Yale University Press, 2004.

Mucciaroni, Gary. "The Study of LGBT Politics and Its Contributions to Political Science." *PS: Political Science and Politics* 44 (2011): 17–21.

Muñoz, Carlo. "'Don't Ask, Don't Tell' Discharges to Receive Full Back Pay from DoD." *The Hill*, January 7, 2013. http://thehill.com/policy/defense/275971-service-members-discharged-under-dont-ask-dont-tell-to-receive-full-back-pay.

Murib, Zein. "Anti-Trans Attacks: Interrogating 'Gender' in Politics and Gender Scholarship." *Politics & Gender* 20, no. 3 (September 2024): 740–744.

National Commission on Terrorist Attacks Upon the United States. *The 9/11 Commission Report*. Washington, DC: U.S. Government Printing Office, 2004.

National Park Service. "Blue and 'Other Than Honorable' Discharges. https://www.nps.gov/articles/000/blue-and-other-than-honorable-discharges.htm.

———. "Women in World War I." https://www.nps.gov/articles/women-in-world-war-i.htm.

New York Public Library "LGBTQ+ Titles Targeted for Censorship: Stand Against Book Banning." June 23, 2023. https://www.nypl.org/blog/2023/06/23/lgbtq-titles-targeted-censorship-stand-against-book-banning.

Newton, Monique, Brian Harrison, and Edward Kammerer. "Political Science & LGBTQ+ Identity: Thoughts & Suggestions for LGBTQ+ Graduate Students." In *Strategies for Navigating Graduate School and Beyond*, ed. Kevin Lorentz, Daniel Mallinson, Julia Marin Hellwege, Davin Phoenix, and J. Cherie Strachan, 371–378. Washington, DC: American Political Science Association, 2022.

Nicholson, Alexander. *Fighting to Serve: Behind the Scenes in the War to Repeal "Don't Ask, Don't Tell."* Chicago: Chicago Review Press, 2012.

Novak, Lisa. "Panel Urges Ending UCMJ's Sodomy Ban." *Stars and Stripes*, October 27, 2009. https://www.stripes.com/news/panel-urges-ending-ucmj-s-sodomy-ban-1.95937.

Novkov, Julie, and Scott Barclay. "Lesbians, Gays, Bisexuals, and the Transgendered in Political Science: Report on a Discipline-Wide Survey." *PS: Political Science and Politics* 43 (2010): 95–106.

O'Brien, Michael. "Lieberman Plans Standalone Repeal of 'Don't Ask, Don't Tell.'" *The Hill*, December 9, 2010. http://thehill.com/blogs/blog-briefing-room/news/133001-lieberman-plans-standalone-repeal-of-dont-ask-dont-tell.

O'Keefe, Ed. "'Don't Ask, Don't Tell' Is Repealed by Senate; Bill Awaits Obama's Signing." *Washington Post*, December 19, 2010. http://www.washingtonpost.com/wp-dyn/content/article/2010/12/18/AR2010121801729.html.

O'Keefe, Ed, and Greg Jaffe. "Sources: Pentagon Group Finds There Is Minimal Risk to Lifting Gay Ban During War." *Washington Post*, November 11, 2010. http://www.washingtonpost.com/wp-dyn/content/article/2010/11/10/AR2010111007381.html.

O'Keefe, Ed, and Paul Kane. "Senate Delivers Potentially Fatal Blow to 'Don't Ask, Don't Tell' Repeal Efforts." *Washington Post*, December 10, 2010. http://www.washingtonpost.com/wp-dyn/content/article/2010/12/09/AR2010120906555.html.

O'Keefe, Ed, and Craig Whitlock. "New Bill Introduced to End 'Don't Ask, Don't Tell.'" *Washington Post*, December 11, 2010. http://www.washingtonpost.com/wp-dyn/content/article/2010/12/10/AR2010121007163.html.

Office of the Deputy Secretary of Defense, Memorandum: "Directive-Type Memorandum (DTM) 19–004—Military Service by Transgender Persons and Persons with Gender Dysphoria." March 12, 2019. https://drive.google.com/file/d/1tQugAtmmg-cDrhwQVRPtCGNBA6c7b3x2/view.

Office of the Under Secretary of Defense for Personnel and Readiness. "DoD Instruction 1300.28: In-Service Transition for Transgender Service Members." October 1, 2016. https://www.defense.gov/Portals/1/features/2016/0616_policy/DoD-Instruction-1300.28.pdf.

———. "DoD Instruction 1300.28: Military Service by Transgender Persons and Persons with Gender Dysphoria." September 4, 2020. https://health.mil/Reference-Center/Policies/2020/09/04/Military-Service-by-Transgender-Persons-and-Persons-with-Gender-Dysphoria.

———. "DoD Instruction 1300.28: In-Service Transition for Transgender Service Members," March 31, 2021, https://web.archive.org/web/20210407095728/https://www.esd.whs.mil/Portals/54/Documents/DD/issuances/dodi/130028p.pdf.

One, Inc. v. Olesen. 355 U.S. 371 (1958).

Orren, Karen, and Stephen Skowronek. *The Search for American Political Development*. Cambridge: Cambridge University Press, 2004.

OutServe—Servicemembers Legal Defense Network. "Fact Sheet About Department of Defense Commission Reports." 2012.

Palm Center. "The Making of a Ban: How DTM-19-004 Works to Push Transgender People Out of Military Service." March 20, 2019. https://www.palmcenter.org/wp-content/uploads/2019/04/The-Making-of-a-Ban.pdf.

Parco, James, David Levy, and Sarah Spears. "Beyond DADT Repeal: Transgender Evolution Within the U.S. Military." *International Journal of Transgenderism* 17, no. 1 (2016): 4–13.

———. "Transgender Military Personnel in the Post-DADT Repeal Era." *Armed Forces & Society* 41, no. 2 (2015): 221–242.

Park, Haeyoun, and Iaryna Mykhyalyshyn. "L.G.B.T. People Are More Likely to Be Targets of Hate Crimes Than Any Other Group." *New York Times*, June 16, 2016. https://www.nytimes.com/interactive/2016/06/16/us/hate-crimes-against-lgbt.html.

Pear, Robert. "President Admits 'Don't Ask, Don't Tell' Policy Has Been Failure." *New York Times*, December 12, 1999. http://www.nytimes.com/1999/12/12/us/president-admits-don-t-ask-policy-has-been-failure.html.

Picq, Manuela, and Markus Thiel, eds. *Sexualities in World Politics: How LGBTQ+ Claims Shape International Relations*. New York: Routledge, 2015.

Pierson, Frank. *Soldier's Girl*. Bachrach and Gottlieb Productions, 2003.

Pimentel, Frank T. "Constitution as Chaperone: President Clinton's Flirtation with Gays in the Military." *Notre Dame Law School Journal of Legislation* 20, no. 1 (1994).

Plant, Richard. *The Pink Triangle: The Nazi War Against Homosexuals*. New York: Holt, 1986.

Quam, Kayla. "Unfinished Business of Repealing 'Don't Ask, Don't Tell': The Military's Unconstitutional Ban on Transgender Individuals." *Utah Law Review* 3 (2015): 721–741.

Resmovits, Joy. "California's Students Will Soon Learn More LGBT History in Schools." *Los Angeles Times*, August 23, 2016. https://www.latimes.com/local/education/la-me-2016-california-act-scores-20160823-snap-story.html.

Rice, Joe David. "Good Lord and Taylor!" *About You*, June 30, 2020. https://aymag.com/good-lord-and-taylor/.

Rimmerman, Craig. *From Identity to Politics: Lesbian & Gay Movements in the U.S.* Philadelphia: Temple University Press, 2002.

Rizzo, Jennifer, and Zachery Cohen. "Pentagon Ends Transgender Ban." CNN. June 30, 2016. https://www.cnn.com/2016/06/30/politics/transgender-ban-lifted-us-military/index.html.

Roe and Voe v. Austin. 947 F.3d 207 (2020).

Rollins, Joe. "Political Science, Political Sex." *PS: Political Science and Politics* 44 (2011): 27–30.

Rostker, Bernard. "50 Years Without the Draft: Behind the Bold Move That Ended Conscription, and What's Next for the All-Volunteer Force." Association of the United States Army, 2023. https://www.ausa.org/articles/50-years-without-draft-behind-bold-move-ended-conscription-and-whats-next-all-volunteer.

———. "A Year After the Repeal of 'Don't Ask, Don't Tell.'" RAND, September 20, 2012. https://www.rand.org/blog/2012/09/a-year-after-repeal-of-dont-ask-dont-tell.html.

Rostker, Bernard, and Scott Harris. *Sexual Orientation and U.S. Military Personnel Policy: Options and Assessment*. National Defense Research Institute. Santa Monica, CA: RAND, 1993.

———. *Sexual Orientation and U.S. Military Personnel Policy: An Update of RAND's 1993 Study*. National Defense Research Institute. Santa Monica, CA: RAND, 2010.

Rummler, Orion, and Kate Sosin. "All the Ways Trump Wants to Exclude Trans People from Public Life." The 19th. March 5, 2025. https://19thnews.org/2025/03/trump-anti-trans-executive-orders/.

Sarbin, Theodore, and Kenneth Karols. *Nonconforming Sexual Orientation and Military Suitability*. Monterey, CA: PERSEREC, 1988.

———. "Nonconforming Sexual Orientations and Military Suitability." In *Gays in Uniform: The Pentagon's Secret Reports*, ed. Kate Dyer, 3–97. Boston: Alyson, 1990.

Satow, Julie. *When Women Ran Fifth Avenue: Glamour and Power at the Dawn of American Fashion*. New York: Doubleday, 2024.

Savage, David. "Military Poised to Accept Transgender Troops, Despite Trump Tweets, as Courts Block Ban." *Los Angeles Times*, December 26, 2017. http://www.latimes.com/politics/la-na-pol-transgender-military-20171226-story.html.

Sax, Geoffrey. *Christopher and His Kind*. BBC Two, 2011.

Schaefer, Agnes, Radha Iyengar, Srikanth Kadiyala, Jennifer Kavanagh, Charles Engel, Kayla Williams, and Amil Kress. *Assessing the Implications of Allowing Transgender Personnel to Serve Openly*. National Defense Research Institute. Santa Monica, CA: RAND, 2016.

Schmidt, Michael, and Charlie Savage. "Eric Fanning Confirmed as Secretary of the Army." *New York Times*, May 17, 2016. https://www.nytimes.com/2016/05/18/us/eric-fanning-army-secretary.html.

Schogol, Jeff. "The Military Spends More on Giving Retirees Erections Than on Transgender Troops." *Military Times*, July 26, 2017. https://www.militarytimes.com/news/2017/07/26/the-military-spends-more-on-giving-retirees-erections-than-on-transgender-troops/.

Secretary of Defense. "DoD Instruction 6130.03: Medical Standards for Military Service: Appointment, Enlistment, or Induction." March 31, 2021. https://web.archive.org/web/20220318183306/https://www.defense.gov/News/Releases/Release/Article/2557220/dod-announces-policy-updates-for-transgender-military-service/.

———. Memorandum: "Directive-Type Memorandum (DTM) 16-005 Military Service of Transgender Service Members," 2016, https://web.archive.org/web/20181021195834/https://dod.defense.gov/portals/1/features/2016/0616_policy/dtm-16-005.pdf.

———. Memorandum: "Policy Regarding Human Immunodeficiency Virus-Positive Personnel Within the Armed Forces." June 6, 2022. https://media.defense.gov/2022/Jun/07/2003013398/-1/-1/1/POLICY-REGARDING-HUMAN-IMMUNODEFICIENCY-VIRUS-POSITIVE-PERSONNEL-WITHIN-THE-ARMED-FORCES.PDF.

Secretary of Defense Ash Carter. "Remarks on Ending the Ban on Transgender Service in the Military." U.S. Department of Defense, June 30, 2016. https://www.defense.gov/News/Speeches/Speech/Article/821833/remarks-on-ending-the-ban-on-transgender-service-in-the-us-military/.

———. "Statement by Secretary of Defense Ash Carter on DOD Transgender Policy." U.S. Department of Defense, July 13, 2015. https://www.defense.gov/News/News-Releases/News-Release-View/Article/612778/.

Seefried, Josh. *Our Time: Breaking the Silence of "Don't Ask, Don't Tell."* New York: Penguin, 2011.

Sheingate, Adam. "Institutional Dynamics and American Political Development." *Annual Review of Political Science* 17 (2014): 461–477.

Shilts, Randy. *Conduct Unbecoming: Gays & Lesbians in the U.S. Military*. New York: Ballantine, 1994.

Shneer, David, and Caryn Aviv. "The Birds and the . . . Birds: Queer Love, Sex, and Romance in America, Now and Then." In *American Queer: Now and Then*, ed. David Shneer and Caryn Aviv, 91–94. Boulder, CO: Paradigm, 2006.

———. "Bulldykes, Faggots, and Faires, Oh My!: Calling and Being Called Queer in America Now and Then." In *American Queer: Now and Then,* ed. David Shneer and Caryn Aviv, 1–4. Boulder, CO: Paradigm, 2006.

Silverberg, Helene. "Gender Studies and Political Science: The History of the 'Behavioralist Compromise.'" In *Discipline and History: Political Science in the United States,* ed. James Farr and Raymon Seidelman. Ann Arbor: University of Michigan Press, 1993.

Silverman, Victor, and Susan Stryker. *Screaming Queens: The Riot at Compton's Cafeteria.* San Francisco: Frameline, 2005.

Sjoberg, Laura. "Towards Trans-Gendering IR?" *International Political Sociology* 6, no. 4 (2012): 337–354.

Smith, Charles. "Gay, Straight, or Questioning? Sexuality and Political Science." *PS: Political Science and Politics* 44 (2011): 35–38.

Smith, Rogers. *Civic Ideals: Conflicting Visions of Citizenship in U.S. History.* New Haven, CT: Yale University Press, 1997.

Somashekhar, Sandhya, Emma Brown, and Moriah Balingit. "Trump Administration Rolls Back Protections for Transgender Students." *Washington Post,* February 22, 2017. https://www.washingtonpost.com/local/education/trump-administration-rolls-back-protections-for-transgender-students/2017/02/22/550a83b4-f913-11e6-bf01-d47f8cf9b643_story.html?utm_term=.3994e6430c68.

Somerville, Siobhan. *Queering the Color Line: Race and the Invention of Homosexuality in American Culture.* Durham, NC: Duke University Press, 2000.

Southern Poverty Law Center. "Report: FBI Hate Crime Statistics Vastly Understate Problem." January 31, 2006. https://www.splcenter.org/fighting-hate/intelligence-report/2006/report-fbi-hate-crime-statistics-vastly-understate-problem.

Stanely, Liz, and Sue Wise. *Breaking Out Again: Feminist Ontology and Epistemology.* 2nd ed. New York: Routledge, [1983] 1993.

Steinhauer, Jennifer. "House Votes to Repeal 'Don't Ask, Don't Tell.'" *New York Times,* December 15, 2010. http://www.nytimes.com/2010/12/16/us/politics/16military.html.

Steinmo, Sven, and Kathleen Thelen. "Historical Institutionalism in Comparative Politics." In *Structuring Politics: Historical Institutionalism in Comparative Analysis,* ed. Sven Steinmo, Kathleeen Thelen, and Frank Longstreth, 1–32. Cambridge: Cambridge University Press, 1992.

Stentiford, Barry. "Selective Service: Before the All-Volunteer Force." *Military Review,* November–December 2023. https://www.armyupress.army.mil/portals/7/military-review/Archives/English/Nov-Dec-23/Selective-Service/Selective-Service-UA1.pdf.

Stolberg, Sheryl. "Obama Pledges Again to End 'Don't Ask, Don't Tell.'" *New York Times,* October 11, 2010. http://www.nytimes.com/2009/10/11/us/politics/11speech.html.

Stoumen v. Reilly. 37 Cal. 2d 713 (1951).

Stryker, Susan. *Transgender History.* Berkeley, CA: Seal, 2008.

Stuart, Douglas. *Creating the National Security State: A History of the Law That Transformed America.* Princeton, NJ: Princeton University Press, 2012.

Subcommittee on Investigations to the Committee on Expenditures in the Executive Departments, 81st Congress. *Employment of Homosexuals and Other Sex Perverts in Government.* Washington, DC: U.S. Government Printing Office, 1950.

Sutton, Matthew Avery. *Jerry Falwell and the Rise of the Religious Right: A Brief History with Documents*. New York: Macmillan, 2013.
Swokowski, Sheri. "Trump's Anti-LGBT Army Secretary Nominee Thinks Veterans Like Me Have 'a Disease.'" *Washington Post*, April 21, 2017. https://www.washingtonpost.com/post everything/wp/2017/04/21/trumps-anti-lgbt-army-secretary-nominee-thinks-veterans-like-me-have-a-disease/.
Sylvester, Christine. *Curating and Re-Curating the American Wars in Vietnam and Iraq*. Oxford: Oxford University Press, 2019.
———. *War as Experience: Contributions from International Relations and Feminist Analysis*. London: Routledge, 2012.
Symons, Johnny. *Ask Not*. Persistent Visions, 2008.
Tadlock, Barry, Jami Taylor, and Maria Brettschneider. "Where Has the Field Gone? An Investigation of LGBTQ Political Science Research." In *LGBTQ Politics*, ed. Maria Brettschneider, Susan Burgess, and Christine Keating, 212–233. New York: New York University Press.
Tandanpolie, Tatyana. "'Flood' of Anti-LGBTQ Bills Show GOP Wants to 'Eradicate Trans People from Public Life': Advocate." *Salon*, January 6, 2024. https://www.salon.com/2024/01/06/flood-of-anti-lgbtq-bills-shows-wants-to-eradicate-trans-people-from-public-life-advocate/.
Taylor, Jessica, and Danielle Kurtzleben. "Clinton's Comments on Nancy Reagan and HIV/AIDS Cause an Uproar." NPR, March 11, 2016. https://www.npr.org/2016/03/11/470141514/clintons-comments-on-nancy-reagan-and-hiv-aids-cause-an-uproar.
Thiel, Markus. "LGBTQ+ Politics and International Relations: Here? Queer? Used to It?" *International Politics Review* 2, no. 2 (2014): 51–60.
Thomas, Queer J. "Celebrating Fifty Years of LGBTQ+ Scholarship: Kenneth Sherrill, an LGBTQ+ Leader Who Has No Trouble Finding Followers." *Political Science Today* 3, no. 3 (2023): 3–4.
Tippet, Alex. "What the 9/11 Commission Found: Slow Confirmations Imperil U.S. National Security." Center for Presidential Transition. December 16, 2020. https://presidentialtransition.org/blog/what-the-9-11-commission-found-slow-confirmations-imperil-u-s-national-security/.
Tiron, Roxana, and Russell Berman. "House Votes to Repeal 'Don't Ask, Don't Tell' Policy on Gay Service Members." *The Hill*, May 28, 2010. http://thehill.com/homenews/house/100397-house-votes-to-repeal-dont-ask-dont-tell.
Title 10. U.S. Code 654. Public Law 103–160. 107 Statute 1671. November 30, 1993.
Title 10. U.S. Code 654. Public Law 111–321. 124 Statute 3515, 2516, and 3517. September 20, 2011.
Title 10. U.S. Code Chapter 47. 1950.
Title 50. U.S. Code 37. 40 Statute 217. June 15, 1917.
Title 50. U.S. Code 37. 40 Statute 553. May 16, 1918.
Title 50. U.S. Code 401. Public Law 80–253. July 26, 1947.
Tran, Bach Xuan, Hai Thanh Phan, Carl Latkin, Huong Lan Thi Nguyen, Chi Linh Hoang, Cyrus S. H. Ho, and Roger C. M. Ho. "Understanding Global HIV Stigma and Discrimination: Are Contextual Factors Sufficiently Studied?" *International Journal of Environmental*

Research and Public Health 16 (2019). https://pmc.ncbi.nlm.nih.gov/articles/PMC6603743/pdf/ijerph-16-01899.pdf.

Tritten, Travis. "Trump Army Nominee Under Fire for Newly Uncovered Transgender Comments." *Washington Examiner*, April 20, 2017. https://www.washingtonexaminer.com/news/792140/trump-army-nominee-under-fire-for-newly-uncovered-transgender-comments/.

Trump, Donald. "Transgender Tweets." July 26, 2017.

Turner, William. "'Adolph Reagan?' Ronald Reagan, AIDS, and Lesbian/Gay Civil Rights." SSRN, July 13, 2009. https://papers.ssrn.com/sol3/papers.cfm?abstract_id=1433567.

UN AIDS. "HIV and Stigma and Discrimination." Human Rights Fact Sheet Series 2024. https://www.unaids.org/sites/default/files/media_asset/07-hiv-human-rights-factsheet-stigma-discrmination_en.pdf.

U.S. Department of Defense. "The History of the Department of Defense." 2021. https://www.defense.gov/Multimedia/Experience/The-History-of-the-Department-of-Defense/.

———. Memorandum: "Transgender Service Members." July 28, 2015. https://web.archive.org/web/20171105172248/https://www.defense.gov/Portals/1/features/2016/0616_policy/memo-transgender-service-directive-28-July-2015.pdf.

———. "Statement by Secretary Robert Gates on Senate Vote to Repeal 'Don't Ask, Don't Tell.'" December 24, 2010. http://archive.defense.gov/releases/release.aspx?releaseid=14154.

———. *Transgender Service in the U.S. Military: An Implementation Handbook*. Washington, DC: Author, September 30, 2016.

U.S. Department of Justice. Office of the Solicitor General. Letter to Speaker Nancy Pelosi. June 6, 2022. https://www.justice.gov/oip/page/file/1510856/dl#:~:text=Austin%2C%20No.-,18%2Dcv%2D641%20(E.D.,Va.).

Valelly, Richard. "LGBT Politics and American Political Development." *Annual Review of Political Science* 15 (2012): 313–332.

———. *Two Reconstructions: The Struggle for Black Enfranchisement*. Chicago: Chicago University Press, 2004.

Vallegra v. Dept. of Alcoholic Beverage Control. 53 Cal. 2d 313 (1959).

Vergun, David. "Legislation Changing UCMJ, Especially for Sex Crimes." U.S. Army. January 8, 2014. https://www.army.mil/article/117919/legislation_changing_ucmj_especially_for_sex_crimes.

Vicinus, Martha. "'They Wonder to Which Sex I Belong': The Historical Roots of the Modern Lesbian Identity." *Feminist Studies* 18, no. 3 (1992): 467–498.

Villarreal, Yezmin. "Donald Trump: Allowing Trans People in the Military Is Due to 'Political Correctness.'" Advocate. October 4, 2016. https://www.advocate.com/election/2016/10/04/donald-trump-allowing-trans-people-military-due-political-correctness.

Wagner, Laura. "Senate Confirms Eric Fanning, First Openly Gay Leader of Military Service." NPR, May 17, 2016. https://www.npr.org/sections/thetwo-way/2016/05/17/478456199/senate-confirms-eric-fanning-first-openly-gay-leader-of-military-service.

Walker, William. *National Security and Core Values in American History*. Cambridge: Cambridge University Press, 2009.

Wamsley, Laurel. "Pentagon Releases New Policies Enabling Transgender People to Serve in the Military." NPR. March 31, 2021. https://www.npr.org/2021/03/31/983118029/pentagon-releases-new-policies-enabling-transgender-people-to-serve-in-the-milit.

Weber, Cynthia. "Queer Intellectual Curiosity as International Relations Method: Developing Queer International Relations Theoretical and Methodological Frameworks." *International Studies Quarterly* 60, no. 1 (2016): 11–23.

———. "Why Is There No Queer International Theory?" *European Journal of International Relations* 21, no. 1 (2014): 27–51.

White House. "Fact Sheet: President Biden Signs Executive Order Enabling All Qualified Americans to Serve Their Country in Uniform." January 25, 2021. https://www.whitehouse.gov/briefing-room/statements-releases/2021/01/25/fact-sheet-president-biden-signs-executive-order-enabling-all-qualified-americans-to-serve-their-country-in-uniform/.

———. "A Proclamation on Transgender Day of Visibility, 2021." March 31, 2021. https://www.whitehouse.gov/briefing-room/presidential-actions/2021/03/31/a-proclamation-on-transgender-day-of-visibility-2021/.

Williams, C. J., and M. S. Weinberg. *Homosexuals and the Military: A Study of Less Than Honorable Discharge*. New York: Harper & Row, 1971.

Women's Army Corps. "Sex Hygiene Course." Pamphlet 35-1. Washington, DC: Department of War, 1945.

Wong, Kristina. "Confirmation Hearing for Army Secretary Pick Eric Fanning Next Week." *The Hill*, January 17, 2016. http://thehill.com/business-a-lobbying/266200-confirmation-hearing-for-army-secretary-pick-eric-fanning-next-week.

Worsencroft, John. "'We Recruit Individuals But Retain Families': Managing Marriage and Family in the All-Volunteer Force." In *Managing Sex in the U.S. Military*, ed. Beth Bailey, Alesha Doan, Shannon Portillo, and Kara Dixon Vuic, 95–118. Lincoln: University of Nebraska Press, 2022.

Yerke, Adam, and Valory Mitchell. "Transgender People in the Military: Don't Ask? Don't Tell? Don't Enlist!" *Journal of Homosexuality* 60, no. 2 (2013): 436–457.

Zane, Sherry. "'I Did It for the Uplift of Humanity and the Navy.'" MIT Press Podcast, September 18, 2018.

———. "'I Did It for the Uplift of Humanity and the Navy': Same-Sex Acts and the Origins of the National Security State, 1919–1923." *New England Quarterly* 91, no. 2 (2018): 279–306.

INDEX

9/11, 101; post-, 38; pre-, 106
9/11 Commission Report, 101, 165n46
A4TE, 172n33
abortion, 119
academic(s), 2, 12, 132; activist, 34; books, 26, 31; inquiry, 6, 27; peer-review, 121–22; space, x
accession, 111–12, 163n15; of queer people, 94, 114–16, 118, 136n14
Acquired Immunodeficiency Syndrome (AIDS), 11, 71, 84, 87–89, 90–95, 123, 129, 159n81, 160n94, 161n97, 163n13, 176n18; activists, 88
activist(s), 34, 41, 52, 88, 89, 90, 97–98, 102–3, 145n89, 165n48
administrative discharges, 61–3, 65, 67, 78, 81, 104
Afghanistan, 101
African American(s), 37
agencies, 45, 75, 117; federal, 5, 75; intelligence, 5, 70; monitoring, 45
AIDS Coalition to Unleash Power! (ACT UP!), 88–89, 161n98, 176n17
AIDS Memorial Quilt, 98

Air Force (US), 82, 133n2, 151n87, 167n5, 167n65
Al-Qaeda, 101
Alabama, 104
Algonquin Roundtable, 146
all-volunteer force, 80–81, 128, 151n88, 159n72, 166n48, 173n46
American(s), 1, 29, 37, 102, 140n10, 160n93, 172n40
amendment(s), 69, 70, 85, 102–3, 105, 119; First, 158n70; Murphy, 102–3, 105
American Civil Liberties Union (ACLU), 167n65, 171n30, 167n65, 171n30
American politics, 12, 14, 17–18, 22, 37, 124, 126–27, 138n50
American Psychiatric Association (APA), 84, 156n37
American political development (APD), 13, 17–22, 35, 125–26, 138n51, 139n58
American Political Science Association (APSA), 13, 15, 125
anal sex, 61, 93
androgyny, 52
antigay, 89–95, 100, 145n89

anti-LGBTQ+, 2–5, 10, 23, 26, 28, 34, 39–68, 70, 72–82, 89, 106, 126, 143n87, 162n10
anti-trans, 171n23
Arabic, 101, 106
Arab oil crisis, 82
Arizona, 103, 166n55
Armed Forces (US), 8, 10, 25, 34, 46, 57, 67, 73, 89–90, 93–5, 98–9, 104–6, 109–11, 114–15, 119, 121, 129, 166n55, 170n17
armed services, 73, 102; *see also* Armed Forces
Armed Services Committee, 102
Army (US), 58, 63, 91, 100, 110, 113–14, 133n2, 162n4, 165n39; Department of, 11–12
Army Nurses Corps (US), 67
Army War College (US), 33, 37, 134n9, 166n48
Articles of War, 39, 41, 58–59, 62
ashes (scattering of), 88
Assessing the Implications of Allowing Transgender Personnel to Serve Openly, 47, 111, 136n28, 146n103, 187n8
Australia, 33

ban(s), 2–5, 8–9, 23–24, 32–33, 47, 57, 61, 71, 77–78, 87, 91, 96, 118, 122–24, 140n5, 158n70, 159n81
Baptist leaders, 86
barring, 18, 77, 126, 158n70; *see also* ban(s)
barracks, 8, 98
base(s), 57, 59, 98, 113
Baum, L. Frank, 146n1
Berube, Allan, 10, 16, 42, 134nn13–14, 135nn19–20, 138n47, 139n69
Biden, President Joe, 118–19, 124, 127, 172n39, 173n40, 174n49; administration of, 2, 12, 25, 109, 117, 119, 124
bipartisanship, 74, 105
bisexual(s), 2, 13, 50, 77–78, 91–92, 124n11, 136nn30–32
Berlin (Germany), 41, 52, 71, 147n17
Berlin Wall, 71
blackmail, 24, 71–73, 76–80, 83, 86, 123

blue discharge, 63, 151n84, 153n108, 157n48
blue ticket, 151n84
Board of Inquiry (US Navy), 17, 78–79, 135n22, 145n99, 157nn51,54
bodies, 33, 41, 57–58, 61, 63–64, 66, 68, 80, 97, 149n52
Bolshevik Revolution, 37, 142n46
Bolshevism, 37
bottom(s), 38, 51–52, 50, 143n55
bottomed, 61
bottoming, 56, 61
branches (military), 12, 79, 92, 95, 99–100, 103–4, 118–19, 133n2, 162n5
Breaking Out Again: Feminist Ontology and Epistemology, 29, 140nn14–15
breast tissue, 58, 64
Britain, 33
British, 72
budget (defense), 64
bureaucracy (government), 74–5
Bush, President George H. W., 88
Bush, President George W., 97–101, 128, 164n4, 171n23; administration of, 99–101, 128, 165n38
butch lesbian, 43, 50, 55, 66–67
butterfly ballot, 164n34

Caggins, Lieutenant Colonel Myles, 114
campaign(s), 1, 56, 88–9, 91, 99, 102, 113, 129
Canada, 33
Canadian military, 67,
Capitol Police (USCP), 74–6, 104
Carter, Secretary of Defense Ash, 109–11, 168n1, 169nn4–6, 170n17
Carter, President Jimmy, 82; administration of, 82–84
Catholic Church, 88
Cauldwell, David, 148n23
Center for the Study of Sexual Minorities in the Military, 58, 101, 149n56, 158n63
Central Intelligence Agency (CIA), 5, 45, 68, 70, 72, 74–81, 87
"change we can believe in," 102

Chevron doctrine, 119, 174n47
Chevron USA, Inc. v. Natural Resources Defense Council, Inc., 119, 174n47
Choi, Dan, 91, 105, 161n3
Christian Right, the, 85
cisgender, 7, 11, 13, 141n20, 142n87
cisnormative, 13, 143n55, 149n43
cisnormativity, 15
civil liberties, 37–8, 81
Civil Liberties Union, American, 115
civil servants, 82, 132
Civil Service Commission, 82
civilian(s), 1, 34, 82, 93, 129, 133n3, 162n10, 163n15
class, 37, 51, 54
classifying, 56, 139n58, 155n24, 156n37
Claytor, Jr., W. Graham, 82
clearance (security), 71–3, 83, 85–87, 136n24, 154n3, 159nn83,86
Clinton, President Bill, 32, 89–90, 93, 164n27; administration of, 89, 98–99, 101–3, 106, 171n171; as governor, 88
Clinton, Hillary (First Lady, Senator, and Secretary of State), 98, 112, 161
clitoris, 64, 149n52, 152n93
closeted, 103, 166n55, 167n57
Coats, Daniel, 99
Coast Guard (US), 82, 133n2, 162n5
cocksucker, 59
codification and codifying, 5, 22, 37, 39, 41, 46, 48, 57–62, 65, 68, 78
Collins, Susan, 105
Collins v. United States, 167n65
Cold War, 4, 8, 10–11, 21, 23–24, 43–47, 49, 65–66, 68, 70–81
colonialism, 36, 141n42
Colorado, 85
Columbus (Georgia), 1–2
Columbus (Ohio), x–xi
Columbus State University, x
comic book(s), 29, 100, 165n39
Coming Out Under Fire: The History of Gay Men and Women in World War II, 10,
42, 62, 134n13, 135nn19–20, 138n47, 139n69, 144nn73–76, 145n96, 149nn50–51, 151nn82,89, 152nn94–95,105,107, 153n108, 114,118–19,125
Committee on Appropriations (US Senate), 73–74
Committee on Expenditures in the Executive Department, 76, 156
Committee on Government Operations, 76
Committee on Naval Affairs, 60, 61, 63, 150
communism, 10, 43, 72–73, 75, 123
communist(s), 70–89
Comprehensive Review of the Issues Associated with a Repeal of "Don't Ask, Don't Tell," 102
compromise and compromising, 32, 89, 91, 98–99, 106, 141n21, 166n51
Compton's Cafeteria Riot, 81, 158n64
Conduct Unbecoming: Gays and Lesbians in the US Military, 45, 145n93, 158n66, 159nn74–78,81, 161n99
Congress (US), 32, 44, 64, 80, 104–6, 116, 119–20, 150n64
Congressional Record, 153n2, 155nn22–23,25–27, 156n44
Connecticut, x–xi, 13, 105, 131
consciousness raising (feminism), 29
conscription, 82, 159n72
Constitution (US), 91, 119
contractor(s), defense, 87
Cooch, Lieutenant Lester, 56
costs, 1, 32, 97, 99, 114–16, 124
courts (federal), 104, 115–17, 129, 157n65
court-martial and courts-martial, 10, 22, 46, 59–61, 78, 80
covert operations, 39, 59
COVID-19, 117, 127, 131
credible information, 118
Creating the National Security State: A History of the Law That Transformed America, 64, 152nn96–99, 127nn127–28
crime, 37, 39, 42, 162n10
criminalization, 39, 166

Crittenden, Jr., S. H., 135n22, 145n99, 157nn51,55,57–58, 159n84, 160n87
Crittenden Report, 46, 79–80, 84
cultural consciousness, 155n20
culture, 29, 34, 40, 51, 54–55, 66, 90, 104, 106, 146nn1–2, 158n68; heteronormative, 149n43; military, 93, 96; open, 52; sub-, 43, 51, 54, 67–68, 76
Curating and Re-Curating the American Wars in Vietnam and Iraq, 131, 141n17, 171n1

defects, 57–58, 135n17
Defects Found in Drafted Men: Statistical Information Compiled from the Draft Records, 57, 135n17, 144n76, 145n94, 149nn44,47–48, 151n79
demise of DADT ("Don't Ask, Don't Tell"), 95, 97–98
Democrats, 75, 112, 167n69
Department of the Army, 11, 162
Department of Defense (DoD) (US), 1, 5, 47, 63, 70, 84, 116, 122, 134n2, 136n29, 146n103, 151n87, 157n62, 160nn87–88, 165nn40–41, 168n72,1, 169nn5,7, 170n16
Department of Energy (DoE), 82, 159n77
Department of Health and Human Services (HHS), 118
Department of Homeland Security (DHS), 134n2
Department of Justice (DoJ), 39, 134n2, 176n19
Department of State (DoS), 24, 44, 73, 134n2
Department of Treasury (USDT), 82, 134n2
Department of Transportation (DoT), 82
Department of Veterans Affairs (VA), 128
Department of War (DoW), 64, 151n87
desegregation of the military, 98
deviant, sexual, 56, 62, 164n24
Dewey, Thomas, 75
Diagnostic and Statistical Manual of Mental Disorders (DSM), 84–86, 155n24, 156n37

Dignity and Respect: A Training Guide on Homosexual Conduct Policy, 100–101, 161n4, 162nn5,40–41,43
Director of Central Intelligence Directive (DCID), 11, 47, 84, 145, 159n80
discharge, 32, 66, 77–78, 82–83, 94, 99–102, 105, 151n84, 152n107; administrative, 61–65, 67, 81, 104; dishonorable, 59, 81
disclosing, 85, 92, 100, 165n43
disclosure, 33, 73, 85, 92, 100, 159n86, 160nn86, 88, 165n43
discrete secondary source material, 17, 26, 36, 46
discrimination, 2–9, 20–21, 23, 30, 41–42, 55, 64, 77, 80, 86, 90–91, 106, 108, 122, 129, 133n3, 161n3
Dobbs v. Jackson Women's Health Organization, 118, 173n46
DoD Directive, 79–82, 119, 157n62
"Don't Ask, Don't Tell" (DADT), x, 2, 4, 7–8, 11–12, 21, 23–24, 32–35, 46–47, 71, 87–111, 114, 116–17, 122–24, 128, 136, 141n23, 162n5, 163n20, 165–66n48, 166n55, 167n57, 167n65
"Don't Ask, Don't Tell" Repeal Act of 2010, 8, 35, 105
draft, the, 57–78, 66, 80–81, 91, 117, 135n17, 149n51; *see also* conscription
drag, 67, 148n43, 149n43
drug use, 56, 59, 88
Dubbs, Julie, 83, 87
Dubbs v. Central Intelligence Agency, 47, 84, 86, 135n24, 145n101, 159nn79–80, 160n92, 160n95
durable shifts, 71
dyke, 50, 55

effectiveness, 96–97, 102, 105, 110, 163
effeminacy, 52
Eisenhower, President Dwight D., 78; Executive Order 10450, 113
Eisenhower administration, 44, 78–9, 82
election(s), presidential, 88–9, 90–91, 99, 117, 164n34, 175n14

employment, 75, 77, 82, 170n18
Employment of Homosexuals and Other Sex Perverts in Government, 77, 156nn40,42–44,46–47, 157n48
enlisted service, 34, 57, 92, 94, 148n43
enlistment, 63–64, 66, 72, 94, 163n15, 166n48, 173n42
entrapment, 60–61
environmental activism, 82, 140n2
erasure, 40, 140n2
erectile dysfunction, 115
espionage, 37, 39, 60, 72
Espionage Act (1917), 37, 60
evidence, 10, 14, 24, 28, 32, 34, 41, 59, 61, 66, 74–75, 77, 79–80, 93, 96, 123, 165n43; blindness, 28–29, 137n36
exclusion (LGBTQ+), 2–4, 7, 16–17, 20, 22, 30, 32–33, 35, 41–48, 57, 61, 70, 85–86, 104, 122, 126, 133n3, 134n7, 137n32, 141n23, 176n66, 160n87, 161n3, 162n8
exclusionary policies, 22, 30, 35, 42, 46, 57, 61, 86
executive orders, 5, 119; Executive Order 9835, 75, 155,; Executive Order 10450, 43–44, 46, 78, 80, 113, 144n81, 157n53

Faderman, Lillian, 11, 42–43, 65, 67, 77, 135n20, 136n25, 144nn77–80, 146n5, 148nn27,34, 151n83, 152nn101–2,105–7, 153nn110,119–26, 158n71, 153nn108, 119–23,126, 155n31, 156n45, 158n71
fairy (slur), 50, 54–55
Falwell, Sr., Jerry, 96, 160
Farsi speakers, 101
fashion studies, 43
fears, 11, 37, 57, 72, 74, 84, 87, 92, 95, 113, 123, 155n20, 170n17
Federal Bureau of Investigation (FBI), 5, 11, 45, 65–66, 75–76, 101, 134n2; Hoover's War on Gays: Exposing the FBI's "Sex Deviates" Program, 135n22, 145n90, 153n108, 156n39, 162n10
Federal Employees Loyalty Program, 75

federal government, 10, 44, 74–77, 79, 84, 86, 96, 101, 133n2, 134n13, 144n83, 155n20, 156n39, 157n48, 163n13
female, 137, 148n43; friendship, 144n80; -like, 64
female Impersonators, 57, 67
Female Masculinity, 53, 144n80, 147n19, 148n25, 152n93
feminine (being), 52, 54, 58, 64
feminism, 6, 35
feminist consciousness, 29
feminist scholarship, 6–7, 13, 17, 22–25, 27–31, 35, 46–47, 122, 131, 133n4, 134n5, 137n36
Feminist Inquiry: From Political Conviction to Methodological Innovation, 28, 133n4, 139n1
feminist praxis, 6–7, 23, 46, 131, 134n5
feminist research ethic, 28, 30–31, 134n5
filibuster, 103, 166
film(s), 42, 146n1, 147n17, 152n94, 156n45, 162n6, 164n28
First Amendment, 158n70
Florida, 99, 155n20, 164n34–5
Florida Gulf Coast University, x
Food and Drug Administration (FDA), 88
Ford, President Gerald, 82; administration of, 82–83, 100, 113
foreign policy, 71, 74, 128
Fort Benning, 31
Fort Moore, 31
frameworks, 5, 6–13, 17–28, 30–32, 34–37, 40–48, 121–26, 138n51, 138nn58,66, 143n57
free speech, 37
Freedom of Information Act, 79, 101
Freedom to Serve guidebook, 117, 132, 172nn37–38, 176n14, 177n2
Friend of Dorothy, 146n1
Führerbunker, 72

Gallup, Inc., 29
Garland, Judy, 146n1
Gates, Robert, 102, 104–5, 168n66, 168n71

gay (people), 2, 4, 9–11, 13, 32–33, 36, 38, 40–41
Gay Berlin: Birthplace of a Modern Identity, 52, 144n72, 147nn14,15–16, 18,20–21, 148nn14,26,31–32, 151n83
Gay New York: Gender, Urban Culture, and the Making of the Gay Male World, 1890–1940, 9, 40, 134nn13–14, 138n47, 139n69, 143nn65–68, 144nn69, 77, 146n5, 147nn6,10,12–13,20,29–33, 36–38,41, 149n43, 150n72, 151nn75–76,83, 153nn124–25, 156n45
Gay-Related Immune Deficiency Syndrome (GRIDS), 87, 129n71
Gay Revolution, 11, 135n24, 136n25, 158n71
Gays in Uniform: The Pentagon's Secret Reports, 11, 135n23, 136n24, 145n100, 154n4
gender, 1, 27–29, 32–33, 38, 41, 44, 50, 52–56, 58, 61–62, 67, 72, 92, 97–98, 111–20, 137n32, 146n43, 163n20; *see also* cisgender, transgender
gender dysphoria, 111, 116–17
gender expansive people(s), 11–12, 77, 80, 106, 108, 119
gender expression, 28, 50, 52–54, 67, 163n20
Germany, 41, 52, 63
Gore, Vice President Al, 99
government (US), 1, 4–5, 9–10, 21, 24, 37, 43–5, 56, 57, 61–2, 67, 72, 74–7, 79–80, 84–8, 96–7, 101, 114, 123, 133n2, 155n20, 156n39
Government Accountability Office (GAO), 101–2
Gilded Age, 36
Goodbye to Berlin, 147n17
guidebooks, 10, 22, 57, 117

hanging chads, 99, 164n34
harassment, 81, 99–100, 112; anti-, 165n39
health care, 98, 111, 115, 124
hearings, 44, 52, 56, 61, 63, 80
heteronormativity, 13, 15, 96, 143n55, 149n43
heterosexual(s), 51, 85, 103
heterosexual masculinity, 11

heterosexual privacy, 33
heterosexuals, 85
Hitler, Adolf, 72–73
HIV/AIDS epidemic, 11, 84, 87–88, 90, 94, 160n97, 161n97, 163n13
Hinojosa, Ramon, 163n17
Hoey, Clyde, 77–80, 135n22, 145n98, 156n37
Hoey Committee, 77–80, 135n22, 145n98, 156n37
Holocaust, the, 72
homophobia and homophobic language and reactions, 87, 92–95, 135n22, 144n84, 158n68, 162n10
homosexual(s), 24, 29, 33, 38–44, 50–61, 63–64, 66, 71–85, 91–92, 99–100, 123, 134nn6,8, 135nn16–17,22, 136nn2427, 140n10, 141nn25–29, 142n35, 143n53, 144nn71,84,87, 145nn94,99, 147nn6,9,21, 149n56, 150nn56,64, 162n91, 153 108, 155nn20,24, 156nn40,42–44,46–47, 157nn48,51,54,63, 158nn63,67–68, 160n93; anti-, 162n10; as "consensual sodomy," 58; as domestic enemy, 43; the word, 51–52; history of, 53; *see also* homophobia
homosexuality, 11, 29, 39–40, 42, 44, 51, 53, 58–59, 64, 71–73, 75–84, 153n108, 155n24
Hoover, J. Edgar, 66, 76
Hoover's War on Gays: Exposing the FBI's "Sex Deviates" Program, 45, 135n22, 138n47, 145nn90–91, 153nn111–13, 156n39
House of Representatives (US), 78, 105
How We Won: Progressive Lessons from the Repeal of "Don't Ask, Don't Tell," 142n38, 166nn51–54, 167nn63–64, 168nn66–70
hypersexualization, 97
Human Immunodeficiency Virus (HIV), 11, 71, 84, 87–95, 123, 129, 159n81, 160n97, 161n97, 163n13, 176n18
Human Rights Campaign, 102, 104, 171n24, 174n49

identity and identities, 4, 6–11, 13–14, 23, 28–31, 37–44, 48, 50–56, 58, 73, 75, 85,

91–92, 85, 98, 110–12, 115, 127, 134n11, 135n16, 137n40, 143n53, 145n89, 147n9, 149n51, 155n20, 160n88, 163n22, 175n9
ideology, 37, 73, 75–76, 145n89, 155n20
immorality, 56–8, 123
inclusion, x, 32–33, 35; intersex, 47; LGBTQ+, 8, 24, 95, 98, 121, 126–27; queer, 93–97, 103, 142nn36,40, 163nn13,20, 166n35; trans-, 1, 12, 106, 108–12, 114, 119–20, 170n17
incompatible with service (conduct), 11, 39, 77, 83
Indiana, 99
Institute for Sexual Science, 53
intelligence community, 3–7, 9–11, 16–17, 20–24, 26–8, 30, 36, 41, 43–48, 69–72, 74–83, 85–86, 89–92, 96, 98, 101, 106–7, 108–9, 111–15, 118, 121–23, 126–27, 133n2, 145n89, 159n81, 161n3
intercepted conversations, 101
interdisciplinary research and scholarship, 5–7, 9, 23, 26–36, 122, 128–29
international relations, 7, 14–15, 30, 127–28, 128
intersectionality, 4, 6, 28
intersex people, 4, 24, 48, 55, 58, 64, 78, 106, 108, 123, 142n36, 143n61, 144n87, 149n51
inverts, 53, 62
inversion (sexual), 53
investigations, 44–45, 65, 75–77, 83, 92, 99, 101, 117, 155n20
invisibility, 28–29, 40
Islamophobia, 113
Israel, 8, 32–33
Israeli Defense Forces (IDF), 8, 32, 96
Iraq, 101, 131

Japanese attack on Pearl Harbor, 64–65
Japanese Breakfast, xi
Johnson, President Lyndon B., 81
Joint Chiefs of Staff, 102, 123
Judge Advocate General, 56, 59
judicial fiat, 104
judiciary, 76, 114–15

Kaiser Wilhelm II, 42
Keisling, Mara, 116
Kennedy, President John F., 81
Kenneth Sherrill Prize, 16
Kentucky, 104
known homosexuals, 66, 73, 76

Lady Gaga, 12, 104, 167nn61–62
Lambda Legal, 115
language, 24, 42, 44, 49–50, 55–56, 62–63, 70, 81–84, 86–87, 101, 106, 140n11, 147n9
lavender bans, 4–5, 23, 47, 122, 129
Lavender Scare, 44–46, 72–76, 78, 145n89
The Lavender Scare: The Cold War Persecution of Gays and Lesbians in the Federal Government, 10, 43, 79, 134n13, 144n83, 154n3
laws (sedition), 39
Law and the Gay Rights Story: The Long Search for Equal Justice in a Divided Democracy, 45, 135n22, 136n26, 145n 92, 153n113, 156n39, 158nn70–71, 159n73, 161n98
leadership, 75, 79, 93, 96, 104, 118
legal battles, 81, 117
legislation, 80, 105; anti-trans, 118
lesbian(s), 2, 33, 43–45, 47, 50–51, 55, 63, 65, 67, 77–79, 85, 87, 91–92, 134nn7,11, 157n48, 160n87
lesbian, gay, bisexual, queer (LGBQ), 2, 8, 10, 16, 24
lesbian, gay, bisexual, queer (LGBT), 14, 141n22
lesbian, gay, bisexual, transgender, queer (plus) (LGBTQ+), x, 2–17, 19–36, 48–50, 52–59, 61–73, 78–98, 102, 104, 106, 110, 113–14, 117, 121, 123–26, 128–29, 133n3, 134n11, 136n32, 137n32, 139n66, 140nn2,5, 11, 141n20, 144n87, 145n89, 146n2, 147n17, 155n20, 158n70, 160n86, 161n97, 175nn7–10; anti-, 4, 41, 44–45, 48, 63, 68, 72–73, 80, 82, 89, 106, 119, 126–27, 132, 133n2, 144n7; exclusion, 3–4, 7, 16, 45, 122, 126, 133n2, 161n3; *see also* inclusion

lesbianism, 65, 144n80, 152n93
libertarian ideas, 86
Lieberman, Joe, 105
little black book, 72
LGBTQ+ history, 29, 36, 122, 140n2
LGBTQ+ studies, 9, 12–17, 21–22, 25, 31, 35–36, 44
Log Cabin Republicans, 99, 165n36
Loper Bright Enterprises v. Raimondo, 119, 174n47
Lord & Taylor, 67

Maine, 105
male(s), 58, 60, 67–68, 85, 97, 137n40, 146n1, 149n51, 158n68, 163n13, 164n24
man/men, 4, 9–10, 36, 40, 42, 58, 60–61, 64–65, 77–78, 129, 134n11, 157n48, 158n66, 160n87
Manual Enterprises, Inc. v. Day, 81, 158n69
Marine Corps, 114, 133n2, 162n5
marriage, 16, 100, 102, 127
masculine (ascription), 52, 67, 95
masculinity, 11, 53–54, 67, 95–96
masculinization, 64, 66
Massachusetts, 85
Matlovich, Leonard, 82, 158n66
Mattis, James, 114, 170n17
Mayhew, David, 18, 138n55
McCain, Senator John, 103–5, 166n55
McCarthy, Senator Joseph, 73, 76
McCarthyism, 72
McConnell, Senator Mitch, 104
McDaniel, Michael, 85, 136n24, 159nn80,85, 160n88
media, 12, 34, 73, 75, 87–88, 115
medical costs, 1, 114
medical providers, 52–53, 111–12, 115
memoranda, 5, 12, 73, 88, 111, 116
mental disorders/illness, 11, 42, 58, 74, 84, 155n24
mental health, 128, 155n24, 156n37
mental instability, 83–86, 90
methodology, 7, 13–21, 22–24, 28, 35, 125–26, 138n51, 139n58

Middle East, 95, 101
military, 3–6, 8–12, 16–17, 20–21; experts, 1, 114; policies, 2, 5, 34, 40, 43, 55, 73, 111
Military Times, 12, 115, 170nn20–21, 171n29, 172n39
militarization, 63–64
Miller, Representative Arthur L., 74
misremembering, 9, 29, 122
Modern Military Association of America (MMAA), 117–18, 127, 132
morality and immorality, 56–57, 59–62, 64, 66, 123, 148n43, 165nn48–49
Moral Majority, 86, 160n93, 161n98
morale (troops), 33, 96, 148n43
Mullen, Michael, 102
murder(s), 98–99, 106, 164n28, 165n39
Murphy Amendment, 102–3, 105
Murphy, Patrick, 105
Muslims, 113
myths and mythologizing, 40, 72, 97, 164n24

National Archives and Records Administration (NARA), 5, 22
National Center for Transgender Equality, 116
National Commission on Terrorist Attacks Upon the United States, 165n44
National Defense Authorization Act (NDAA), 102–3, 105, 119, 166, 174n48
National Military Establishment (NME), 70
National Mall, the, 88, 132
national security, 6, 36–40, 45, 49, 60, 62, 64–66, 68–72, 77, 79–80, 101, 119, 128, 131,
National Security Act of 1947, 37, 68–70, 72, 80
National Security Agency (NSA), 24, 101, 104, 109, 133n2
National Security and Core Values in American History, 36, 142nn41–47
national security state, 36–37, 64, 66, 79–80
Navy (US), 39, 46, 58–59, 61, 63, 70, 78–80, 84, 133n2, 135n21, 162n5; bases, 10, 59; Naval Academy, 140n5
Nazis, 72

Nebraska, 71, 74, 153n110
New York City, 81
Nixon administration, 45, 76, 82
nonbinary, 12, 142n36
Nonconforming Sexual Orientations and Military Suitability, 136n24
Newport (Rhode Island), 59–61, 65, 150n59

Obama, President Barack, 98, 102, 105, 113, 119; administration of, 1–2, 98, 104, 105, 108–10, 115, 118, 126, 142n40, 171n23
Odd Girls and Twilight Lovers: A History of Lesbian Life in Twentieth-Century America, 42, 65, 135n20, 144nn77–80, 146n5, 148nn27,34, 151n83, 152nn101,102,105–7, 153nn110,119–23,125–26
Office of the Director of National Intelligence (ODNI), 109
Office of the Quartermaster General, 67
One, Inc. v. Olesen, 81, 158n69
ONE magazine, 46, 158n69
open transgender service, 2, 7, 17, 106–7, 108–9, 118–20, 121, 124, 126, 128–29
oral sex, 60
Out of the Past: Gay and Lesbian History from 1869 to Present, 72, 134n12, 135nn20, 22, 140n12, 144n82, 147n9, 151n89, 152nn104, 107, 153nn110,126, 154nn7–8, 15,19, 155n35, 157nn48,58, 158n66
OutServe, 11, 102, 104, 117, 160

Palm Center, 8, 31, 115, 117, 171n29, 172nn35–36
Parameters: US Army War College Quarterly, 19, 33, 135n9, 142n33, 162n6
Parker, Dorothy, 146
pathology, 58; *see also* mental disorders and illness
Pearl Harbor, 63–65, 68
pedophilia, 164n24
Pentagon, the, 11, 32, 85, 93, 98–99, 101–2, 104, 106, 111–12, 114–15, 118, 128, 134n6, 142n40, 160nn88,90, 165n39

percentages, 14, 29, 103, 111, 137n35, 165n48, 168n48
performance, 33, 75, 85, 92, 96, 103
Personnel Security Research Center (PERSEREC), 47, 84–85
pervert(s), 39–40, 60, 62, 75, 77
perversion (sexual), 38–39, 57, 77–78, 80–81
Peurifoy, John, 73–74
phallus, 58, 64, 149n52
phenotypes, 10, 39, 42, 58, 143n61
Philippines, the, 36
physical features (morphology), 39, 42, 57–58, 64, 78
physical fitness, 116–17, 123
pinkwashing, 127–28
police, 39, 74–76, 81, 93
political science, x, 7, 12–18, 20–23, 25, 27, 31, 47, 121, 124–27, 132, 137n32
politics, 1; American, 37, 124, 126–27, 128nn50–51,55; geo-, 96; LGBTQ+, 17, 19, 124–25; morality in, 56; Republican, 86
port cities, 59
positionality, 13, 31
post-DADT, 34
power bottoms, 143
predators (sexual), 33, 97, 164n24
Preservice Adjustment of Homosexual and Heterosexual Military Accessions: Implications for Security Clearance Suitability, 85, 136n24, 159nn80,85, 160n88
primary source material, 5, 8–12, 22, 45–50, 55, 141n23, 158n7
privacy, 8, 24, 33, 91–92, 95–97, 100–101, 124
Progressive Era, 36
providers (medical), 52–53, 76
psychiatry, 42
psychology, 16, 83
psychological scars, 32
psychopath(s), 39
psychopathic character, 39, 57
public consciousness, 52, 61
public health, 88, 118, 129, 163n13, 176n18

Public Health Service Commissioned Corps, 118
public opinion, 16, 34, 93, 103, 127
Puerto Rico, 36

qualitative methods and sources, 5, 13, 15, 17–19, 21–22, 24, 138n51, 139n66
quantitative methods and sources, 15, 19, 139n66
queer(s), 2, 7, 9–11, 14–15, 23–24, 27–28, 30, 32–34, 39–44, 46–68, 70–87, 90–101, 103–6, 108, 110, 113, 123, 137n32, 140nn2,9, 141n20, 142n36, 143n61, 144nn71,87, 145n89, 146n1, 147nn9,17, 152n93, 156n39, 157n48, 158nn70–71, 159n81, 160n88, 161n3; educators, 155n20, 164nn22,24, 165n49; employees, 159n71, 161n2, 163nn13,20, 166n55, 170n17, 172n38, 175nn7–8, 176n14; military history, 36, 158n68

rationales, 3–5, 8–10, 12, 17, 20, 22–24, 33, 47–48, 49–50, 57–59, 62–66, 68–69, 70–71, 77–87, 89, 91–97, 103, 108–9, 113–14, 116, 118, 122–24, 126–27, 159n81, 160n87, 161n3, 166n55
readiness, 33, 64, 90, 92, 95–96, 105–6, 110–11, 116–17, 169n13, 172n36
Reagan, First Lady Nancy, 161n97
Reagan, President Ronald, 84, 159n81; library, 160n93
Reagan administration, 86–8, 94, 160n97
Reconstruction, 36
recruits, 40, 58, 61, 64, 114, 165n48, 166n48
Red Scare, 10, 72, 78, 145n89, 155n20
redacting, 85
reliable persons, 87, 100–101
religion, 21
repeals, 8, 11, 34–35, 91, 97–98, 102–6, 108, 110, 124, 167n57
reports, 11, 47, 59, 84–85, 110; vice, 38–39, 57
representatives, 104; *see also* House of Representatives

Republicans (GOP, Party), 75, 99
research questions, 3–7, 15, 17, 20, 24, 121–22, 126, 129
Research and Development Corporation (RAND Corp.), 89–95, 111, 115, 119, 162n10
revisions of anti-homosexual and anti-LGBTQ+ regulations, 63–64, 81–83
Rhode Island, 123
Rideout, Harrison Allen, 56
Roaring Twenties, 63
Roosevelt, President Franklin D., 59, 61, 65–66, 76
Roosevelt, President Theodore, 36
rumors, 73, 75
Rumsfeld, Secretary of Defense Donald, 100, 165n38
Russia and Russians, 57, 71, 142n46

sailors (in Newport), 60–61, 164n22
San Francisco, 81
sanctioned ignorance, 28–29
Sanders, Sarah Huckabee, 114–15
Sarbin, Theodore, 84–85, 136n24, 159nn80,85, 160n87
scandals (sex), 10, 41–42, 52, 56, 59–60, 65
Schroeder, Patricia, 85
Section A group, 59–61, 164n22
security clearance, 72–73, 83, 85–87
security studies, 23, 25, 27, 31–35, 44, 46–47, 22, 128, 132, 141n23
security threats, 27, 33, 56, 58, 63, 77, 83, 84, 92, 163
Sedition Act of 1918, 37, 60
Selective Service System, 82
Senate (US), 10, 52, 60–61, 63, 73–75, 98–100, 102–3, 105, 110, 150n64
separation from armed forces, 73, 91, 100, 111, 167n65
September 11 (2001), 1, 101
Servicemembers Legal Defense Network (SLDN), 11, 102, 104, 110, 117

Sessions, US Attorney General Jefferson, 104
sex acts, 38, 52,
Sex Deviates Program, 76
sexologists, 51-3
Sexual Behavior in the Human Male, 73, 154n11
Sexual Orientation and US Military Personnel Policy: Options and Assessment, 47, 89, 90, 93, 136n24, 145n102, 150n56, 151n78, 151nn85,87,89, 153n126, 154nn6,13, 159n78, 161n103, 162nn9-12, 167nn56-59
Sexual Orientation and US Military Personnel Policy: An Update of RAND's 1993 Study, 135n18, 146n103, 149n55, 154n4, 157n56, 158nn64,67, 169n76, 161n1, 163n15
sexual perversion, 38, 78, 80
sexuality, 15, 27, 29, 31, 38, 46, 50-51, 53, 60, 72, 92-93, 98, 100, 103, 106, 143n55, 156n37, 162n6, 163n20, 165n43
Shaver, Dorothy, 67
Shilts, Randy, 45-46, 145n93, 158n66, 159nn74-78,82, 161n99
social movements, 15
society, 30, 32, 43, 51-52, 54, 61, 71-72; American, 43, 58-69, 62, 66, 81; civilian, 129
sodomy, 39, 58-60, 62-63, 166n51; being found guilty of, 59-60, 62
soldiers, 8, 33, 57, 98, 100, 162n5
Soviet agents, 24, 71-73, 78-80, 83, 123
Space Force, 118, 133n2, 162n5
Speakes, Larry, 87, 160n97
special counsel, 117
spies, 71-73
Stalin, Joseph, 72-73
state, the, 37, 63, 66
stigma, 94, 129,
Stonewall Inn, 81, 158nn70-71
Stonewall Riots, 81
Stoumen v. Reilly, 81, 158n70
straight people, 7-8, 13, 15, 22, 33-34, 51-56, 67, 73, 76, 84-85, 93, 95-98

The Straight State, 134n13, 135nn15,19, 138n47, 139n65, 143nn57,59-61, 144n69, 145n94, 148nn36-39,42, 149nn44-48, 51,54, 151nn77-81;85, 152nn90,92, 153n10
The Strange History of Don't Ask, Don't Tell, 100, 156, 161nn102-3, 162n6, 163n16, 164nn25,32, 165nn42,47-48, 166nn48-49,52,55, 168n70
Studds, Gerry, 85
student protests, 81-82
subcommittees (Senate), 74-76, 156n40
Subcommittee on Appropriations for the District of Columbia, 74
subcultures, 40, 43, 51, 54-55, 67-68, 76, 146n1, 158n68
Supreme Court (US), 99, 118-19, 164n34, 166n51, 174n51
surveillance, 45, 66
switching sexual positions, 52, 60-61

tabloids, 72-74
terrorist attacks, 101
testicles, 58, 64
Time magazine, 82
tops (sexual), 38, 60-61, 143n55
trade (sexual orientation term), 50, 54, 60
Trans Ban 2.0, 116-18, 132
transition (Medical, Social, In-Service), 10, 111-12, 115-18, 121, 141n20, 169nn13-14, 170n15
transgender, 1-2, 4, 11-13, 15, 16-17, 24-25, 27-31, 35, 47, 53, 55, 77, 80, 87, 91, 107, 108-20, 121-24, 126, 128-29, 134n11; history, 7, 9, 140n2; inclusion, 12, 24, 106, 108-12, 114, 119, 126, 142n40, 170n17; nonbinary, 12, 142n36; policies, 91; woman, 7, 30, 98
Transgender Day of Visibility, 118
Transgender Service in the US Military: An Implementation Handbook
Transsexualismus, 71
tribade and tribadism, 152n93
TRICARE, 119

Truman, President Harry, 70, 75, 98; administration of, 44, 75, 78
tweets and Twitter. See Trump
Trubshaw, Harold J., 59–61, 150nn58, 71–72
Trump, President Donald, 1–4, 108, 113, 119–20, 141n23, 142n40, 170nn17,19–20, 171nn23–24,26–31, 172nn32,36, 174nn50,51; administrations, 12, 21, 23, 25, 108–9, 114–18, 122, 124, 126–28, 132; tweets, 1–2, 114–15, 133n1, 171nn26,31

Un-American Activities Committee (US House of Representatives), 145n89
unfit for service, 24, 39–40, 115, 117
Unfriendly Fire: How the Gay Ban Undermines the Military and Weakens America, 101, 165nn45–48, 166n49
Uniform Code of Military Justice (UCMJ), 46, 63, 166n51
unit cohesion, 8, 24, 32–3, 89, 90–103, 105, 109, 113–16, 124, 166n55
University of Connecticut, ix–xi, 13, 131
University of Tennessee at Knoxville, x
urbanization, 40–41, 68
USSR, 72; *see also* Soviet spies

Vallegra v. Dept. of Alcoholic Beverage Control, 81, 158n70
Valelly, Richard (Rick), 12–13, 17–22, 125–26, 136nn30–31, 138nn48–49,52,55, 139nn59,67, 141n22, 174n3, 175nn11–12, 176n13
venereal disease, 57, 65
veterans, 42, 46, 91, 97, 118, 128, 131–32, 161n3, 171n22
vice squads, 10, 39, 56–57, 59, 75, 149n43
Victorian era, 56
Vietnam Veterans Memorial, 131
Vietnam War, 82
vigilantism, 92, 99, 101

violence, 32, 89–95, 123, 162n10
voters, 128

waivers (criminal and moral), 165–66n48
wars, 49, 63, 131
War as Experience: Contributions from International Relations and Feminist Analysis, 30, 131, 140n17
War on Terror, 101, 128
Washington, DC, xi, 22, 76, 98, 131
Weimar Republic, 41, 52, 147n17
Weinberger, Caspar, 88, 159n81
Wherry-Hill Investigation, 74–75
White House, 1, 12, 65, 81–82, 87–88, 98–89, 102, 114, 118, 158n71, 172n40, 173n41
Wilson, President Woodrow, 37, 150n63
Winchell, Barry, 98–99, 106, 164n28, 165n39
witch hunts, 98
The Wonderful Wizard of Oz, 146n1
woman and women, 4, 6, 10, 27–29, 30, 32–23, 42–43, 51, 58, 64–67, 69, 77–78, 82–83, 87, 93, 98, 118, 134n11; cis-, 7
Women's Army Corps (WAC), 43, 65–66, 153n110
Women's Army Auxiliary Corps (WAAC), 43, 65–66, 153n10
workplace rights, 81
World Trade Center, 101
World War I, 3–5, 9–10, 17, 21–24, 30, 36, 38–43, 45–54, 57, 62–74, 77–80, 93, 108, 122–23, 126, 163n22
World War II, 4, 10, 21, 23–24, 36–43, 45–48, 49, 53–54, 58–74, 77, 80, 83, 89, 96, 122–23, 134n13, 148n43, 151n87; post-, 152n91, 155n24

YouTube, 12, 104

zero tolerance, 93

GPSR Authorized Representative: Easy Access System Europe, Mustamäe tee
50, 10621 Tallinn, Estonia, gpsr.requests@easproject.com

www.ingramcontent.com/pod-product-compliance
Lightning Source LLC
Chambersburg PA
CBHW031244290426
44109CB00012B/429